Long Rider
To Rome

Also by Mefo Phillips:

Horseshoes and Holy Water: On the Hoof from Canterbury to Santiago de Compostela (2005)

Long Rider To Rome

1400 MILES BY PILGRIM HORSE FROM CANTERBURY

Mefo Phillips

Signal Books
Oxford

First published in 2018 by
Signal Books Limited
36 Minster Road
Oxford OX4 1LY
www.signalbooks.co.uk

A catalogue record for this book is available from the British Library

ISBN 978-1-909930-67-4 Paper

Cover Design: Baseline Arts Ltd
Typesetting: Tora Kelly
Cover Images: Mefo Phillips
Photographs supplied by Mefo Phillips
Printed in India by Imprint Digital Ltd

Contents

Written in memory of my mother
Dickie Pares
(also known as author Judith Campbell)

And dedicated to

My husband Peter
My horse Leo
Bessie the Bedford

And the wayward Via Francigena,
together with all the associations and individuals
who work tirelessly to improve its signage
and create safe paths for its pilgrims

Paths of the
Via Francigena

ENGLAND

CANTERBURY

BELGIUM

GERMANY

Arras

Laon
Reims

Châlons-en-Champagne

Troyes
Bar-sur-Aube

FRANCE

AUSTRIA

Dijon
Besançon
Pontarlier
Lausanne
SWITZ.
ITALY

Cluny
Mâcon

Annecy
La Clusaz
Lyon
Aosta
Beaufort
Ivrea
Bourg-St-Maurice
Susa
Pavia
Piacenza
Col de l'Iseran
Col du Mont Cenis
Torriglia
Bra
Ovada
Pontremoli
Lucca
San Gimignano
Siena
San Quirico
Bolsena
Viterbo
Sutri
ROME

SPAIN

Mediterranean Sea

N

Via Francigena
(*principal route*)

Via Francigena
(*secondary route*)

Via Francigena
(*author's detour*)

FOREWORD
by Robin Hanbury-Tenison

Mefo Phillips and her beguiling spotted horse Leo have already
delighted us in 2005 with their book, *Horseshoes and Holy
Water*, about their pilgrimage from Canterbury to Santiago de
Compostela in Spain. Then they rode with her sister Susie on
another Appaloosa, Apollo. When their brilliant mother died
of Alzheimer's, Mefo took another Sabbatical from her day job
working in criminal law to ride Leo on her own from Canterbury
to Rome and to raise money towards finding a cure for that
hideous disease. Once again her stoical husband Peter provided
the backup, driving their ancient and unreliable Bedford lorry,
Bessie. He would really have preferred to be playing golf, but
found some solace in the vineyards along the route, which are far
more plentiful than golf courses. They share a childish sense of
humour, essential for overcoming the many frustrations of long
distance riding; the inevitable irritations and grumpiness, which
are vital ingredients of all good marriages, rang lots of bells with
me and are well evoked.

This is a hard book to put down: I read it at a sitting on a long
flight. It rattles along, a page turner full of all the best ingredients
of a cracking travel book. From day one we are informed and
entertained by stories relating to this great pilgrimage route,

the lifeline of Christianity through the Dark and Middle Ages. We share the inevitable dramas of all long distance rides as the pilgrimage, quite properly being done on a shoestring, lurches from one potential disaster to another. We meet a plethora of mostly kind characters, who almost always will react hospitably to a lone traveller on a horse; while at the same time there is always the imminent likelihood of catastrophe that accompanies equine travel, whether from inconsiderate speeding traffic hurtling past and often unable to resist the temptation to blow a terrifying blast on the horn; the constant predicament of wondering where you and your horse are, as maps and rare signs let you down; and the nagging worry about where you are both going to spend the night.

This book is very funny, often unintentionally, I suspect. Mefo has to a well-honed degree the ability to make friends and encourage them to be nice to her. As a result, she is able to bring alive the characters she meets along the way. Reading between the lines, I suspect that they often found her as entertaining as she did them. Although we are not spared the hardship and travail of the ride, the author makes every mile intriguing, observing as she goes the scenery, the buildings and the people. And she has an insight or, at least, an opinion on everything. She did her homework well before departure, which is all too rare in travellers today. Without having it thrust down my throat, I learnt about the Via Francigena and visited just enough of the innumerable churches and sites along the way never to feel sated.

There is laughter and tears in equal measure. Mefo's mother, Dickie Pares, who was the spur for the journey, shines through as a vibrant personality, much loved, but also discovered and better known as a result of the journey, even though no longer there in person. The Epilogue, in which Mefo discovers, in a long-lost letter, an astonishing link with her mother's own desire to ride across Europe, is deeply moving.

But it is Leo, to whom Mefo chats unabashedly as they ride together, who steals the show. All horses have personas, although they are often hard to discern, but Leo comes across as exceptionally self-possessed and, while wilful, so that life is never boring, also impressively willing. The perfect travelling companion.

PROLOGUE

'Silence! All rise!'

Exhibit lists were shoved inside road maps of Holland as the barristers, defendants and legal clerks sighed to their feet at the end of another airless Crown Court day.

The Judge had been the only one on the ball at the brain-dead time of 3 p.m., while in front of him several members of the Bar leant forward with brows propped on their hands to conceal their closed eyes, and the note-takers' slow pens dribbled words off the page. Another hour passed before his enthusiasm for questioning the witnesses himself finally tailed off, and by then some counsel had lines of playing cards displayed on their laptops, and half the jurors were asleep.

The trial was into its third week. There were seven defendants charged with a smuggling conspiracy: organisers, middle-men and lorry drivers, but today's evidence had concerned only one of them, and even the Customs officer in the witness box appeared bored by his painstakingly compiled schedules of phone calls and vehicle movements.

Luckily for me, the evidence hadn't concerned my client at all, so there was no need to fight cramp in my fingers while trying to take a legible longhand note at top speed. But I wasn't napping; in fact, had the Judge's eyes strayed to my unusually alert attention to the maps as I sat behind defence counsel in his frayed black gown, he might have wondered how it was that Holland had sprouted a range of mountains.

But the flat network of motorways from Amsterdam to Calais didn't feature on the maps I was studying. They were of south-east France and I was trying to puzzle out the path across the Alps of the Via Francigena, the mediaeval pilgrim road that runs to Rome, because in a few weeks' time I'd be setting off from Canterbury Cathedral to follow it with a travel-mad companion – Leo, my spotted horse.

1

To Be a Pilgrim

'You can't want to go off on another adventure.'

'Yes I do.'

'But it's only three years since you rode to Spain, isn't it?'

'I know. But Leo wants another trip. He's bored.'

'*Leo's* bored?'

There were plenty of conversations like that, but a ride to Rome wasn't a new idea for me. In 2002 my sister Susie and I had travelled with our spotted Appaloosa horses along the pilgrim Way of St James to Santiago de Compostela in north-west Spain, and on the way I'd hatched a plan to take Leo to the Vatican one day. I wanted to follow the Via Francigena, the second of the three great mediaeval pilgrim routes that thread through Europe – the third one goes on to Jerusalem, but I wasn't tempted to go that far and my husband Peter certainly wasn't. Not that he was very keen on the idea of Rome either, and I did my best to put no pressure on him to come too; but it got to the point where I needed to know if he'd consider following Leo and me in Bessie the Bedford horsebox, just as he had patiently trailed us all to Santiago, because I wanted to set off in the spring of 2006 which was only six months away. The alternative was for me to go on my own with Leo and a pack horse – more complicated, but possible if I had time to work out a different kind of plan.

My employers had only one thing to say when they heard of my latest idea: 'Mefo, you're mad. It could be dangerous. Surely your husband wouldn't let you go alone?'

I reported this to Peter.

'Yes I would,' he said.

But at Christmas he said he was coming.

Travelling by horse is addictive and every spring since the Santiago trip I'd had itchy feet, a longing to go off again with Leo, to lead a vagabond life, setting out each morning with probably only the vaguest idea where we'd be by the evening or where we'd stay. It had been consigned to the back burner, though, because I was sure my solicitor employers wouldn't allow me to take another sabbatical. But then my job disappeared when the firm gave up state-funded criminal defence work, and for the first time in my life I was self-employed, an outdoor clerk working in the Crown Courts for other firms – and free to take the time to gallop off to Rome, if I could afford it.

There was another, important reason for going, this one concerning my elderly mother. She'd developed Alzheimer's Disease not long before Susie and I went to Santiago, and when we came back she couldn't remember that we'd even been away. But a strange thing had happened. We used to joke on our way through France that we were taking her with us in spirit; she'd always been a great traveller, rider and writer, and even during her confusing move into a care home she was still clued up enough to know that we were planning a horsy adventure. When we'd called in to see her with our horses on our way to

Dover she'd looked as though she was ready to come as well, her slippers amazingly transformed into riding boots, her wheelchair equipped with hooves. When we got home again four months later she was speaking to everyone in French, not a language she'd ever learned – new staff at the home even thought *she* was French. Had she escaped her batty mind and joined us? Just a batty notion of ours – but we couldn't explain it.

Everyone at the nursing home was wonderful with Ma, but I hated to see her there even though there was no alternative. She'd been such a free spirit, so funny and talented, and then horribly aware that something was going wrong when suddenly she was scared of the house she'd lived in for sixty years – it wasn't a familiar overcoat any more, but an alien place where the doors had to be locked to stop her wandering off.

When clearing out the family home, on the market now that my mother was in care and my father in a cottage in my home town of Faversham in Kent, I found a piece of paper still curled round the roller in her old typewriter. I pulled it out and read what it said:

> *Type-writer and paper, both fly away!*
> *Their services are certainly not required for today!*
> *Now it is obvious what all and sundry do suspect –*
> *I'm as dotty as a Magpie*
> *Which is what the most suspect!*
> *So tear off the paper and adjust your sight.*
> *Your eyes and silly mind are both girding for the fight!*

But it was the last thing she ever wrote. The Alzheimer's had won.

In the care home Ma developed a protective shell, and mostly she lived inside it in a parallel universe of life as it used to be: writing books and articles, travelling, looking after Pa and a succession of hairy horses. Of course it was all pretend, but while I noticed some residents deteriorating into inarticulacy, sometimes keening with a terrible, uncomprehending despair, others had defence mechanisms like hers and took refuge in the past. Occasionally they'd jump back into the present – there was one old man who sat in a chair all day, as thin as a scarecrow in empty trousers, but when I bent down to say something to my mother he was quick to lean forward and pinch my bottom, and when I turned round his eyes were sparkling with naughtiness.

As for Ma, she often thought she was at the Royal Mews where she'd researched one of her books, and she ordered the nursing home staff (in French) to see to the horses. She made it to her ninetieth birthday, and then it seemed she'd had enough. She went to bed and didn't get up again, and when I went to see her she threw her arms wide and said, *Et voilà.* That's it. Three days later she exited on a cloud of Beethoven symphonies ringing out from her stereo, and we buried her in the churchyard near my parents' old home, high on the escarpment above Romney Marsh and the sea, with a black horse in a black plumed bridle posing against a savage sunset.

But for me it was unfinished business. I still felt bad that she'd ended her days in a nursing home, squashed in with dozens of noisy people when she'd loved nothing more than to be alone in the quiet countryside. Forgetful all her life, my three sisters and I had joked for years that if she lost her marbles we'd put her in a home. *No you won't*, she had vehemently told her family, rising to the bait every time. But we had.

No great believer in God and an afterlife, I didn't think Ma would hang around now and haunt me, but I still wondered in off-key moments if somehow she really had travelled with Susie and me in spirit to Santiago, and I thought that if I did another long distance ride, something I believed she would have loved to do herself, it would be a proper ending. And it also seemed fitting that I should make this journey for charity, as Susie and

I had done last time, so I contacted the Alzheimer's Society to say I would ride to Rome to raise funds for research into this hideous disease.

The next practical step was to join The Association Via Francigena whose motto, *Omnes Viae Roman Perducunt*, roughly translated (predictably enough) as All Roads Lead to Rome. The Association's map showed the one that started in Canterbury. It travelled south-east to Reims and Besançon before passing through Switzerland to climb the Grand St Bernard Pass into Italy and then follow the Aosta valley down to Piacenza. From there it went south to Pontremoli in the Apennines before turning south-east again through Tuscany and its cities of Lucca and Siena, names redolent of warm nights and scented breezes to my romantic imagination, and on through Bolsena and Viterbo to Rome.

But at Châlons-en-Champagne, 200 miles south of Calais, I noticed the map showed a secondary route branching off in a line of red dots, and it was this one that intrigued me. It went through Troyes, with no further cities marked until Lyon which seemed to leave me free to choose which way to ride. Then it turned abruptly south-eastwards and crossed a big tranche of the Alps in an impossibly straight line over the French/Italian border to Susa, using the Mont Cenis pass, before dog-legging to re-join the primary route near Piacenza. I liked the idea of avoiding Switzerland, which sounded expensive and perhaps complicated, as a non-EU country, for someone whose companion was a horse, and I thought a ride from the top to the bottom of Burgundy would appeal to my wine-loving husband. On the way through we could visit Cluny with its gigantic abbey, now mostly demolished, which was once the most powerful seat of Christianity. The Cluniac monks, responsible for building the Way of St James in Spain to Santiago, had also colonised my own local Faversham Abbey which now lies buried under school playing fields.

And when I began to look into who in the past had travelled along the Via Francigena all the way from Canterbury along this minor route, I couldn't identify anyone in particular who'd done it, let alone by horse. It added a certain frisson followed by alarm when, poring over my maps in Maidstone Crown Court, I couldn't find an equine-friendly way to Mont Cenis. My map of the Pèlerinages Europe showed a path like an arrow from Chambéry to Mont Cenis, but in reality there wasn't one, and certainly no road. What was Leo supposed to do – glue on some Pegasus wings and fly over Mont Blanc? But I was sure it would be all right. Just a few mountains to circumnavigate – first the Jura, then the Alps, and then the Apennines.

Susie had taken one look at an Alpine map, steely with glaciers, and had turned green. A long-time sufferer from vertigo, there was no way she was going to come on this trip, and anyway she had family commitments at home in the summer. We also felt the journey we'd made together to Santiago de Compostela had been a one-off, that we could never repeat the sense of wonder at doing something we'd never done before. And although in many ways this had left Santiago in its own perfect bubble of recollection, the fact was that it hadn't always been easy for someone with no great sense of time passing (Susie) to travel alongside someone whose life was generally driven by the clock (definitely me).

So I would ride alone on what promised to be a more difficult trip – very little infrastructure for pilgrims as far as I could see, probably not much signage, and 500 miles of mountains. Meanwhile everyone continued to say I was mad, which of course made me even more determined to go.

As for the Via's history, the primary route was famous for having been walked in 990 AD by the newly consecrated Archbishop of Canterbury, Sigeric, who travelled to Rome to receive his pallium from the pope. I had no idea what a pallium was but Wikipedia provided a picture of Pope Innocent III wearing one: a narrow woollen band looped round his shoulders, with a pendant piece hanging down in front. It seemed an archbishop couldn't take up his office until he had received it.

Sigeric's journey became famous because he kept a detailed chronicle that included all his stopping places on the way home – but in fact it looked as though the Via Francigena might be a collective term for a number of paths, and I stopped worrying that I wasn't going to be an authentic pilgrim if, for example, I took a direct line from Susa to Pontremoli instead of riding east to Pavia in order to loop back again. Even doing that, this was going to be a journey of more than 1200 miles since there was no useful short cut over the Alps.

I decided I'd turn east at Mâcon, above Lyon, so I wouldn't get caught up in the industrialised areas around Grenoble, and after weeks of scouring the road map I thought I'd found a promising route round the top of Lake Anneçy that Bessie and Peter could follow as well. It went through La Clusaz, where I'd often been skiing, over the Col des Aravis and down to Beaufort, right in the middle of the Alps. I convinced myself it would be fun to travel from one ski area to another (praying there was no snow) – Les Arcs, Tignes, Val d'Isère, and then a long haul up to the Col de l'Iseran, at almost 9000 feet the second highest road pass in the Alps. And not just Leo, but seven and a half tons of elderly wooden-bodied horsebox as well – hopefully only a minor consideration.

The Via Francigena (in all its forms) had never been simply for pilgrims. The Romans built roads across the Alps, and over the following centuries, armies, traders, emigrants and smugglers used them too. The first hospice to shelter travellers was built on Mont Cenis in the ninth century and others quickly appeared on other passes, perhaps all on trails known as the Via Francigena. By the Middle Ages pilgrims were tramping them not just to

Rome but from Rome to Santiago de Compostela, while some went south from the Holy City to the coast to catch a boat across the Adriatic and so carry on to Jerusalem.

But it wasn't until the late 1900s that the Via Francigena caught the imagination of the public and the media, and in 1994 the Council of Europe made it a designated cultural route. And then it became something of a political hot potato in Italy, with successive governments promising to improve and define it, to divert it from the original Roman roads (now thunderous truck-laden, pilgrim-squashing highways) to safer countryside tracks.

I was often asked if Leo and I were going to follow in Hannibal's footsteps over the Alps. I didn't think anyone had pinpointed exactly where Hannibal had crossed; I hoped it might have been at Mont Cenis, but it wasn't – theories seemed to suggest the Col de la Traversette, further to the south. But I did find out that Hannibal's brother Hasdrubal had marched over Mont Cenis in 207 BC, which seemed good enough.

Who else had crossed that way? Emperor Henry IV for one. A fiery character who'd fallen out with the pope, he found himself excommunicated in 1076 and in danger of being deposed as emperor as well if he didn't travel to Rome to receive urgent absolution. Unfortunately this meant a trip over Mont Cenis in the middle of winter. With family, followers, guides and pack animals he struggled to the top – only to face a skating rink down the other side. The men slipped and fell and slithered all the way, dragging the ladies perched on ox-hides with them (and inventing tobogganing in the process, I dare say), but the animals weren't so lucky. Henry decided the best way to get them down the hairpin bends was to drag them as well – on their sides with their hooves tied together, which resulted in a tangle of dead and injured horses at the bottom.

Probably best if Leo and I didn't risk reaching the Alps before the end of June.

Next came the practicalities of preparation. I'd thought I had all the equipment I needed, left over from the Santiago pilgrimage, but then I decided to take a bit of camping gear this time so I didn't tie my golf-loving husband to a rendezvous with Leo and me every single evening. My father bought me a tent, and I bought Leo a portable electric fence – a collection of folding aluminium poles, tent pegs, bungee elastic, insulators, tape, battery and an earth rod, all stuffed in a bag. It looked so unnervingly fiddly that I also bought a tethering line for Leo just in case, along with a corkscrew a foot long. It was for winding into the ground to anchor your dog, and I just hoped its horse-restraining abilities wouldn't be put to the test.

I thought about the mundane problem of travelling once again with a horsebox that had no loo. We'd taken trowels on the pilgrimage to Santiago, and personally I was quite happy to set off again with mine, but this time I decided Peter deserved the luxury of a Porta Potti, a mini-throne accompanied by bottles of chemicals and oceans of instructions. My only concession to spoiling myself was a hot water bottle that was going to be stuck in a saddlebag if Leo and I went off camping on our own.

Maps. As always, the French hiking maps, the IGN Série Bleue, were a delight of precision and clarity. They were expensive, but Stanfords in London willingly sponsored half their cost as they had done for the Santiago trip. But the Italian maps were a nightmare. I had a complete set of the Association Via Francigena's impressive daily itineraries, but they didn't seem to conform to any particular scale and I had a feeling I might have trouble with them. They should help me as far as Châlons but then I'd be diverting on to the secondary route which they didn't cover, and I wouldn't be relying on them again until Pontremoli.

I was advised by some horsy adventurers that Italian military maps were the best, and eventually I tracked down some websites that supplied them. Distracted by the unexpected need to create a password to get on to the sites, I typed in the first one that came into my head, *longrider2rome*, which seemed appropriate since Susie and I were now members of the Long Riders Guild, an inspiring organisation reserved for horsemen who make a continuous journey of more than 1000 miles.

From the internet description, some of the maps looked as though they'd be very useful, but I was foxed by their prices: some were very cheap and others quite expensive. When they arrived it was obvious the cheap ones would look wonderful framed and hung on a wall – they dated back to World War II and showed mule tracks and major roads with nothing to tell you which was which. The expensive ones ranged from 1982 to 2002, but all appeared to be based on a 1960 edition, and all were covered in orange snakes of roads that looked so similar I still found it difficult to distinguish between a quiet lane in the hills and the scary Via Aurelia and Via Cassia, the arterial roads leading to Rome. So I bought every series of map I could find: Kompass cycling guides, Ecotrek, Carta dei Sentieri e dei Rifugi, Carta Turistica Stradale, Euro Map; even Michelin, obviously designed to help four wheels and not four hooves.

Peter was unsympathetic about my sleepless nights spent worrying.

'Just follow the sun south,' he said, 'and in the end you'll get there.'

What if the sun wasn't shining?

Bessie ungracefully failed her MOT and I had to go on bended knee to my father again, because 'its brakes aren't quite right'

turned into 'it needs a new master cylinder', which cost £1000 I didn't have. Pa provided it because he wholeheartedly supported the Alzheimer's cause, having watched his adored wife change from someone who supported and indulged him into a personality spiky with irritation and mistrust. In the final weeks before she went into a home, Ma said something to him that ordinarily she wouldn't have dreamed of saying: he was under her feet trying to help her prepare a meal, and she told him to fuck off out of the kitchen. For all my sisters and I knew, she might have been bottling that one up for years – we thought it was understandable, but Pa was appalled. And she would tell him she'd been out riding that morning even though her final pony, The Fiddler, had died more than two years ago. When my father pointed this out she snapped at him, and tension twanged in the air. He remembered those miserable days very clearly, and he was happy to help fund my trip as long as I promised to keep in touch and let him know how it was going.

Although I wanted to be as self-funding as possible, my earnings from criminal defence work were now only spasmodic, so I made some last minute approaches for sponsorship in kind. These resulted in P&O standing Bessie an open-ended ticket across the channel (with a confirmatory email listing the passengers as Mr Phillips, Mrs Phillips and Leo the Horse), Faversham Joinery sponsoring Bessie's expensive Green Card, and the manufacturers of Farrier's Formula sending Leo forty kilos of their vitamin-packed pellets to boost his thin-walled feet, along with a jacket, vest, sweatshirt and a five-foot banner from their Cherokee HQ for me.

Leo's digestion could be as problematical as his hooves, resulting occasionally in acute cramp in his hindquarters if he was suddenly switched from one kind of food to another, as could well happen in the months ahead. I contacted Saracen Horse Feeds for advice, and they presented him with 300 kilos of Re-Leve, a special concentrate nutritionally balanced to avoid the risk of cramp, and in return he became the Face of Saracen as well as the Face of Farrier's Formula – rather different from the famous Face of l'Oréal, for which he probably wouldn't have qualified due to his hairy ears, long nose and bad attack of spots.

I still had the now battered English saddle that I'd used on the Santiago pilgrimage, with its bum-preserving sheepskin on top. I added two layers of foam between the saddle and the sheepskin to take into account that I was now four years older and creakier, but I wondered about taking a Western saddle as well, better for carrying heavier loads like a tent and horse food because of its greater weight-bearing surface. These saddles were expensive, but Ed from Rawhide, a Western riding shop in Kent, came to the rescue. After the surprised Leo had put up with fittings involving unfamiliar breast straps and cinches round his belly, Ed lent me a new saddle that was top of the range, with instructions to soften the leather with oil, and brace the stirrups with a broom handle wedged through them to turn them out when the saddle wasn't in use so I wouldn't end up riding pigeon-toed.

I swapped Leo's conventional bridle for a hackamore, a bit-less affair that had steel shanks and a very efficient braking effect on his nose. Leo approved of this because it left his mouth empty of ironmongery, ready for some unimpeded grazing whenever he had the opportunity. And in the attic I found a beautiful leather headcollar that had belonged to The Fiddler. It seemed right to take such a typical piece of Ma's life with us, so I had its nameplate turned over and Leo's name engraved on the other side.

Things-to-do lists were all over the house. There'd been no prolonged and careful planning for this trip given that I'd made the final decision to go only at Christmas. I'd left it very late to try and raise ordinary sponsorship, but I did have time to set up a JustGiving website, and the Alzheimer's Society helped as well. Leo and I featured in promotional photographs together: me in a logo-emblazoned T-shirt trying not to make it obvious I was freezing to death in a March gale, and him posing insouciantly in his Western kit as though he'd been a cow pony all his life. I also did the rounds of the long-suffering friends who'd sponsored Susie and me last time, resulting in several cheques in advance and more by way of promises-to-pay *if* we got to Rome.

The Association Via Francigena sent a pilgrim passport, ready for stamping in the town halls of France and Italy, and I contacted DEFRA for Leo's export certificate. I knew this had to state a destination address, and luckily the only one I could dream up appealed to their sense of humour. The certificate arrived with the destination duly printed on it: c/o The Pope, The Vatican, Rome. It also showed our departure date in black and white for the first time – 3rd May 2006. It was only ten days away.

I started buying last minute necessities: a screechy whistle for emergencies; tungsten studs for Leo's shoes to prolong their life on the road; stereo jack plugs for the lorry so we could listen to some restorative music in the evenings; and Minnie, an old folding bike I bought just in case Leo was incapacitated at any time. Peter's golf clubs were piled into the lorry along with all the pots and pans from my boat, and its saloon cushions migrated into the house for my daughter Clara to sleep on at home since I'd pinched the mattress off her bed for Peter and me.

And finally, two important purchases – new badges for my squashily comfortable pilgrim hat: the crossed keys of the Vatican and the Canterbury cross, pinned either side of my St James scallop shell. I packed my proper hard riding hat as a gesture, but I didn't intend to wear it – I knew it wasn't logical, but I was superstitious about my pilgrim hat and I reckoned Leo and I would come to no harm if I wore that instead.

I'd remained a consultant with my old firm of solicitors, and the day before we left I was still in their office writing notes on the files I was handing over to Fred, the partner who'd tolerated my previous absence on pilgrimage for more than four months. He was in chatty mode, embarking on a golf monologue knowing he could still wind me up with tales, tall or otherwise, of how he was allowed to take his Labrador dog round the Royal St George's course but not his wife. But I was in too much of a panic to rise to the bait.

'Have you remembered I'm going to be away until the end of July riding to Rome? I'm leaving all my files with you.'

'What? Oh, of course, so you are. Well, good luck, old...'

'Don't call me Old Girl! I'm supposed to be fit and lithe and stuff.'

I was about to switch off my computer when Fred circulated an email to Canterbury Office Staff: 'You are all welcome to attend the Cathedral at 10 a.m. tomorrow to say goodbye to Mefo when she leaves for Rome for her extended holiday.'

Extended holiday?

2

The Teaspoon and
the Dressage Whip,
and Sundry Small Adventures

Canterbury Cathedral's massive Christ Church Gateway fills my vision, its central bronze sculpture of Jesus gleaming faintly with a patina of green. Leo and I trot through its archway – and back again, and through, cloaked in its shadow as the cameramen try to get a clear shot for the local TV news.

Déjà vu. We've been here before, four long years ago, when we set off to Santiago with Susie and Apollo. My sister's here today but she's on her feet, come to say goodbye. It all feels very strange even though the first step I take is just the same as last time, a step that's more emotional than physical: when we left in 2002 Susie persuaded Patrick the Archdeacon to bless us, and although I'm not religious I've asked for a blessing once again – for muddled reasons of superstition and fright I suppose, plus a feeling I'll need all the help I can get. And while I should be asking the Via Francigena's patrons St Peter and St Paul to keep an eye on our ride to Rome, I expect I'll still be relying on St James in times of crisis. Once a Santiago pilgrim, always one.

Patrick blesses Peter, Leo and me in the sunshine outside the cathedral. Really the one who most needs a benediction is the unpredictable Bessie, but she's taking up four spaces in a car park down the road because I couldn't work out how to get her into the cathedral grounds. Anyway, it might be stretching the archdeacon's goodwill to ask him to bless the horsebox as well as the horse.

It's time to go. They're all here again to see us off, my family, friends and work mates – but this time I'm giving Susie a farewell hug too while Leo, oblivious to the absence of Apollo, dances on the spot and snorts impatiently when I apply the hackamore's brake to his nose. Full of excitement, he bounces through the cathedral gateway again and this time there's no turning back; noisy goodbyes and shouts of encouragement follow us down the street and are swallowed up by the sound of the traffic on the city's ring road.

At least I know which way to go ... or I should do, as this is the same route towards Dover that Susie and I took last time. But I'm distracted by the effort of keeping Leo under control and take a wrong turning almost at once – not a great start, but we've left our supporters far behind so at least there's no one to watch as I do a bit of backtracking to find the right lane. And when I do, to my surprise there's a Via Francigena sign in front of my nose, and then another one: a little yellow pilgrim with a staff, walking his way to Rome.

So far so good, though while I'm musing that a solo pilgrimage might be different from riding with another human companion for all sorts of reasons, a very basic one starts bothering me urgently because I never thought about the consequences of gulping down a pint of tea before I left. This time there's no Susie to hold Leo while I look for a concealing ditch, and since he's still breathing fire I daren't tie him up in case he jumps back and breaks his headcollar. So we have an embarrassing moment in full view of the busy A2 while I try to hide behind his conspicuous white legs and hang on to his bridle at the same time.

Leo's also struck by the difference when he finds himself alone in a borrowed paddock outside Dover for the night. He hasn't noticed Apollo's absence because he hasn't seen him for some time, but he certainly registers that his friends from his field at home aren't here. Peter and I are no substitute and, worse still, we're abandoning him as well because we have to go home and load Bessie with the sacks of horse food that have been piled on the sitting-room carpet for the last month. But by the next morning he's settled down, already adjusted to a lone existence and happy to be distracted by the hay net waiting for him in the lorry. Horsy friends forgotten, he sails peacefully across the Channel in the bowels of the car deck while I'm anxiously pacing round the duty-free shop buying bottles of gin.

I don't fancy riding through a line of stationary HGVs at Calais port so it's a short horsebox journey to tonight's gîte outside the town, but after today Leo and I won't be cadging any lifts in Bessie even if it pours with rain from here to Rome. And I'm determined to ride right into St Peter's Square when (or possibly if) we get there – a severely scary thought, but for now there are more immediate things to worry about, like the state of the gîte's horse accommodation. It's a field full of poisonous yellow ragwort plants, but fortunately Leo usually senses what's good for him and what is not; anyway, I daren't say anything because our hostess has evicted her own horses so she can cater for mine, and she's also invited Peter and me to supper with her family. We've just spent two hours scrubbing every mucky trace of Leo out of Bessie and redistributing our belongings round the horse section, so I'm thankful I don't have to ferret about for the baked beans.

Full of wine and chicken pie, we pile into our bed in the lorry's Luton head, more comfortable and cosy than any hotel room. It's pure nostalgia for me and I'm flooded with rose-tinted memories of the Santiago pilgrimage, though when I look at

19

Peter I can see his expression has more resignation than nostalgia about it: here we go again, more months of spitting toothpaste out of the groom's door every evening.

Leo survives the night, the ragwort untouched, and on a grey morning we set off down long tracks and country lanes with me absentmindedly chatting away to an invisible Susie. There's a chance to talk to a real person when an old man at the roadside waves me down, but all he has are two short questions:

'Is it true the English don't eat their horses?'

'That's right. They don't.'

'Won't you eat yours when he dies?'

'Certainly not. He's my friend.'

But I have reason to curse my friend over the next twenty miles, and it doesn't take long for a monologue aimed at Susie to turn into a dialogue with Leo, limited to one topic:

'Will you *please* walk on the right hand side of the road!'

'No I won't. I'm English, I always keep to the left.'

'Will you *sodding* well walk on the right, or we'll get run over.'

'No! I'll gallop sideways up the middle if you wind me up!'

Fancifully anthropomorphic as it may seem, it isn't difficult to converse with horses – they're expressive, emotional creatures, and you can understand what they're saying even without words. In Leo's case, after seven years together we know each other very well and like all good friends we're sometimes prone to arguments, though I could do without one today – I'm worn out and still tetchy by the time we arrive at the second of the three horsy lodgings I managed to arrange in advance. But Leo wanders out contentedly into a field of proper grass, our disagreement forgotten, and when the sun comes out Peter and I relax in the recliner chairs I thought we ought to bring this time so yes, this is the life – bangers and mash before the sausages go off, a dose of *The Best of Rod Stewart*, and a quiet dusk when I swap my chair for a recline against my husband's chest.

In the morning the gîte's owner rides with me down the road towards Lumbres on a lively mare. The flirtatious Leo is entranced with this new lady in his life, but he has a job to keep up with her – she goes like the clappers, and by the time they leave us to return home he's starting to go lame. The tungsten studs in his shoes certainly stop them wearing down, but they're very unforgiving to his hooves and legs when we're on tarmac. A long-forgotten childhood ditty surfaces in my brain:

> It ain't the 'untin' on the 'ill that 'urts the 'orses' 'ooves,
> It's the 'ammer 'ammer 'ammer on the 'ard 'igh road.

So no more of that, then, and I turn off on to the nearest track.

There's no trace of sunshine today, and when a haze of drizzle turns to a deluge the map starts falling soggily to bits, making it almost impossible to decipher, although according to our compass direction it looks as though we must be almost back on the road. I can hear an odd pinging noise nearby – what on earth's that? It's a ... for God's sake, Leo, we're on a driving range. His interested gaze follows the arc of a golf ball whistling past his ears, and when I tie him up to what looks like a sodden shack so I can go and ask someone exactly where we are, I'm told this is St Omer Golf Club and we shouldn't really be here. Peter turns out to be waiting a mile away in a supermarket car park.

Our final pre-booked night is at a farm on the other side of Lumbres, but when we get there all is not what it seems. Monsieur's gîte is cavernously empty, mournful toys discarded under the beds. I apologise for arriving so early in the season when the gîte's still closed, but Monsieur says it won't be opening again, not ever, though we can use its loos and basins and Leo's welcome to graze in his big field, which I notice is full of sprayed buttercups dying in the grass.

Monsieur has two Barb Arab stallions stabled in his yard, one with a terrible dent in his nose bone from the days when a previous owner kept him strapped in a headcollar that was too tight. The other is sixteen years old and Monsieur used to ride him eighty kilometres at a time in endurance competitions, but now he has retired. He is *l'ami de mon coeur*, says Monsieur – the friend of my heart. I like that. I tell Peter that Leo is *l'ami de mon coeur* and he looks put out. 'I thought I was,' he says. 'Well, you're *l'amour de ma vie*, the love of my life. I expect you'll be the friend of my heart when we're eighty-five-ish, too old for anything more energetic than a doddle round the garden.'

By early evening a stream of cars is pouring into the farmyard. We wonder if Monsieur's having a party, but the sign hanging over the gate should have given us a clue – it says *Speed'zza*, and we realise he's swapped his gîte business for take-away pizzas. The customers wait patiently for boxes bulging with dough and cream and cheese while the stallions entertain them by leaning over their stable doors to lunge at each other with bared teeth. And for us, Monsieur's new line of work proves to be a bonus – I still don't need to look for the baked beans because we can gorge ourselves to obesity on Pizza Savoyarde.

The rain dumps down on Bessie's roof all night, and I tell myself Leo needs a rest after going lame on the hard road yesterday. He hasn't keeled over from buttercup poisoning yet so he'll probably survive another day in his field. For Peter and me, life's already pared down to a pilgrimage microcosm: Major Event of the Day concerns the adventures of the teaspoon and the dressage whip. Having emptied a spoon down the yard drain with the washing-up water, we manage to make it leap out again when tempted by the magnet buried in the handle of my dressage whip (there for the proper purpose of storing it hugged to a metal saddle rack). Repetitive sessions of the jumping teaspoon provide fascinating entertainment for most of the afternoon, with interruptions from the fluffy farm cat who keeps trying to creep past me into Bessie and get in our bed. Eventually I realise why she's so insistent – her swollen belly's rippling with imminent kittens, just what Peter would like to find under his pillow. None of my efforts at kindly discouragement has any effect, but in the end she gives herself a fright by taking a short cut over the gas stove; a horrible smell of burnt fur fills the lorry, followed by departure of scalded cat, and then I have no further distractions to prevent me from doing what I've been avoiding all day, which is route planning.

The problem is that I can't reconcile the Via Francigena map with the IGN one. Topofrancigena stresses that its data is only indicative, and indeed it has some little grey roads that tail off artistically into nothing, which obviously I'm not supposed to follow. Instead there's a choice between the continuous red line of the historic route (main road, not good with a horse), the red dots of the recommended route (minor road, better, might have a grass verge) and the green stars of the excursion route (inviting but convoluted mixture of lane and track, difficult to work out what's where). When I compare it with the brittle remains of yesterday's IGN map, my eyes start revolving – I have to turn one of them upside down because Topo progresses from the bottom to the top, and IGN from the top to the bottom.

To be fair, I don't suppose the Association Via Francigena had horse riders in mind when designing its individual maps with day-sized chunks of travel set out on each, and it looks as though my best bet will be to ride parallel to the dots or stars, sometimes using the IGN guides to cut across country on footpaths and cart tracks. Some of the Association's symbols aren't likely to assist Leo, much as he would appreciate bed and breakfast in the middle of a town, but some are definitely helpful: a blue cow means a farm, hopefully with pasture, and three crosses in a square indicate a cemetery. The importance of this to an equine pilgrim is the cold water tap for the flowers – or a drink for a thirsty horse travelling with his collapsible bucket. I hope I never need a small cross (hospital) or blue steam train (railway station), but on the other hand Peter might appreciate the tall flag in a hole that marks a golf course.

So far I haven't met another pilgrim nor seen a single Via Francigena sign since leaving Canterbury, even though I've tried to stay in touch with the official route. I was expecting this expedition to be a lot trickier than the Way of St James, which has numerous yellow arrows to point you in the right direction, but I didn't expect there to be no fellow pilgrims. Where are they all? Maybe it's too early in the year, too unappealing; I can empathise with that, as we look through Bessie's window at the rain coursing down silently all day.

But then there's a clear dawn, not a cloud fluffing across the cold sky, and the path to Leo's field is studded with snails copulating in heaps of passionate froth. Thirty minutes later it's tipping down and I notice the cat has tucked herself up in the spare cushions in the back of the lorry, but I can't be bothered to check if she's given birth before I get back into bed.

Eleven o'clock and it's still pouring, so I might as well get going. I climb on Leo shrouded in my son Oliver's oversized mac, Peter's oversized waterproof trousers and my own wellies. Although it remains a miserable dank day of driving rain, Leo is cheerful and adventurous, pleased to be on his way and not lame at all as long as we don't trot on the tarmac.

At least it's raining in England too, as my secretary tells me when she phones with a question about a case file, and on balance I'd rather be here than there even though the wind's howling across the naked hectares of farmland we're crossing and there's blood from a cut finger adding rusty contours to the map. I can't see exactly where we are as a result of those and we end up at the bottom of a hill face to face with a mile of barbed wire fencing and no gate.

But it turns out not to be a problem because St James puts in the first of many appearances, today disguised as a small farmer in a boiler suit who takes the fence apart to let us through. Arguably, I suppose, he's really just another local who might like a perfunctory chat:

'Is it true the English hate the French really?'

'Er...'

'Or is it just made up by the English newspapers?'

'Yes! It's a story, that's all.'

He uproots a support post, creates a horse-sized gap and waves us through with a beatific smile.

We've run out of pre-arranged accommodation, and when I arrive in Fléchinelle there's nowhere to stay and no one about except Peter and Bessie who've been waiting so long they've taken root. I have two short questions for my husband:

'Have you tried to find somewhere for us?'

'No.'

'Why not?'

'You'll have better luck with a horse.'

I shoot him a gimlet look but I suppose he's right, and after a weary clop up the road and back again a kind Monsieur takes pity on us and says I can put up our electric fence in the grounds of a house he's building. Leo checks anxiously that the food-bearing Bessie is parked on the road next to his personal building site, and I check firstly that the farm cat is not still on board and secondly that there's somewhere suitable for me and my trowel, far from the public eye. Well, I think I've found a place, but my trip up the village slag heap in the morning is swiftly truncated when I discover there's something like a motorway up it as well.

Now Leo and I are trudging over a bleak landscape of dead mining villages and more slag heaps coated in scrub; there are no little shops, no bars, no *mairies* with busy town clerks, nothing. After several hours we stop disconsolately for lunch, and our conversation afterwards leaves me filled with guilt. Leo's snuffling at my hands.

'Where's my Mars Bar?'

'Nowhere! What Mars Bar?'

'You've eaten one! I can smell chocolate! Where's mine?'

He's rummaging in my pockets.

'I'm sorry, you're right, I did have one and I didn't leave you any ... you were eating grass and I thought you wouldn't notice.'

I'd better not do that again.

In the cheerless afternoon I skirt round a copse reeking of putrefaction, as though there's a decomposing body in there somewhere. And for all I know that might once have been the case – we've nearly reached the battlefields of World War I, and on a lonely track I come across an unexpected shrine: to a teenage sentinel, shot down by a sniper.

It's the first of many.

3

On the Pathways of War

Lest we forget.

There's no danger of that here – cemeteries dot the landscape, village churchyards are crammed with slaughtered soldiers, and each hamlet has its own monument carved with the names of its dead from the two World Wars: *morts pour la France.*

At Ourton, an unassuming village that once was the base of Canada's Machine Gun Brigades, we're allowed to camp right next to the cemetery with its tap. With my holy sister Susie in mind I check the church, but it's locked. Apparently the bell rings the angelus at 6.30 a.m. to wake up the workers (Peter's going to love that), at midday to summon them for lunch, and at 7 p.m. to send them home for dinner; practicality before religion, it would seem.

Our arrival provides entertainment for the local children, Bessie because in a moment's inattention I set fire to a cushion, resulting in black smoke pouring out of her windows, and Leo due to his novelty spotted coat and good-natured tolerance of dozens of tiny hands patting him on the knees. The children shouldn't be in his improvised field with him at all, but they're impervious to electric shocks and hooves like breeze blocks. Peter and I settle down in the scorched lorry for a supper of tinned Kit-E-Kat stew (at any rate, that's what it looks like)

and another evening's diet of Rod Stewart, humming along
with the lyrics.

'How can you say lorry living isn't the best?'

Peter says nothing, but in the steamed-up mirror above the
kettle he traces a heart with an arrow through it and our initials
at each end. So it can't all be bad.

The angelus rings in a sunny day and a beaming Madame
with a posy of lily-of-the-valley for us; she says the flowers bring
good luck, and asks me to say a prayer for her in Rome. Luckily
I'm saved from a complicated conversation about my hazy
religious beliefs because her attention shifts from what I might
be saying to what I'm doing, which is clearing up the horse shit,
les crottes, using rubber gloves and a bucket. This is a word Susie
and I learned early on during our journey to Santiago and we
jokily anglicised it to crots. The word was adopted by pilgrims
we met of all nationalities, who would tell us they didn't need
to look for the yellow arrows pointing toward Santiago – they
simply followed the crots.

This morning, cheerful Madame is swiftly diverted from
religion to practicality, and she rushes off to fetch her own bucket
so she can pile every smelly crot into it for her garden.

Today's countryside is no more picturesque than
yesterday's; thin paths crisscross the hills with their slag
heap silhouettes, and ahead of us lie Arras and the lines of
the Western Front nearly a century ago. The Via Francigena
goes straight through a town but I see no point in queueing
with the rush hour traffic, so we skirt round it on a lane that
should cross the Route Nationale at the village of Hermaville,
according to the map. But it doesn't – it ends in a cul-de-sac
and when I divert to a busy main road intersection to pick up
our route again the other side, we find ourselves in the middle
of the fire station.

'Leo, this can't be right.'

But it is. We squeeze past the fire engine and the inspection pit under the gaze of Mademoiselle Fire Officer, who beckons us through.

'*Cheval!*' she shouts nonchalantly over her shoulder, and eight muscular firemen leap up from their mattresses where they were sound asleep in the sunshine, all stripped to the waist and all lobster-coloured with sunburn or embarrassment. Mademoiselle's expression says triumphantly that *she* wasn't caught snoozing on duty, and it seems best to smile politely at them all and urge Leo into a quick canter, hard road or no hard road, so we can make a tactful exit.

Hermaville has no gîtes, no campsites, no horsy lodgings and no discernible communal land nor cemetery. There's a farm, but horrified Madame la Fermière says only chickens are allowed here. She tells me to ask the mayor's father-in-law for advice since the mayor himself is unavailable – on Wednesdays the *mairie* is shut, and needless to say today is Wednesday. I'm still hunting down his in-laws when Peter phones to say that Madame's husband is a lot more hospitable than his wife and we can stay there after all – Leo in a field with 3000 chickens, and the rest of us in an open barn.

My evening is spent on the phone tracking down both an equestrian centre and a gîte near Arras so Peter and I can take a day off soon to visit a nearby Commonwealth cemetery, where his Great-Uncle Reggie is buried. Unfortunately the gîte is in one village and the horse centre is in another but possibly Saints Paul, Peter, James and sister Susie combined are all looking after us, because by chance Madame Equestrian Centre owns a field down the road from the gîte I've pinpointed in Agny, and Leo's welcome to camp in it.

Somehow Battlefield and Commonwealth Cemetery Tours got missed out of my education, but I'm about to make up for it now. When we get to Agny, Leo's paddock turns out to be next to a military cemetery designed by Sir Edwin Lutyens, and the perimeter fence has gaps that a horse could stride through and then cause havoc among the pristine graves. There are more than 400 here including 118 with unidentified bodies, their headstones inscribed *To a soldier of the Great War, known unto God*, and I'm compelled to walk up and down every row, reading them all with a growing sense of desolation at the waste of life. By the time I've finished, Leo is already eyeing up the fence, his practical mind registering that the grass is much greener on the other side among the graves, and there's no more room for melancholy as I run up and down with the electric tape, blocking off the holes.

The staff at the Commonwealth War Commissions Bureau at Beaurains don't turn a hair when Peter and I arrive in an elderly horsebox to enquire about the grave of Bertram Reginald Baker, 2nd Lieutenant, 17th Battalion The Royal Fusiliers 2nd Division, killed in action south of Béthune on 3rd May 1916. Their computer instantly confirms his details and his burial site at the Tranchée de Meknes Cemetery near Aix-Noulette, so called by the French troops in honour of the expeditionary corps sent to Mequinez (Morocco), and used by the British from the beginning of 1916. Great-Uncle Reggie's commemorative medal, scroll, and letter from King George V inscribed *I join with my grateful people in sending you this memorial of a brave life given for others in the Great War* were sent to his relatives after his death; the scroll and letter have long since vanished but Peter has the medal at home, one of more than a million christened the Dead Man's Penny by the troops and sent to the families of soldiers killed in the war. The Penny is made of heavy gunmetal, more than four inches across; Britannia and the British Lion are carved on it together with Reggie's full name and the words *He died for freedom and honour*, and at the bottom there's a smaller carving – another lion, this one crunching on the German Imperial eagle.

There's another poignant reminder of him that still exists: a description of the way he died, set out in a letter to his father from his commanding officer. It says: 'I cannot tell you how deeply I regret the death of your son, who was killed by a German rifle grenade at 9.40 this morning. This grenade had stuck in the side of the trench and failed to explode, and your son considering its position constituted a menace to the safety of his men tried to remove it, and it exploded as he was doing so killing him instantly. Your son was an ideal officer, gallant, cheerful and very keen on his work. He was immensely popular with all the officers in the battalion and we all mourn his loss more than I can say...'

In careless sunshine we rumble off to Aix-Noulette where the main cemetery contains English, French and Canadian soldiers. Among the Canadians buried in it are two who were shot at dawn for desertion in 1917; it seems impossible now to justify such a punishment for young men perhaps too terrified and battered by war to do anything but run away blindly with their fear, but in the unimaginable horror of that war, I have to accept that mercy might have been the path to mass desertion and defeat.

Bessie lurches down the half mile of rough track to the Tranchée de Meknes graveyard. Here is literally a corner of a foreign field that is forever England – a tiny square in the middle of rolling hectares where the farmer's chugging past on his tractor, spraying the young corn. Once there must have been trenches around here, and now God knows how many fragments of young men have been ploughed into the soil. A wall enfolds the immaculate little cemetery, and we find 2nd Lieutenant Baker's grave among the rows where some of the headstones are grouped in fours and sevens, as though the explosions that killed the soldiers blew them into so many bits you couldn't tell who was who. Peter leaves a poppy, and there are flowers here on other graves too; visited, mourned and nurtured still. We read the epitaphs: *At the going down of the sun ... we will remember them*, and *He laid down his life for his country*; nothing politically incorrect, no *What passing bells for these who die as cattle?* One inscription hints at the agony: *In memory of our son, our beloved only child.*

I climb on the wall, look across the ranks of headstones shining in the sunlight, and feel completely choked.

We move on to the Canadian National Memorial site at Vimy Ridge, where on 9th April 1917 the Canadian Corps of the British Army attacked the massive German defensive position here, forcing it off the crest of the Ridge within hours. By 12th April the whole Ridge had been taken, a victory that was a turning point in World War I – but at a heavy price; more than 3500 Canadian soldiers were slaughtered and another 7000 wounded. The Memorial site was opened in 1936, a haunting reminder of the 11,285 Canadians killed in France whose bodies were never found or never identified.

Rows of coaches are disgorging tourists eager to walk round the trenches and tunnel systems that have been preserved. Peter and I stick to the footpaths of the park itself, with its avenues of fir trees planted to either side; the shell craters and trenches here are gently disguised now by grass, but the red danger signs warn you not to stray. During the war the tunnels were filled with mines planted by both sides and then exploded, but the legions of those that didn't detonate are still volatile enough to catapult you to oblivion.

In the distance we can see two huge pillars of Dalmatian stone, symbols of Canada and France, piercing today's calm sky – but all through the night torrential rain and hail bombard us at nearby Agny, and the crump and crash of thunder crack open a memory of hell.

'I'm ready to go. Ready-ready-ready.'

'Leo, will you *stop that!* Now!'

He's pawing at the gravel in the gîte courtyard, grinding down his front shoes, completely re-energised by his day's rest. We fly out of Agny but half an hour later we're almost back there again – the IGN map leads me to tracks that don't exist any more, and now I come to check it properly, the TGV line we've crossed isn't marked either. What date is this map? 1977, wonderful. If I try riding by compass direction instead, we might manage not to go round in circles. This works better, and we make it from Arras to Bapaume with frequent pauses to unclog Leo's feet with the hoof pick – the soil round here is solid clay with stones from the railway tracks embedded in it, and he's tottering, 'ow, ow! there's another one stuck to my sole, look, I'm holding up my hoof, can't you see?'

'For God's sake, Leo, you're such a wooss. You'd have been a hopeless war horse.'

But to be fair, he's coping well with the pace and effort of our pilgrim days. Our routine is to travel for three hours without a break, stop briefly for lunch and then carry on for another two hours or more. That seems to dispose of fifteen to twenty miles a day; we're progressing quite quickly, but I have to be careful that in my driven way I don't forget to stop to get mayoral stamps for my pilgrim passport. That's if I can find any *mairies* in these little villages where often the only substantial buildings are the churches.

We leave the main roads behind as we approach the Somme, and now the view is filled with potato furrows streaming away to the foggy skyline. I pause on a little humpbacked railway bridge – perhaps I'll take a photo of the line, cold and straight as far as the eye can see. Oh *Jesus* perhaps I won't – that hissing – God what an idiot, stand still Leo, we haven't got time to get off the bridge ... the TGV whistles underneath at 200 m.p.h. at least, but my horse gazes vaguely after the departing rocket and doesn't move a muscle, while in my case my teeth have nearly chattered themselves out of my mouth.

When the map indicates a short cut through the middle of a forest, unfortunately I don't notice there's a vital word missing from its written description – *domaniale*. It turns out this isn't public woodland, and before long there are signs nailed to trees telling me this is *propriété privée*. We carry on anyway, although the short cut takes a long time to navigate – huge machinery has created ruts and quagmires, and the path is buried under brutally felled trees. Leo tiptoes carefully over the tops of the trunks, and while I'm concentrating on helping him keep his balance he transports me straight into a tidy garden, something I certainly wasn't expecting to see, which has a notice outside saying *Garde Forestier*. There's a proper Range Rover parked by the house but the Ranger himself must be asleep is all I can say, since the presence of a bright white horse in his flowerbeds goes unremarked.

So it's a guilty scramble out through nettles to reach a respectable road, and in the late afternoon we meet up with Peter and Bessie, hoping to find a stopping place in the hamlet of Bussu. But it's just another village with not much in it, so I suppose I'll have to carry on to Cartigny, the other side of a distant swamp, which looks bigger, but … well, maybe I'll just flag down this car and ask.

'Madame, excuse me, do you know if there's a horse riding centre at Cartigny?'

'There's one here in Bussu, Madame, and you're standing right beside it. I'm the Secretary. Are you looking for somewhere to stay?'

Leo and I have both missed the obvious – the line of stabling, the gently steaming muck heap – but in his paddock beside the manège he suddenly realises there are other horses all around. He leaps into action, galloping to and fro, sweating till his spots turn blue, leaving a trail of crots I'll have to clear up in the morning and definitely not winding down after a long day.

Equestrian centres are a relatively easy option for Peter and me, a rest from the usual daily worry of Where To Put The Horse, but they're a bit too stimulating for Leo who sometimes still misses his friends from home. On balance, though, it's worth it for the warm welcome we always receive, and Bussu's no exception – octogenarian Monsieur takes me to see his elegant Selle Français mare, 24 years old (too old for him to ride her any more, he says, drawing no inferences from his own age), and then the centre's owner arrives with his basset hound, a cockerel, two bantams and some light reading for me in French: *PERONNE 1535 Le Siège Héroïque*. I've nearly finished *The Da Vinci Code*, so that should keep me occupied for a week or twelve. He directs a lengthy monologue at Peter concerning the history of the village, insisting he must visit the World War I Museum in Péronne tomorrow while Leo and I are spending the day hoofing it towards Laon via the swamp.

Bussu in the evening is a noisy place where every household's Barkalot goes racing round its garden, and even when they're called indoors and all the shutters are closed against the night there's no silent, seamless transition into sleep for Peter and me. The church clock bongs out every hour and a disorientated cuckoo shouts 'Cook! Cook!' imperiously in the darkness; the last straw is when Leo starts neighing at dawn for his stabled pony friends, at which point I give up, get up and get going.

It's 15th May, his thirteenth birthday, and still bursting with excitement he speeds through the swamp and then across country on horse-friendly tracks, until they end on a lane with another World War I cemetery stretched alongside it. I stop to look at the headstones and find an English name with a carving above it that shifts my train of thought from World War I to World War II.

The carving is instantly familiar: it's the spoked wheel of a gun carriage, the crest of the Royal Artillery, and a reminder for me of my father's regiment. When he came home on leave in 1945 he gave my mother a Gunner brooch with diamonds set in its tiny gold wheel, and she wore it every day until she was so incapacitated by dementia that she was likely to lose it. Then she was persuaded to lend it to me, and now I wear it on Crown Court days to pin down my collar.

My father's war years were spent in Italy, Greece and the Middle East, and at home he has a silver cup to commemorate his spell in Iraq; it celebrates a victory over the home side at the Inter Troop Football League match at Kirkuk in 1943, a result he still treasures. As for Ma, for most of those years she stayed on in that same vulnerable house overlooking Romney Marsh and the English Channel, close to the front line airfield at Lympne. During the clear-out of the family home I came across her account of that time, when private cars were banned in this military restricted area and she relied on her pony Smith for transport. She wrote of her shopping trips to the nearby town of Hythe, rucksack on her back:

It was a tricky moment when, not for the first time, I was returning home after curfew and a sentry jumped from a hedge to challenge us. As Smith whirled round and galloped off I was shouting 'Don't shoot! I'll come back!' And so we duly did, only to be arrested and marched off to the nearest Army H.Q where an embarrassed Commanding Officer failed to find regulations for dealing with a recalcitrant female on a horse.

When the curfew wasn't in operation she rode to Hythe in the evenings to go to the cinema, leaving Smith at local stables. It was always late when they left to come home:

Then we were off through the darkened streets of the town, taken at speed to avoid any attentions of the ruder soldiery, and up the track to the lane along the crest of the escarpment. There would be no sound but the drumming of Smith's hooves, nothing between us and the sea but the dark mass of the Marsh below the hills, no company but the arms of the searchlights ceaselessly combing the sky. Once I saw an aircraft caught in those beams. Like a dazzled moth it failed to escape, then plunged, engine screaming, down into the sea where moonlight illuminated the great spurt of water that marked its grave...

She was there all through Dunkirk, all through the Battle of Britain and all through the onslaught of the doodlebugs, the unmanned V1 bombers fired by the Germans at twenty minute intervals to be greeted by the roar of the British ack-ack guns.

Her descriptions were raw and vivid, and at the end of her account she wrote:

> *For me World War II is like an alien volume amongst a collection of similar books. It is a tome bearing no relation to the others, but if removed it would leave a big gap on the bookshelf of my life.*

4

Men Go First, to Show the Ladies the Way

I'd rather do anything than go to the dentist – to me, crossing the Alps on a horse is far less frightening. But I'll have to go – there's a crater in one of my teeth left by a filling that erupted into my Mars Bar. Not that we're anywhere near a dentist-inhabited town at the moment, or a town at all; today's track fizzles out on the D32, and when a steam roller follows Leo and me down some strangely smoking tarmac it occurs to me the road might be closed for resurfacing. The driver's carefully ironing out the hoof prints.

While Peter's still in Péronne visiting the museum, I come across a farm at Roupy which is smack on the green stars/red spots recommended-and-excursion route of the Topofrancigena map. Kind Monsieur and his mother say we can stay here, even though Leo tactlessly drops a crot in their tidy courtyard, and when Peter arrives he's delighted to find he can tune in to Radio 4 and listen to the Test Match. But for me there's no competition between the cricket commentary and an offer of a hot shower in Monsieur's house, a lot better than our usual scrub in the washing up bowl with water from the kettle. Life's *really* good now, except for the hole in my tooth.

But a day or so later there's a chance to get it fixed thanks to an unscheduled visit to the dreary town of La Fère. Leo and I have already spent long hours on tracks and clanging metal bridges over the St Quentin canal when Peter phones to say he's found a campsite at La Fère, wisely omitting to add that getting there will add another five miles to the twenty we've already covered. Eventually we slog through the town just as the school day is finishing and the streets are full of cars, buses and small boys neighing in our direction, and Leo's pitch at the site is a little piece of land bristling with toxic horsetail plants. But he's much too sensible to eat them, and at least this busy town has a dentist.

Given that Madame Campsite's considerable powers of persuasion have convinced the mayor that an equine guest is acceptable, she has no trouble in arranging an appointment for me with her own dentist at nil notice. As I quake into his surgery I notice he's about sixteen years old. And is this his surgery, or is it his office? 'Madame, it's both,' he says as I'm trembling flat on my back in his tilting chair. He swings a computer screen in front of me while dextrously inserting a scaffolding tower into my mouth, and suddenly the Alps are parading before my eyes. Except they're not mountains, they're my teeth, and that shrouding of snow on every peak represents each of my numerous fillings, the result of a misspent childhood of lemon sherbet addiction. I'm trying to choke out that I'd like an injection, but you can't form consonants when your mouth's jammed open, and anyway it's all over in seconds – he drills, fills, and hands me a bill for 51 euros, to be paid now, Madame, you are able to reclaim it from your English health service. Well, I don't think I'll bother – I'd have paid more than that to the NHS in the first place, so thank you, Monsieur Child Dentist, it didn't hurt at all.

La Fère has a shop selling local hiking maps from which I can see I'm still on the Via Francigena and close to its route through the St Gobain Forest. I set off in that direction after a frenzied mosquito-slapping night which has left Peter's and my blood from the exploding bugs smeared over Bessie's white planks, our first experience of the torture of a warm night in a lorry with gappy seams.

St Gobain is the largest forest I've ever ridden in, and it's probably not a good idea to try following any tracks; the Via Francigena is marked in red dots down the D55 road through the middle and I decide that authenticity is more attractive than adventure today. The map highlights the little church at St Nicolas, but when we get there it's locked. The village *mairie* is also locked because it's only open between 10.30 and midday on a Wednesday, and since today is Thursday this means I can't get my pilgrim passport stamped. And the fourteenth-century abbey further on consists of two pillars and a visiting cow. So come on, Leo, this is getting boring. Let's try a track after all.

'OK, yes, yes! Let's go, let's gallop…'

And he thunders off knowing I haven't had time to shorten the reins, zipping along the nearest path until the track sprouts other little tentacle trails, when I manage to slow him down. By now we could be anywhere, but the forest is too magical for worrying, full of light and dappled shade from the silky leaves of springtime. We shuffle through the layers of dead leaves from winters past, and from the top of an escarpment I can see the road below us winding away to Cessières at the edge of the woodland. Leo sits back on his hocks to toboggan down the hairpin tracks to the prettiest village I've seen so far, and here's another one, little Laniscourt, where we could stay if we could find someone to hover over, looking pathetic. Muddy horse and splattered rider seek accommodation…

But it's no good. Every door and gate is shut, and the notice on this *mairie* says it's only open between 5.30 and 7.00 p.m. on a Friday, so today there's no one to ask.

The Via Francigena is bending eastwards now into Laon, 160 miles from our starting point in Canterbury if we'd trotted straight down the motorway – though we've probably covered closer to 200 given the squiggly tracks we've followed so far. And since there's hardly likely to be a horse paddock in the middle of the city, I carry on riding through the woods, hoping to re-join the Via to the south of Laon tomorrow.

'What's that, Leo?'

I pull him up in surprise, for suddenly there's a dark shadow on this sunny day – another cemetery, but this one is different. Underneath the sombre oaks, lines of plain black crosses are stretching back into the forest. There are no flowers, no elaborate inscriptions, nothing but grass and unadorned symmetry, row upon row. German soldiers lie buried here, perhaps killed when the French army seized St Gobain back from enemy hands in 1918, a vital move because the trees held a secret: the Paris Gun, the largest piece of artillery used during World War I.

There were several of these super-cannons operating from here with a range of more than seventy miles, lobbing 100-kilo shells at the capital. The first was fired in March 1918 and caused absolute terror because the Parisians thought they were being bombed by a new kind of zeppelin; the shell had dropped out of the sky without warning, the explosion as it detonated at faraway St Gobain masked by the sound of smaller weapons being fired at the same time. Despite its enormous size, or perhaps because of it, relatively few people were killed because it was impossible to aim properly – but it was a brilliant propaganda weapon. Between March and August 1918 about

360 shells were fired, but as the Allies advanced the guns were either destroyed or hauled back to Germany, and no trace of them was ever found.

There's an emplacement site still in existence somewhere around here, but I'm not going to take Leo on a search for it because apparently you can't see it until you fall into it. Instead I settle for a photograph of the silent cemetery, taken from Leo's back with his cheerful spotted ears in the foreground, and then we move away from this sad place.

At Clacy-et-Thierret the *mairie*'s actually open and the lady mayor is sitting at her desk, just as she should be. She needs no persuasion when I ask if there's anywhere here we could stay; her husband's a fellow *randonneur*, a long distance rider with two horses of his own. She jumps on her bike and takes me to the churchyard with its water tap, next to communal land big enough for both Bessie and Leo. Monsieur Randonneur appears within minutes, full of rapid-fire conversation about his horses, the cockerel on the church's weathervane which is something to do with Napoleon, my work in defence of criminals (*Ah! Les crapules!* Well, yes...) and all kinds of roundabout routes he could work out for me on my maps, much better than the roads and tracks I've painstakingly picked out and highlighted for the next week. I'm not going to tell him I think mine are better than his, though, because he's handing over a bottle of 1999 St Emilion.

'Thank you, Monsieur, we shall enjoy it very much.'

'*C'est la France!*'

And he cycles off.

Tonight's storm arrives with a mattress-juddering crack of thunder right overhead. Peter stirs, wondering vaguely if his lucky night has also arrived as he registers that I'm wide awake, but I'm preoccupied with peering out of Bessie's window to see if Leo's been struck dead. He hasn't – he's standing patiently with his back to the hail and the wind, lit up in a giant celestial flash photograph, and by morning the only trace of the storm's passing is the wet grass. Monsieur Randonneur appears promptly at 9 o'clock with his horse Diego, a charming Andalusian who sniffs Leo's nostrils ecstatically, instant best friends. Leo's in show-off mode, prancing down the road in front of him, but Monsieur's having none of it – men go first, to show the ladies the way. However, he reckons without his horse: Diego doesn't think that's right at all, and he flatly refuses to pass us. An uncontrollable giggle is pulling at my face as the Gallic swearing reaches full volume behind me, and then Monsieur consoles himself by shouting directions instead, followed by non-stop chat and companionable singing.

We cut across country. Laon Cathedral is dramatically silhouetted on a hill just a mile away but there's no time to go and take a look, so I put it on a growing list of places I'll have to come back and visit one day by car.

This GR track is getting very narrow. Very faint, too ... and suddenly almost perpendicular as we ride into the woods.

'Monsieur, it's blocked at the top, see? Where we come out into the field? There's been a landslip, it's all loose earth on the path ... Jesus, it's *moving*...'

And it is, thanks to the tipper truck tipping an avalanche of rocks and mud at us as we speak.

'*Merde! Tenez-moi mon cheval!*'

He leaps manfully off Diego, throwing me the reins, and scrambles over the moving mass to go and remonstrate with the truck driver. The poor man has no idea he's damming an equine highway and there's not much he can do about it now, so we're going to have to slog through the wobbly morass on foot, dragging the horses behind us. Now I fervently wish Monsieur Randonneur could persuade his horse to go first so they can't witness my feeble efforts to stride up the gluey incline without having a heart attack mid-mud, but Diego's rooted to the spot. It's Leo who saves my face – he decides to gallop up, dragging me with him. My arm does its best to detach itself as I cling grimly to a stirrup leather, but all Monsieur can see from behind are my feet, skimming lightly and athletically over the top of the mound.

We're out on the road again, and our companions turn regretfully for home. Leo grumpily drags his feet in the other direction, through Martigny-Courpierre, where the war-ravaged church has been replaced by an attractively angular art deco one, and on to Neuville-sur-Ailette where there's a campsite marked on my map.

Except it's gone. Had I bothered to ask Monsieur's advice about the area he would no doubt have told me there's a massive Center Parcs complex under construction here, and saved us the trouble of fighting our way through the lorries across a main road bridge. The wind's funnelling down the lake below us, whipping it into peaks and crests and long streaks of foam, hardly a good advertisement for all those pedalo and water ski enthusiasts who'll be holidaying here in a year or so. But on my flailing map I can make out the thread of the GR12, so we disappear along a blissfully quiet track lined with Early Purple orchids, scattering an assortment of deer, partridges and hares en route to the next village.

The notice board says this *mairie* is only open on a Thursday, which would have been great if we'd got here yesterday. Unluckily for the mayor, though, it also gives his home address. Half an hour later Leo is munching grass in the shadow of the church and a very elderly Madame in darned stockings is struggling up the hill, homing in on Peter and me. She demands a chair and settles into a monologue for the rest of the afternoon: her grandmother was a journalist who lived to be 113 years old, she says, and she herself is ninety-nine. Or perhaps eighty-nine. And her granny predicted that commercialism would destroy the little villages, and the supermarkets would kill the butchers and the bakers. So now there are only sixty people left. My brain's boggling at the thought of murderous supermarkets, but I think I know what she means. Eventually she toddles off, and ten minutes later she's hobbling up the hill again with an egg each for Peter and me, laid by her hens today.

I watch her stumpy figure receding into the distance once more, and it's hard not to feel a bit wistful. She's about the same age as my mother was when she died, and her cheerful independence reminds me of how Ma used to be before dementia silted up her brain. This old lady's still firing on all cylinders – why is it she's kept all her marbles, while my mother's were scattered in all directions, taking away her memory, her reasoning, the essence of the person we knew?

One look at the sky next morning, and it's clear this is going to be a day of wet-weather-everything for me, and of trying to share the skirts of Oliver's mac with my fussy-fair-weather-horse so they cover his haunches as well as mine. Not quite yet, though – the clouds are still holding their breath when we turn south through the heart of the Vauclair Forest.

The ruins of Vauclair Abbey come into sight by the side of the road. It was founded in 1134 by St Bernard but its days of power and glory ended long ago – or at least until the recreation of its chessboard pattern medicine garden in the 1960s, since when it has become one of the most visited sites in the region. There's an orchard of rare species of apples and pears here, too, but it's the ruins I'm curious about – a whole series of imperious arches and pillars crowned not by carved stone capitals but by grass headdresses, and with a savagely truncated look. What happened here?

Leo's happy to fall asleep tied to the railings as I clomp round in wellies with the camera, alone in the misty morning until a man with brooding eyes materialises out of nowhere. I wonder if he's a ghostly monk, albeit one with driving skills if the car with Belgian number plates suddenly stationed next to Leo is anything to go by. The man says he passed us on the road (did he? I haven't seen anyone all morning) and he'd like to know what we're doing.

'My horse and I are making a pilgrimage to Rome to raise money for the Alzheimer's Society,' I say.

'A *pilgrimage!*' His eyes light up.

'I'm not religious,' I add hastily, 'I just like the sense of history.'

'Madame, it doesn't matter, tell me about your pilgrimage...'

So I tell him about my mother dying because of Alzheimer's, and then I get on to Susie's and my journey to Santiago de Compostela, and then he talks to me, and talks and talks in excellent English, and takes a photo with a very unghostly digital camera of Leo checking me out for peppermints.

'Madame, a few minutes speaking with you has meant the world to me.' And he looks quite cheerful suddenly. Typical British embarrassment is threatening to envelop me, but that's stupid, I should just be glad that whatever's troubling his soul has lifted for a while.

I turn in my saddle to wave goodbye, and he's still standing there smiling as we go off to our next stop – the place that Monsieur says accounts for the abrupt razing of this abbey in World War I: the Chemin des Dames, scene of some of the bloodiest fighting of all. Burrowed into its ridge is the Caverne du Dragon, the quarry converted into underground barracks by the Germans.

Drachenhöhle.

5

Le Chemin des Dames

Baa. Baa. Baa baa *baa baa baa...*

Not sheep, but soldiers – the sound of the French mutineers of 1917 cynically bleating as they were herded into battle, lambs sent to slaughter by a general desperate to save his reputation after his disastrous attack on the Chemin des Dames ridge.

As Leo and I leave the shelter of the forest and turn along that ridge, a gale howls down the road behind us, battering the rain clouds across the sky - but it's nothing compared to the driving snow and sucking seething mud that the French 5th and 6th Armies struggled through on their way to annihilation on 16th April 1917.

The road's romantic name stems from the eighteenth century, when Louis XV had it cobbled so that his daughters, the Dames de France, could travel along it without lurching through potholes on their way to visit their governess near Vauclair. But as I scurry along the crest between the Aisne and Ailette valleys, and wide views open up in every direction, it's easy to see how strategically important it was and how it became associated with conflict. Caesar's army was fighting here in 57 BC, and Napoleon's troops were taking on the Russian and Prussian armies in 1814, but it's the tragic events of World War I that have really soaked into memory.

The area is riddled with underground stone quarries, and in 1915 German troops began to create a vast barracks in one of them, complete with a hospital and chapel – the Caverne du

Dragon, or *Drachenhöhle*. It often changed hands, but in April 1917 it was under German occupation – and General Nivelle's 'surprise' attack against the enemy's very strong, fifty-mile-long position along the Chemin des Dames was no surprise at all. This arrogant general, bolstered by victory at Verdun thanks to his newly-invented technique of despatching infantry right on the heels of rolling artillery barrages, had made no secret of his plan to use the same strategy on the Chemin. The Germans knew the details well in advance, and the results were devastating.

At dawn on 16th April the barrages and troops surged over the top in terrible weather, buoyed by Nivelle's total confidence in success, and poured their bombardment on to ... nothing at all. The Germans had moved from their forward trenches and were dug in above the French, lying in wait. The confused soldiers milled around in the open, sliding in the mud and blinded by sleet, easy targets in a bloody abattoir; whole battalions were wiped out by machine guns, entire regiments destroyed, 120,000 men dead in one day.

But their general wouldn't accept that his plan had failed this time because the element of surprise was gone, and he sent the troops back over and over again for a month. The number of casualties climbed towards 187,000, and the rising death toll caused a rebellion. On 28th April every member of a battalion of the 18th Infantry Regiment refused to take his place in the front line. Some were shot, some were imprisoned, and when the remainder of the battalion finally obeyed orders, it was to the sound of their bleating before most of them were wiped out.

Inevitably word got back, and mutiny spread through the troops until some 40,000 men refused to go on the offensive at all. The panicking government brought in General Pétain to replace Nivelle, and gradually he rebuilt the French Army's shattered morale, abandoning the disastrous tactic of continuous attacking action that caused such slaughter, and instead waiting for reinforcements before launching into major battles.

As for the Vauclair Abbey, the Germans used it as an ammunitions dump and it was Nivelle who caused it to be blasted almost to infinity, never to be restored.

I stop in the car park of the museum at the Caverne du Dragon. I'd really like to explore this re-creation of daily life in the underground barracks but the information office says it's two-hour guided tours only, and I've a feeling my bored horse would untie himself from the road sign outside and set off for home or Rome without me. So I add it to the places-to-see list and we carry on along the ridge, the wind swirling Leo's tail through his legs as the clouds balloon into one vast leaden mass.

Halfway down the hill towards Craonnelle the first needles of rain slant across from the west, and through its advancing curtains I can make out rows of crosses in the French National Cemetery lining the slope behind us, whole regiments of them piercing the grass with not a flower in sight. Further along, the old village of Craonne is marked only by a soaked arboretum. The village itself was completely destroyed in the war.

'Leo, this is really depressing.'

'I agree! I'm stopping now.'

'What do you mean, you're stopping?'

The road's snaking back on itself and we're heading right into the wind. Leo's ears are flat with displeasure as the rain lashes us both in the eyes, so he turns his rump to the weather and plants all four legs firmly in the middle of the lane.

'For God's sake! What d'you think you're doing? We can't stand here for hours hoping the rain will sod off!'

'Yes we can.'

So we have an argument about it, which I win by a narrow margin, and go crabbing sideways over the River Aisne and on for several miles before the rain does clear off. But there's no time to relax – once we're into open countryside there's nothing to shield us from a hurricane bellowing across the flattened fields. We gallop up the verge, trying to keep ahead of the next stampede of clouds, and the gale weasels its way into the gap between the outer skin of Oliver's mac and its lining until it's so fully inflated that I must look like Michelin Man, bouncing across the landscape.

Peter's waiting at Guyencourt, a cheeringly pretty village which is miles to the west of the Via Francigena, but to hell with it, I'm not going to follow the authentic route – it goes straight down the N44 to Reims, and even the starry excursion track runs too close to the suburbs for equine comfort. I just need to skirt round the city and catch up with the Via the other side somewhere near the imposing sounding Montagne de Reims – and hopefully near a congenial course for my golf-starved husband.

An old man is waving, beckoning us over. He says his son runs a livery yard here, and he's so keen to help and so enthusiastic about his beautiful stables I haven't the heart to tell him Leo's claustrophobic and can't bear being shut in.

'You'll have to lump it, Leo.'

'I won't! Lemme out of here! Or I'll jump out!'

He's on his hind legs glaring over the partition, his spots blue with sweat and rage, but there's hail crashing down outside and we all have to lump it in here for half an hour except for Peter who's still in Bessie, trying to jam her window shut with a spoon while the ice cubes rattle through regardless, filling up the washing-up bowl in readiness for the gin.

And then the clouds sail off at top speed, the sun springs out and larks go pinging into the sky. Mr Claustrophobic is released into a clover patch, and we don't need to take to the gin – Monsieur and his son present us with a bottle of champagne straight from their fridge. Our dinner is unexpectedly successful as a result, even though the cupboard is almost bare: omelettes made from Madame's hens' eggs (and some English ones several weeks past their sell-by date) crammed with fried potatoes, onions and cheese, and all washed down with champagne.

Every rambler, scrambler and *vélo* bicycle racer from Reims has descended on the soggy countryside for an energetic Sunday, passing Leo and me in their skin-tight Lycra suits, mud sprayed up their calves and backs. Some of them pause, curious to know where we're going, and with all my fingers crossed I tell them we're following the Via Francigena to Rome. Except that we aren't, at the moment – I'm heading straight for a golf club sign on my IGN map that says Golf de Reims Champagne, though I'm concerned about the word Champagne as it's suddenly occurred to me there won't be much horsy pasture around the vineyards.

I'd like to stop before we edge any closer to Reims – the buffeting of yesterday's long ride was so wearing that I'm in dead donkey mode today, just like Leo, although in his case it's caused by his busy night spent eating the clover. We need somewhere to stay, but the vineyards are crowding in and when I pause in a village to ask about *petites patûres* the residents are preoccupied with their annual fête, happy to think briefly about our dilemma before turning back to their funfair with Gallic shrugs. Leo freaks out when he wakes up to the fact that he's surrounded by dodgem cars, and plops so many manifestations of fright down the street that I have to divert into the vineyards themselves, armed finally with the phone number of an equestrian centre that's in the wrong direction. The number turns out to be wrong as well, so either it's going to be a night by the rubbish dump, the *déchetterie*, where there's a smidgen of grass, or a ride to the horse centre to ask if we can stay.

Still powered by fright, Leo hurtles along between the rows of vines. At the stables we're met by smart Madame who is actually quite helpful and says *pas de problème*, although there's no grazing land here and no question of a foreign horse being turned out in the carefully raked sand arena. So Leo really does have to lump it in a stable this time, for 20 euros for the night, although Peter, Bessie and I can stay for free. After two hours he's still walking round and round his loosebox, and the hay I've had to buy for an extra 5 euros is well and truly buried in his bedding. Madame Poseuse appears in Bessie's doorway, teetering on the ladder in her white winklepicker boots, and warns us that Voltaire, her Doberman, is a very dangerous guard dog who's left loose at night. But Voltaire's no fool – he waits till his mistress has disappeared for the evening, and then he whines and smiles at us ingratiatingly until we strike a bargain that if I give him some of our supper, he won't kneecap me if I have to nip out to the stable yard loo in the dark.

Peter's probably still dreaming of his day of golf when Leo and I speed off the next morning. My horse has box-walked all night, eaten nothing, and is on full throttle as we gallop into the forest of Reims with me struggling to roll back my sleeve and check the compass. It's wrong direction, wrong track, then wrong Route Forestière; but here are St James and other Disciples dressed as ramblers who, it so happens, also trekked to Santiago in 2002, and who have a useful map with them which sends me off south and then east to Bouzy, a village I can't resist because of the name.

We shouldn't be riding in these vineyards, but it's too far round by the road. Little pegs stuck in the ground tell me they belong to Mercier and Moët et Chandon, and as we tiptoe between them over the hill, the rumbustious wind whips their rows of supporting metal wires into a tinny song. Bouzy's a village breathing wealth, all manicured *caves* and restored stone houses, and no grass anywhere. However, the *mairie* here is open every day, and among its lists of *caves* selling stupendously expensive crates of champagne there's one list of *chambres d'hôte*. I select a place that advertises Bouzy Rouge for sale as well, and ride into its elegant courtyard. Leo beams at chic Madame who runs it, and thank you again, St James – it turns out she owns the only horse field for miles around. I book Peter and me into an entire suite of luxurious rooms for two nights, and we celebrate his successful day on the golf course with a greedy dinner at nearby Tours-sur-Marne. Tuna steak, and what's for pudding? Sorbet, that's great, a light dessert ... sorbet in Marc de Champagne, what's that? Let's have it anyway. Oh my *God!* It's pure alcohol, distilled from champagne ... my throat's on fire, *aaaaargh*, can't breathe ... what? You're going to drink it *neat?* Peter sends half a pint in pursuit of his sorbet which is already chasing the bottle of wine he's consumed, and we lurch back to our sumptuous accommodation with the lorry rolling and rollicking all over the road.

Bessie's puking diesel the next day and I feel as though I'm doing much the same – that was far too much rich fare after our recent basic rations. Monsieur Garage Man arrives in a van to spend five minutes tightening various inaccessible nuts and bolts, so that fixes Bessie; and Peter's and my hangover cure is a therapeutic tour of Reims, ostensibly to admire the cathedral but in reality to dump a load of washing at the *laverie.* We leave it flopping round in a yawning tumble-dryer while we go off to walk the aisles of the cathedral with its extravagantly gothic exterior, tempered by lofty simplicity inside. Vivid stained glass by Marc Chagall blends with the classical rose windows, all backlit by sunshine that throws an illuminated path through the open doorway down the length of the nave. Susie's here in spirit, reminding me of the names of various bits of ecclesiastical architecture, just as she did when we travelled together, and then she's sympathising with us back at the *laverie* because, as ever, our clothes are still wringing wet after an expensive two hours in the dryer. Peter and I slump in the nearest bar for another hour, crowded in with men in berets playing cards, their floor mop dog perched on a table beside them to check if they're cheating.

I get back on the Via Francigena at Ambonnay, which is right on the Topo excursion route; it's only a champagne cork's throw from where we've been staying, as it turns out, but there's no mention of Bouzy on the Via map – maybe it's too sinful to be marked, reeking of money and fleshpots. I observed when I left that Peter was making the most of it, wedging enough bottles of Bouzy Rouge down the back of our mattress to keep us pissed from here to Rome.

Just past Ambonnay, I notice a place on the Topo map called Poteau St-Sulpice. We appear to be almost on top of it. In *The Da Vinci Code* I noted that St Sulpice Church in Paris might have held the keystone to unlock the Holy Grail, so the Post of St Sulpice sounds promising. But I can't find it; it's not marked on the IGN map at all, so whoever St Sulpice was, maybe he upped his post and removed it. Anyway, Leo and I will soon be abandoning the enticements and distractions of the Association Via Francigena maps for the rest of our time in France, because we're almost at Châlons-en-Champagne where the primary and secondary routes divide. These maps have been a mixed blessing so far – although they're beautifully drawn and presented, I've found them lacking in perspective and very hard to follow. Maybe they'll be easier in Italy when we rejoin the primary route at Pontremoli, the gateway to Tuscany, and perhaps I'll even see some yellow VF signs again – I still haven't seen a single one since leaving England.

For now we manage to amble down the Via to Isse without getting lost and we cross over the Marne canal, leaving the pilgrim route at Aigny to weave its way into Châlons and on towards Switzerland. For Leo and me there's a long stretch of towpath to a turning south over the River Marne itself, but what would have been a beautiful ride on cart tracks is wrecked by the howling head wind that blows Leo's ears flat back again and makes my eyes stream so much I can't read any map at all.

St James, could we have some springtime now? It's so cold that Peter and I take our freezing selves to bed early, complete with woolly socks and books. After *The Da Vinci Code*, what next? I'm not sure I'm ready to take on *PERONNE 1535 Le Siège Héroïque* just yet, so I opt for something totally different – an old unpublished manuscript of my mother's which I found when clearing out the family house. It's a novel called *There's a Divinity*, worlds away from her twenty-seven factual books which were all published under her *nom de plume* of Judith Campbell, a combination of my sister Tessa's and my middle names. For this one she switched to Clea Drayton; I've no idea where Clea comes from, but Drayton's the name of an old family pile in Kettering. It sounds an exotically romantic writing name – and before I've even finished the first sentence it's obvious this is a naughty love story. Or maybe a story of lust. When did she write it? The typewriter ink's very faded so I would guess it was a long time ago, and I'll bet Pa's never read it. The heroine is the blue-blooded Miranda, but it's the anti-heroine who seems more real – a suitably buxom Kentish girl, only thirteen years old at the beginning of the book but full of ripening, disgraceful passion. I wonder if my outwardly cool mother was like that too, under the skin. Intrigued, I read on.

Jesus, this weather! I'm sure it was never as bad as this on the road to Santiago. Leo and I are scuttling along in driving rain yet again as the wind sends smoke from an alfalfa silo swooping down its chimney sides to cover us in greasy fog. We cut across exposed swathes of farmland where the harvesters are struggling to cut crops lying horizontal in the downpour. There's a neat little cart track tunnel under the A26 autoroute, and as we pass through it a sheltering deer bursts out in fright, causing Leo to dance an Irish jig while the HGVs swish and splosh overhead. In fact there's plenty of sodden wildlife around, and I try to keep my numb brain in gear with bad rhyming couplets:

> Red deer and rabbits, plenty of hares;
> Pheasants, and partridges, always in pairs.

But I bore myself with trying to get the scansion right, wondering if the hind we saw was actually a fallow deer, and give up. Nothing's OK with this foul afternoon.

Peter's waiting at an unpromising village and the next one is no better, every door closed, every window shutter streaming rain. And the *mairie*'s only open between 11 a.m. and 12.30 p.m. on a Wednesday and Friday, so naturally today is Thursday. It's a further long hike from here to Poivres, and Leo and I both look so miserable that Peter agrees to do today's recce. By the time we arrive in the village, via the military zone near Mailly-le-Camp which I thought was disused until three monster tanks went clanking past, he has organised a field with grass a foot long in the grounds of a tiny mediaeval house. The builders restoring it have connected the water today and we're welcome to help ourselves, and they take me into the single downstairs room where, oh bliss, there's a roaring red gold orange leaping flames real log fire. I've never been so glad to see anything in my life.

With the slow dying down of the wind, the sky clears for a brief sunset. Hoping for a more upbeat end to the day, I go off to investigate the church which looks as though it might be interesting. But the door's locked, and when I wander into the churchyard to admire the flowers I come across another tale of tragedy: along the back wall there's a row of Commonwealth graves, the first World War II ones I've seen. Thirty members of the RAF and seven of the Australian and Canadian Air Forces are buried here, all shot down on 4th May 1944, their tombstones engraved as poignantly as ever: *he did his best*, and *he died so we might live*; as daylight drains out of the sky the stones still glimmer faintly, quiet reminders of families ripped apart forever.

6

Boozy

Dilemma.

Is this fight, flight, or carry on eating my lunch?

The man I saw walking in the distance has suddenly changed direction and now he's bearing down on Leo and me, looking very intent.

Flight seems out of the question. I'm sitting on the ground, and Leo's unsaddled. I'm far too old to leap on him bareback and go careering off like Tonto and anyway, the bloke might disappear with the saddle while we're steaming round the countryside out of control.

Fight seems a bit extreme, so I might as well continue eating. I expect he's just curious to know why we're riding across country in the middle of nowhere. But what's *he* doing here, on these remote and lonely paths? No rucksack, so he isn't a pilgrim. Black eyes, black eyebrows ... they meet in the middle, a very bad sign. But I don't want to offend him, so I'm careful to ease my Swiss army knife invisibly out of my pocket, flicking open a blade and concealing it in my hand. How *rude*, how very un-British, to suspect the worst.

And of course the man is chatty, charming and full of bonhomie. I feel really bad about the knife edge pressing sharply into my palm as he wishes me *bon courage* and strides back to his original footpath, but then again, you never know. Would I have used it if I had to? Driven by terror, me or him – yes, I think so. Though I might well have speared myself by mistake.

✂

At a crossroads close to the River Aube, Peter has found an enclosed field we can all occupy for the night, 'we' now including our friends Gerry and Penny who are joining us for a few days. Leo's delighted to be right here too, one of the crowd, snuffling at our gin, and since Gerry isn't into horses of course he's the one to get a hairy muzzle resting on his head. At bedtime there's Peter's peppermint toothpaste to be sampled, and then we struggle to fall asleep to the sound of munching under Bessie's window.

On the way to Géraudot (Destination Golf Course for Peter and Gerry, at the exotically named Golf de la Forêt d'Orient) I pass a church like no other church I've ever seen – if it wasn't for the astonishingly tall steeple poking out of its cat-slide roof, you'd think it was just a heavily beamed house. It's a real curiosity, but there's no question of looking inside – it's not only locked, but barred. What's happened to France in the four years since I last rode across it? I don't remember a single church that Susie didn't manage to inspect. But this area looks as though it's full of conscientious, careful citizens; even the cornfields are uniformly tidy, save where the wind strokes the young barley sideways like the pelt of some vast animal. I'm relieved to see seven rebels in it: four are bright blue cornflowers cheekily growing in a corner, and three are furious hares having a boxing match right through the middle.

The campsite at Géraudot is equally orderly. The camp commandant has decreed No Horses On Site, which means Leo is penned in a narrow strip beside the road where every fly and mosquito in the forest emerges to feast on him. The first crot he drops mutates into a heaving black buzzing mass. How *disgusting* – but the word's out. Dung beetles arrive in their hundreds and shape it into little balls to roll back into the undergrowth, and then hordes of orange slugs with eyes on black stalks come oozing out behind them ... that's it. Enough.

'Monsieur Commandant, perhaps I could make an enclosure for my horse further down the verge where it's wider?'

'Why, certainly *not*, Madame.'

'Why not?'

'It's for parking the cars.'

'What cars? There aren't any. They couldn't park there anyway, there's a ditch in the middle.'

'Madame, the ditch is for the frogs and salamanders.'

'The *what?* There aren't any of those either. There's no water. The ditch is dry.'

'No horses, Madame.'

'Monsieur, you are a pain in the arse' (except I don't say that, being English and polite).

Meanwhile Leo's going mad, blood trickling down his coat where the mosquitoes are murdering him. Peter and I walk up the road to the nearest farm.   'Madame! What a beautiful horse! Of course he may stay with us, next to the sheep. Monsieur! I'm so sorry ... you naughty dog.'

This is addressed to Monsieur's fox-terrier Milord who's piddling on Peter's leg to show him who is *le propriétaire* around here, but my husband's in too much of a good mood to mind, after winning his golf match with Gerry. As for the tortured Leo, ecstasy is a day's rest in a field with woolly friends, on higher ground where the breeze keeps the insects away.

Penny and I have a peaceful pottering day while Peter and Gerry go off to do battle again. We clear out Bessie, jam the wobbly Porta Potti into the horse section with sacks of horse food, and get round to eating lunch at 4 p.m. – tomatoes and sardines and feta cheese and baguettes and peaches, our taste buds honed by a warm day out of doors while the sun is actually shining. But there's a certain *froideur* in the air when the golfers return. We daren't enquire who won and who lost, so a trip to the local café for a series of gins and tonics followed by bottles of red wine seems like a good idea. And then there are the *coupes colonel* for the men – ice creams drowning in vodka. Gerry and Peter spoon them up, full of camaraderie again.

Back at the lorry, Peter stands outside talking to his son Sam on the phone. The conversation goes on for a long time and I climb into bed and switch off, transported by my mother's book to a time when the world was sliding into war. Peter's been out there a long time. Oh, he's coming in. Sort of.

'Why are you sitting on the floor?'

'I don't feel very well.'

'What? I can't hear you.'

'I don't feel very well.'

'Why? Are you pissed? I've never seen you really pissed.'

'Where are we?'

Christ. I haul him into bed and he lies there looking confused, asking question after question in a very small voice. But they're all the same questions, and this is the thirtieth time I've told him where we are, why we're here and what he's been doing today (playing an acerbic game of golf with Gerry, by the sound of things). Now I'm getting worried – he sounds like Ma. Perhaps this is instant Alzheimer's. Or perhaps he's had a stroke. I look to see if bits of him have frozen into immobility, but it's hard to tell. Then he stops talking, and I really freak out ... 'Peter, Peter, are you OK?'

'Where are we?'

He *must* be hammered. This has got to be alcoholic amnesia. I'm comforted by this mundane explanation; even more so when the small voice billows into a symphony of snores.

I wonder how Gerry's doing. He and Penny are supposed to be leaving at 5 a.m. to drive back to England. When I surface at 7 o'clock their car has indeed disappeared, and later they phone the surprisingly chirpy Peter to say their journey took a long time because they had to stop on the motorway so Gerry could throw up. As far as I can gather, the consensus is that the ice cream must have been off.

Of course.

Spring has back-pedalled into winter again, into downpours and drowning fields. I'm riding with a plastic cover over my saddle all the time now, no point in taking it off, my pilgrim hat squashed in a pocket and my mac hood pulled forward; if Leo was black I'd pass as a Dark Rider from Lord of the Rings. Riding in wellies is problematical – they fall off in the road if I swing my feet out of the stirrups to rest my legs. Lining Leo up with one of them so I can descend gracefully straight into the boot and then hop round him to rescue the other one is quite a challenge.

But when the rain pauses and the sun flashes out, it's a different story: suddenly, banks of flowers sparkle into life – wild columbine, Solomon's seal, dog roses, blue scabious; and there are clumps of orchids - Early Purples (blooming very late), Pyramidals in neat rows and long-tailed Lizard orchids. When the sun goes in again, they're all just weeds in the hedge.

My mother, an ardent observer of wild flowers, would have loved to see them all. Maybe she can, though I have no sense of her presence except through her manuscript; curled up with Peter in the evenings while Leo braves yet another celestial cocktail of iced rain and sleet outside, rugged up to his ears, I have time to finish the book. Its aristocratic heroine Miranda has found an ethereal love with Anthony, the local landowner, but their gentle conversations take a dramatic turn at the final reality of war:

> *Fight? But of course I'll fight! Who wouldn't fight for his very existence? But if you think that I like the idea – that I want to exchange the sun, and the moon, and the trees, for the so-called glamour of a uniform! For the stink, and blood, and mud; for the retching filthiness of war, then you're very much mistaken! God! To think that we were given a world like this to live in – all the beauty of it, all the satisfaction of growing and creating things – and man has had to employ his superior mind in devising new and more ghastly methods of destroying his own flesh!*

Is that what my Gunner father, called up into the anti-aircraft section of the Royal Artillery, once said to Ma?

Her view of the place of women in the world is disconcerting, if Miranda is her alter ego and Anthony is Pa's. There's a paragraph of Miranda's thoughts that makes me chuckle:

> *She thought of the utter fulfilment of love, both mentally and physically, and of the foolish virgins who cried for a higher education in inessentials, instead of for the life for which woman was equipped. Not all of them had the chance to fulfil their destiny it is true, but how many of them threw away the moon and cried for sixpence! Clamoured for seats in parliament and rights for women, when life itself was laid at their feet, theirs for the taking. Surely the most abused slogan in the world was Equality of the Sexes? Man had his brain, fitted for its own logical uses, and women had theirs, fitted for their part in the world, and the two did not mix. Each to its own calling, each able and competent in its own capacity, but let the male stick to his work, the female to hers.*

I'm left wondering when Ma abandoned this philosophy and became the ambitious writer I remember, though she was always a bit surprised at her own success. This novel must indeed have been written a very long time ago.

As for the anti-heroine, the lusty Emmie now grown up, she barely waits for her long-suffering husband Fred to depart to the war before getting up to no good. The parallel stories of the two women sharpen into tight prose, shot through with the threads of what my mother must have witnessed of the Battle of Britain from our family home on the hill:

> *The sky looked as though some gargantuan child had dipped his paint-brush in white poster-paint, and let his creative fancy rip all over the canvas of blue. Squirls and whirls, loops and lopsided figures of eight were drawn in a fantastic pattern through which the fighters, little hornets of death, weaved their gleaming way. The fight of 'the Few' was on, and the fate of England and the whole world hung in the balance.*
>
> *The staccato tattoo of machine guns was mingling with the more spaced and deeper note of cannon shells; empty cartridge cases rattled on the village tiles, and bullets bit the roadway with a vicious zip...*

In the end, Good has to triumph over Bad, not where the war's concerned because it's still grinding on when the book ends, but in the fates of Miranda and Anthony, Emmie and Fred. The wounded Anthony is invalided home to be healed by his loving wife, but Emmie comes unstuck. When Fred returns on leave and finds her and his neglected little daughter shacked up with Bob the lodger, Ma's writing froths to fury:

> *Madness filled his brain, and madness looked out of his eyes. With a shout, as animal and inhuman as the scream of a charging elephant, he crashed into Bob who was crouching,*

fists clenched, ready to receive him. Dramatically, and as if of intent, a nearby searchlight switched on, and illuminated the two men as clearly as if they fought before the arc lamps of a Hollywood set.

Emmie stood by the window, her hands gripping the wooden frame, her mouth agape, her eyes staring. She drew in her breath with a sharp hiss. She could hear their panting, their quick oaths, the muffled smack when fist met flesh, and the slither and ring of their boots on the road. Her blood raced in her veins, her face was bright and wild with excitement. She did not care who won, she had forgotten all that lay behind this issue, almost she was unaware of their identities. She was caught up in the primitive surge of a fight, when the animal breaks from its bars of convention, and man is the brute revealed...

Fred is the winner, of course, and when the bloodied Bob limps off down the road, he turns to his wife:

He looked into her heart and saw all the meanness of her; all the egoism, the petty vanity, the lies and ill temper; the essential unfaithfulness of mind as well as body. He looked, and saw that truth and honour were not of her, and had never been, and that only the curtain of his love had concealed the poverty of her soul. He looked, and saw her for the slut that she was.

And then he takes the baby and walks away into the night.

Blimey! I'm exhausted, and unnerved that my mother let all that out into 200 pages no one ever saw. I'll never know if she really empathised with Miranda, or secretly with the bawdy Emmie in spite of her bad end.

Leo and I go bowling along through Buxières-sur-Arce, Ville-sur-Arce and then the Arce itself, as it were, tiptoeing through a ford in the chattering river of that name. According to the map, we're still in champagne country which is a worry because I thought we must be well on our way to Burgundy. We've been four weeks on the road and when there have been no available tracks, thanks to the wide verges I've managed to keep off the tarmac about 80 per cent of the time. Leo's shoes have held up surprisingly well, but now they're wearing thin and it won't be long before they work loose and fall off. Next rest stop, farrier.

Tonight's camp is in Courteron, just a name on a map, a dot south of the Lac d'Orient. It borders the Seine, the next of France's great rivers that we need to cross, and not only is it very pretty but the secretariat is actually open, and Madame stamps my passport and says we're welcome to stay on the *terrain communal* because the mayor certainly won't mind. Leo lazes on to a carpet of daisies at the edge of the water sliding quietly by, and Peter's and my only regret is that it isn't 20°C warmer. I walk down to the ancient stone bridge with its boxes of geraniums balanced on the parapet; the map will take us this way tomorrow, and on to a track that runs for fifteen miles through the forest before we get anywhere near another village. Every opportunity to get lost, in other words.

I note there's a gîte in this tiny hamlet where only White Van Grocery Man hoots his way through in the mornings, thrusting baguettes into bits of drainpipe hanging horizontally outside front doors: *Pain S.V.P.* But we don't need a gîte tonight. As the temperature drops, we pile into our Bessie bed and spread all our clothes out on top of the duvet as well. In the morning I haul my jeans under the covers to warm them up while the kettle puffs its way to boiling point with my defrosting bra over its handle, like an aviator's helmet with earmuffs.

The forest is a mass of wild aquilegia, Day-Glo slugs, signs warning of hunting on Thursdays and Saturdays, and elaborate stone hides in igloo shapes – fortunately empty, as today is Wednesday. Some of the trails lead nowhere, and some plunge down escarpments to nameless roads, but Leo and I still manage to meet up with Peter in a designated village square at 3 o'clock precisely, and persuade Jean-Christophe the furniture maker to let us park on the grass outside his factory – a new type of venue to add to Places We Have Stayed With Horse and Lorry. We can use the factory loo and shower block where the water pipes sing when you turn on the taps, and where the thermometer registers 13°C, which feels positively balmy compared to the return of the Ice Age outside. According to our host, it's been the coldest, wettest May in living memory and it'll be even colder tomorrow.

'Gimme your sandwiches!'
Leo's standing over me, wiffling his nostrils into the bread.
'No! Bugger off! Horses don't eat cheese and Marmite.'
'Hmph! Not fair! And you've got more Mars Bars than me.'
This is true, I have to concede – I've been eating two to Leo's one, and he's quite capable of working that out. So we'll have to have one and a half each, every day from here to Rome.

We're standing by the chilly roadside and I'm puzzling over the map which is showing tracks all over the place although, as usual, the reality is that some have fizzled out. For God's sake. Where's this one gone? We're looking at a field of oilseed rape, sticky ramparts of it, and the apparent disappearance of our path means a mile on the Route Nationale instead. No thanks.

But actually the path *is* there – illuminated, even. It must follow the line of the tractor ruts, and those are obvious – the squashed rape has struggled up again and blossomed later, and some of its blaring yellow flowers are still dancing in a double line right through the surrounding forest of stalks and seeds. So we plunge into the field hoping the farmer's nowhere within shouting distance, and now Leo's swimming through seed pods up to his ears, his nose wrinkled at the pungent smell as the scratchy plants split and drag my legs backwards. When we get to the other side we're both soaked and covered in petals; they're stuck in the studs on my gaiters, in my stirrup treads, in Leo's bridle, in his girth, everywhere. Picking off the guilty evidence takes a frantic half hour with me looking wildly back at the motorway of devastation we've left behind us. The tiny seeds cling to Leo's legs, as irritating as the mustard to which they're related, and for miles afterwards he stops every few yards to rasp his teeth on his ankles.

This is a very odd sort of day, Leo.

The contours of the countryside are suddenly rearing up into mounds and hillocks, and in the distance a shaft of light shines down from heaven – a weak ray of sunshine wobbling through the clouds. It must be late afternoon by now, but my watch has been registering 1.30 p.m. for hours. And I've no idea where we are, because my wrist compass went mad just as I reached the end of the map and found I'd forgotten to bring the next one. I turn Leo towards the sunbeam, which must be in the south-west, but the needle swings through two revolutions and settles to point the same way. North, it says. What's going on? We carry on in what must be roughly a southerly direction, and after about six miles the compass abruptly rights itself and my dead watch next to it responds to a whack and starts up again.

Here's another spectral village, one of many we've clattered through today. We're almost at the last lifeless house when two black shapes leap across the road in front of us – quarrelling cats with spiky fur on end. A cockerel crows a signal, another relays it down the valley, and then invisible dogs start barking in response, invisible sheep bleat, disembodied cows moo ... but there are still no people. The final battering to Leo's and my ears comes from a comatose donkey we passed half a mile back, now blasting out a gullet-splitting foghorn of a bray. We push on, Leo swinging his head from side to side suspiciously, and me with the back of my neck prickling. The clouds begin flocking ominously together over our heads and then suddenly they all bolt off in different directions; between them I can see two military jets in soundless flight, the scream of their passing lagging far behind.

Peter and I meet up by luck alone since we're in *un trou*, a black hole where there's no phone signal, but that luck runs out when it comes to finding a gîte for a two-day-rest-and-farrier stop: they're full up round here because there's a local moto rally next weekend. The best we can do is stay in Bessie between a gîte that's overbooked and the communal wheelie bins, though Leo does rather better – a kind farmer loans him two acres of cow field, minus the cows.

We've done nearly thirty miles today and I'm knackered and spooked by our adventures, and to cap it all, the barometer in Bessie is inexplicably low even though the sky's cleared.

'Must be my poltergeist, Peter. It often follows me around when I'm really tired, turning on lights and hiding the bedsheets, stuff like that.'

'Rubbish,' he says, 'the barometer's dropped because I've been lurching round the lanes all day and loosened up its innards.'

And it turns out there's a rational explanation for my loopy compass as well: this afternoon's bumpy horizon hid the remains of disused tin mines, and the ore still in the earth was spinning the needle. But I can't explain the rest.

Anyway, trying to keep off the supernatural and steer in the direction of practicalities, we concentrate on appointments for tomorrow's rest day: one with the farrier, one at the local golf course and one with the goddess Sequana, who guards the source of the Seine.

7

A Stuffed Cat and
a Pregnant Clock

'Farrier? No problem, Madame.'

Monsieur Cow Field arranges it all. For 6 a.m. tomorrow. Six o'clock! Peter and I were hoping for a lie in. We're a bit short on sleep after too many nights parked in the shadow of churches whose bells clang out every hour, and we've been pleased to note nothing ecclesiastical in this village so far.

Monsieur catches sight of my expression and kindly rearranges the appointment for 8 p.m.

Needless to say, the church is hiding just round the corner from our Bessie billet, and before I've had time to wipe the dismayed expression off my face a lady rushes over to take me on a conducted tour. It's a simple nineteenth-century building, restored in the 1960s and with eight stained glass windows, six of them perfectly traditional and two that look as though they've been sploshed by Picasso in a blue period. Still, the overall effect is harmonious, though my concentration isn't great because Madame is a bit of a worry – she keeps on genuflecting, and I wonder if I should be doing the same. Where are you, Susie? I need some advice; I don't want any caustic thoughts from on high about being hypocritical if I start crossing myself, but Madame might think I'm rude if I carry on walking round with my arms buttoned to my sides.

However, she's not at all bothered. In fact, she's overwhelmed to hear I have a holy horse heading for Rome, so she kisses me twice on both cheeks and says she'll pray for me, which is probably what I need after today's cranky goings-on.

By 10.30 p.m. the church clock is still booming out the half hour as well as twice for the hour. Peter's temper isn't improved by this, nor by my absent-minded addition of a heaped tablespoon of chilli powder to our supper which results in the back of his throat catching fire. He puffs off to bed, and when Rest Day dawns to a cloudless sky he tells me the clock, if not the chilli, kept him awake all night. As sleep's now out of the question, we get to our appointment with the river goddess in good time.

Sequana continues to keep an eye on her Gallo-Roman sanctuary where we find the Seine, bearing the French translation of her name, bubbling up through a plug hole in a pool, just a tiny gurgle that within 200 miles becomes the stately river that curls round Paris. The goddess promoted fertility, and effigies of round-bellied women and intertwined couples were discovered in her pool; she had healing powers, too, and in times gone by had a pilgrim following of her own. Models of afflicted arms, legs, heads, internal organs and even whole bodies were sculpted out of wood and bronze, silver and stone, and left in a large pot for her attention. One image of Sequana herself still exists, the only one ever discovered: a bronze statue in flowing Roman robes, standing in a boat with a prow carved in the shape of a duck's head and neck, its tail feathers waving in the stern. Its home now is in a Dijon museum, and here in her grotto she's represented nowadays by a half-naked stone nymph relaxing behind railings.

We carry on to the village of Saint-Seine-l'Abbaye. Its church's austere walls hold a faded mediaeval painting of the Tree of Jesse, Christ's family tree, an image I last saw in Santiago Cathedral where it forms the central marble column of the Pórtico de la Gloria. A seated St James is carved into it, and pilgrims queue to push their fingers into the intertwined roots below his statue in keeping with the tradition of a completed journey. At St Seine there's nobody in the church except Peter and me, and the lady in the tourist office tells me I'm the first Via Francigena pilgrim to call by. She stamps my passport with its best image so far: it shows St Seine, the successor to Sequana, all Christianised not to mention masculinised, riding a smiling donkey who's showing his master the path ahead with a pointy forefoot.

Leo's 8 p.m. appointment with the blacksmith means Peter's afternoon golf session is truncated to half an hour on the driving range, where I fall asleep on the rubber mat next to him and don't hear a single ball clacking off into the distance. But when we rush back to our camping spot, the farrier's not there. A mortified Monsieur Cow Field explains to me, while casually measuring Leo from ground to shoulder height with a metric tape, that the man turned up at 5.45 p.m. when we were out.

'*Ah! Soixante!*' he murmurs, which makes my horse about the size of a Labrador dog. He must mean *cent soixante*, 160 centimetres which, according to my translation into 'hands' of four inches each for proper horse measurement, adds considerably to Leo's actual height. No matter – embarrassed Monsieur is simply trying to veer away from the subject of horseshoes, so I tell him I'll solve the problem by phoning another farrier en route to our next destination outside Dijon. After jiggling around with unobtainable mobile numbers, I track one down who says he'll definitely be there tomorrow at 3.30 p.m.

For once we've booked ahead into a chambre d'hôtes. What a treat this will be – a room with an en suite bathroom and our first proper wash for a month. Getting there, however, might well take a week due to the constant need to backtrack. Trail One on the IGN map goes straight through a forest and then through a bog into running water – puzzling, because the path itself has been well trodden by cows. Small cows. They seem to have dug up the track into muddy heaps here and there ... oh my *God*, Leo! This is a wild boar motorway, we're getting out of here now, here's another field of rape, never mind, we're going right through the middle again.

Which we do.

In the tangled woods on Trail Two, marked as an *itinéraire équestre* but alarmingly bordered by tight contour lines indicating cliffs and ravines, I get hopelessly lost. A chainsaw-waving logger's directions of twenty-five turn-lefts followed by thirty turn-rights take us to the top of the appropriately named La Montagne, where there's a sheer drop of eighty feet right in front of our noses. So it's back to a road, but that turns out to be no good either – it's the D104C when I need the D104K. What's the difference? I'm trying to read the map while riding down a fiendishly steep hill when all the *motos* from the weekend's rallies come roaring past, closely followed by Monsieur le Logger in his Fiat Panda. He squeals to a halt in the middle of a blind bend.

'Madame! Not that way!'

'Monsieur! Please don't stop here! It's *dangereux*...'

But it's a case of *tant pis*, or too bad – he waves his arms and gestures rudely at the motorbikes and cars that have to brake and swerve, all the riders and drivers growling and swearing, and then he sends Leo and me off down the hill again armed with directions for a picturesque but convoluted route via the Château de Lantenay. *Cher* Monsieur, it's kind of you to think we might appreciate some sightseeing, but we've already spent eight hours getting this far and all Leo wants is his dinner, and all I want is a bath. So I carry straight on down the main D104 (minus any letters of the alphabet at all) and catch up with Peter who's backing Bessie into the chambre d'hôtes' driveway at a necessarily acute angle so he can get the ramp down. Two collisions with the gatepost later, he turns off the engine and smiles at the owner who is too polite to say anything.

After I've scrubbed off weeks of mud, rich warm horse honk and aura of crots, Madame does us proud with her home-cooked dinner. There's smoked ham and melon, salmon grilled with red peppercorns, mushroom salad, wild asparagus, and rhubarb and raspberry tart, all so delicious that I later record every detail in my journal. Never mind that Peter hates rhubarb and isn't mad about mushrooms – anything's better than yesterday's searing chilli thrown together out of tins; and the bottles of 2001 Givry and 2000 Mercurey that our hostess magically produces ease it all down very smoothly. Not that there's much opportunity to relax over our meal, because Madame's eating with us and my brain's soon reeling from the non-stop battery of French chat. She flits from subject to subject, from politics and the state of the world to her little wild cat, Gypsy, who came in one day and stayed for ever. Gypsy sits close by, densely spotted and with a tail that has two tight curls in it like a pig. Looking at her leopard-pattern camouflage coat, I start to wonder if she's really a changeling wild boar piglet. Madame says this is her only cat, from which I conclude that the ginger one asleep in its bed under another table must be stuffed.

And there's no time to study the other exotica in her dining-room such as the statues, paintings and candelabra because she wants to whisk us off in her car for a nocturnal tour of Dijon. As we leave the room, the only thing to make itself noticed is her wonderful long case clock with its bulbous stomach which suddenly and thunderously lets rip with the chimes of Big Ben. Here's hoping it shuts up for the night.

Our road to the city is as tortuous as Monsieur le Logger's proposed scenic route earlier today, due to diversions to see the old house of the poet Lamartine and then the source of I don't know what welling up in a trough groaning with flowers. Madame says the water's pure enough to drink, a fact she knows because the mayor has it tested every year. A fox comes trotting up the lane towards us with its jaws clamped round an empty plastic container ... what? Is the water that special?

Dijon at night is probably an amazing sight, but it's hard to take in its beauty when Madame is distractingly driving through two sets of red lights, the wrong way up a one-way street, and the length of a cul-de-sac Peter and I can see is a dead end before she even turns into it. She pulls up at the cathedral just so we can view a stone salamander on the wall and stroke a gargoyle that has to be touched with the left hand only. We escape briefly, walking on ahead while she pauses in her car with headlights blazing and the engine switched off. She is such a long time catching up with us again that we have visions of a flat battery and a twelve-mile walk, but it turns out she stopped to give salamander-and-gargoyle instructions to some unsuspecting passers-by.

By the time we get back to the village my brain's completely numb from the ceaseless barrage of French, delivered with a slightly singsong inflection that has lulled Peter to sleep. I try switching off from the monologue but it's hazardous – you have to watch out for what might be a question, and answer *oui* or *non* appropriately. Due to inattention and fatigue, I find I've agreed it's a bad thing there's no death penalty in either France or England, when in fact capital punishment is my pet horror hobby horse and I wouldn't work in criminal law if we still had executions. But I'm too tired to correct myself, and we move on to a safer question and answer session about the responsibilities of magistrates, which don't seem to include building guillotines at dawn.

Madame's pregnant clock says nothing all night, but in the inevitable church outside our bedroom window tumultuous bells once again ring out every half hour, and Peter's mobile phone, which he forgot to turn off, plays a snatch of electronic music at 4 a.m. to announce the arrival of two gobbledegook texts from T-Mobile plus instructions to delete them.

Not one but three farriers arrive half an hour early next day to attend to Leo by the roadside, pondering in turn over the tungsten studs which have to be drilled into his shoes at a precise angle. To my relief he's a model of patient equine behaviour and we set off afterwards to get a couple of hours further down the road, leaving Peter to load the lorry with kind-hearted Madame's parting presents – an entire vegetable patch of fresh rhubarb, roses from her garden and some marzipan ladybirds, heavy as paperweights. In the meantime, Leo has some complaints for me.

'My shoes are too tight.'

'No they're *not*, you fussy old devil.'

'They are. I'm not walking on the road, it's too hard.'

'You'll have to, there's no verge. For God's sake, Leo! Your other shoes were paper thin, falling off. These ones just feel different, that's all.'

We potter through a hamlet which has just one shop, run by a taxidermist who specialises in African trophies and possibly ginger cats as well, for all I know, and Leo continues to remind me about his feet all the way to Chamboeuf where luckily there's a pony mare grazing in the field next door to our campsite. Pinched toes forgotten, he spends the evening galloping up and down, showing off.

When I have time to look around me rather than ride along with my nose in a map, I start to realise that this part of Burgundy is beautiful, filled with rolling hills and views that stretch into the hazy distance. I wake up to a blue-sky-and-fluffy-cloud day, and it's warm, so warm that I can ride in shirtsleeves. A ribbon of road takes me south to join the GR7, one of the major long-distance walking routes through France, marked out neatly on my IGN map of swirling contours, deep valleys, and famous names: Nuits-St-Georges, Gevrey-Chambertin, Beaune.

When the GR sweeps away to the left an inviting grass track appears in front of me, and never mind that there's a notice saying *interdit sans autorisation*; there's nobody to ask, so I give myself permission and ride along it. It leads to a skinny section of the GR76, a reminder that these Grande Randonnée trails aren't really for horses: the path between ancient walls is so narrow that I have to get off and walk in front of Leo or be squashed. But our magical wandering day threatens to end with some blunt reality when Peter, ahead of us at another campsite, phones to say the manager took one look at Bessie and said he hoped Peter wasn't planning to bring a horse here. Not encouraging. I've already diverted half a mile out of Savigny-lès-Beaune towards this site, and if I retrace my steps and carry on south I'm going to be right on top of the A6, the frenetic Autoroute du Soleil. How about a motorway rest-stop for the night, Leo? No?

But the magic hasn't deserted us after all. We pass a house in mid-renovation and I approach the builder to ask if there's any *terrain* where we can camp. He listens to my accent and then replies in excellent English.

'No, Madame. But I have a place in the valley where there's a lot of grass. You could stay there. I'll just have to drive there first to warn the housekeeper.'

The *housekeeper*? Who is this builder? When Peter arrives, Monsieur sets off in front of him in a car with Swiss number plates, further and further up the valley with Bessie grumbling along the rough road behind him, and Leo grumbling behind her at having to trot to keep up at the end of a long day. And right at the end we reach La Maison du Garde Fontaine Froide, no ordinary house but a fairytale little castle that keeps watch over the cold springs that rise here on the River Rhoin. Monsieur waves his arms expansively; he owns the whole valley, he says, and once he's shut the gates it'll all be enclosed and Leo can go free. My mind boggles – I might never find him again or worse still, he'll eat all the flowers in their neat borders. Monsieur sees me eyeing up the rainbow trout in the river. We never eat those, he says, they just come up to be fed. And trustingly he leaves us to it.

We fence in three sides of a big stretch of grass; the fourth is bordered by the wide Rhoin which means we don't have to bother with buckets of water, and there's so much to eat Leo probably won't stir more than a yard. But he has other ideas.

'Where's Bessie?'

His head's up, eyes bulging, full of separation anxiety. Bessie's on the other side of the river.

'I want to be with my lorry! What about my dinner?'

'*Leo!* Don't you dare ... don't...'

But he does. He sticks a hoof in the shallows, assumes it's safe, plunges in, trips over, and instantly is up to his neck in a torrent. I'm frozen to the spot as he flails his way through, scrambles out, shakes himself violently, and then strolls casually over to the lorry.

'OK, now where's my dinner?'

I can't believe it. The only damage is a small graze on his shoulder. But after that adventure we incarcerate him completely in a tiny chunk of field with the fence fully electrified.

When the tree shadows start to stretch their black fingers down the valley I go for a walk in the top meadow. It ends unexpectedly in a fifty-foot drop into the river, so it's as well I didn't accept Monsieur's invitation to let the accident-prone Leo go roaming. Behind me the château's stone walls are glowing honey-gold in the last of the sun, and everywhere the flowers and grasses of a real old-fashioned field are nodding and dipping their petals and seed heads: garlic, sun spurge, wild lupins, white campion, jack-go-to-bed-at-noon, dotty grass; and pale blue harebells, which I haven't seen for years. On impulse I pick one of each to press between the leaves of my journal, a reminder of a perfect evening, a perfect place.

Tonight we can fall asleep in the darkness of the deep countryside; no light pollution and no noise either save for the rushing of the river waterfalls and the soft churr-churr of the crickets, a contented summer sound.

Not a church bell for miles.

8

From Holy Cluny to the Devilish Bridge

Very unusually for him, Peter's stirring when I heave myself out of bed at 7 a.m.

'Why are you awake?'

'Didn't sleep – it was so quiet. I kept listening out for the bells.'

I'd also spent the night awake, waiting for the splash of Leo falling in the river again. But he's still in his pen, now mown as close as a golf course green, and we walk back down the lane to thank Monsieur for his kindness. I've decided our host must be a Swiss banker, but he tells me he has 'an antiques shop' (full of Old Masters? ancient Persian carpets?) in Geneva, not far away.

Geneva not far away? For weeks now my horizon's been limited to twenty-mile dollops on large scale maps, but when I check the road atlas for the bigger picture I'm astonished to see we're on the same latitude as Zurich, and a long way down through France. Somewhere near Mâcon I'll need to turn left, and then start worrying as we ride towards the mountains of the Jura and the Alps. But I'm *not* going to think about that yet. No.

For now I stick to the GR76, with diversions to photograph all the famous village signs from Leo's back with his ears in the foreground: Pommard, Volnay, Meursault, Chassagne-Montrachet; and its neighbour Puligny-Montrachet, home of my parents' favourite wine before its escalating price took it off their menu. Its name brings back memories of a Sunday lunchtime long ago, when the family watched in fascination while Ma poured gravy into her wine glass instead of the Puligny. Was this a first sign of Alzheimer's? Alarming if so; I've already once measured the milk for my *café au lait* into the plastic bubble for the bio-wash…

Lunchtime is spent in a vineyard, the sun tempting me to sleep under the tracery of summer leaves, the grapes in early June not yet even a tight collection of green full stops. It's a slow day on my grass-stuffed horse and by Chagny we've had enough of toddling along at a snail's pace, but when we get to the town's campsite my heart sinks. It's very upmarket, full of prim pitches and paved paths, but while I'm hesitating at the entrance the wardens see Leo and decide they can't resist him: 'Monsieur, Madame, please stay here with us, there's a pitch for your lorry and two for your horse, and our restaurant is open for dinner.'

Over a fried-squid-and-chips supper, I ferret through some pamphlets and come across a leaflet called La Voie Verte. It describes a cycling route along the converted track of a disused railway line for about sixty miles from Givry to Mâcon, calling in at old stations with names like Saint-Désert and Saint-Boil, and it runs very close to the ruined abbey at Cluny which is high on our list of places to explore.

I'm tempted. It's a lot more direct than the GR76, but at the back of my purist mind I'm wondering if it might be cheating to take such an easy route. So I decide to stick to Plan A after all, keeping a low profile when we leave in the morning because I've just lobbed a stray crot over the hedge behind the site and there was a terrible splash. I hope it went in the river, but it could have been the municipal swimming pool.

Along the path of the GR76 I meet St James, heavily disguised as an elderly lady riding an Austrian Haflinger pony with a mind of its own. It's fat and over-excited, and Madame's fed up with it.

She joins Leo and me, cursing the pony and saying she'll show me a better way to Mercurey than the one I've planned. What better way? She brings us to a cattle grid, a lethal hoof remover. But St Leo obediently hops up on to a wall beside it and tiptoes along the narrow top, while Master Haflinger throws a hissy fit and hurls himself off the wall to land in the vineyard several feet below. '*Quelle comédie!*' says Madame crossly, remaining glued to the saddle. And two minutes later she leaves us to return home.

'Where on earth are we, Leo?'

I can see Mercurey straggling along the road below, but we're at a completely different crossroads from the one I thought I needed. However, it's too much effort to work it all out so I take the line of least resistance – the main road to Givry, empty of traffic in the drowsy hours of siesta. And when we arrive there, I find the best thing without a doubt is to follow the Voie Verte after all.

Is that what you meant us to do, St James/portly Madame? I appease my conscience by convincing myself that maybe this old railway line hides a Roman road, a mini Via Francigena, since the original one's probably underneath the Autoroute du Soleil. Or it could even be a spur of the Jakobsweg, the German route to Santiago de Compostela, given that I passed a road marker yesterday telling me I was on the Chemin de St Jacques.

It turns out to be a good decision and long afterwards, when I conjure up memories of our pilgrimage, I recall our days on the Voie Verte as the most sun-filled, peaceful part of the whole journey.

The Voie runs in a tarmac line with verges on either side, mile after arrow-straight mile with only the whisper of bicycle wheels or the rasp of a skateboard to harmonise with Leo's clippety-clop. The station at Saint-Désert is indeed deserted as the sun hammers down, and in the late afternoon we stop at Buxy for the night, forcing the metal spikes of our fencing posts through the hardcore under the grass in the old marshalling yards, another first for Places We Have Stayed With Horse and Lorry. Buxy station isn't quite abandoned because there's some kind of wine processing place next to it with a steady thump-thump going on, as though the director is energetically bonking his mistress. Peter and I are filled with admiration as dusk falls and he's still at it.

Leo's diet of weeds and sugary clover has a surprising effect on his stomach when we set off next day – a tunefully farted rendition of the opening bars of 'Three Blind Mice'. As I belong to the infantile fraternity that finds farting funny, the next few miles are filled with smutty sniggers and efforts to remember the rest of the nursery rhyme. There's simply nothing more onerous to think about – the Voie stretches on and on, so carefree, so easy, no cars, no lorries to watch out for; and the views unfold to either side, sunshine pouring down on fields striped with rows of vines and hay bales, the epitome of summer. We stroll along a verge packed with Bee orchids, pausing at a dedicated *halte équestre* furnished with hitching rails and a water tap, and continue through the lazy afternoon to a campsite at Cormatin that has proper paddocks for horses and where, once again, an oversized camper van is *pas de problème*.

Privacy is a bit of a problem, though – the site is filled with motor homes whose owners seem to think we're a travelling circus, and they arrive with their children to photograph the chaos in the back of Big Top Bessie. This prompts us to shut up the ramp and drive off to Cluny early next day, leaving Leo behind in his field wearing a fly veil to combat the first batch of buzzing fiends that become the hot weather downside of our travels.

First stop in the town is for maps, but we draw a blank. The Voie Verte pamphlet sends cyclists to the Bois Clair tunnel not far ahead, with a warning in capitals that it's completely unsuitable for horses. There's nothing much on the subject of diversions and Madame at the tourist office doesn't appear to know the tunnel even exists. Our next stop is more rewarding – it's a chocolate shop displaying an eye-catching diploma from the Golden Marmite

Association. No familiar dumpy jars here, though – it sells wodges of glacé orange, caked in black chocolate an inch thick, and we get through 10 euros-worth in less than five minutes.

Finally, the proper reason for visiting Cluny: the abbey, or what remains of it. There are only ruined walls and aisles now, solitary towers and chapels ranging round more than thirty acres of the town's footprint from which to piece together the cohesion of what was once the most powerful abbey in the western world. I can't get any real sense of what it must have been like because the complex was so comprehensively destroyed that its fragmented memories are still an architectural puzzle. The great gates leading to the last, colossal version of the abbey church are long gone, though their double Romanesque archways still straddle the road; they give me just a hint, a shadow of what once was here.

The best impression comes from the computer-generated recreation of the final church, Cluny III, which you can view through 3D glasses – a nave immense beyond imagination comes into focus, 250 feet long and with a vaulted ceiling that is 100 feet high. And in the museum there are two carved capitals which give a clue to one *raison d'être* for such an enormous church – they depict the Gregorian chant's eight tones, an illustration of the Cluniac monks' love of music and the search for perfect acoustics.

Apparently the first Cluny church was just a small wooden affair, built in 910 on the site of a hunting lodge, a gift to a local abbot by Duke William of Aquitaine who was hoping to absolve himself of all his sins before he died. He insisted the monastery should be answerable only to Rome, which neatly sidestepped any future problems with locals who might want a say in Cluny's organisation or try to get their hands on its wealth. The abbey's coat of arms reflected its allegiance: the keys of St Peter and the sword of St Paul.

The successive abbots who ran Cluny often lived for a very long time. One of the first was Odo, whose passion for music shaped the physical structure of Cluny II, a new and bigger church with a vaulted nave roof to suit the acoustics of plainsong chanting; but it was his successor, Abbot Mayeul, who was responsible for most of the work. He brought in an architect from Lombardy in Italy, William of Volpiano, who introduced the soft curves of the Romanesque school, with classical columns and carved capitals, tall towers, and roofs built of stone instead of wood.

Cluny grew rich with gifts of land and money, and its umbrella extended over other monasteries and churches, among them beautiful Vézelay and Moissac on the Chemin de St Jacques, both of them etched forever in Susie's and my memories from our pilgrimage in 2002. Its empire expanded and spread abroad, and one of its most powerful leaders, Hugues de Semur, who was abbot for sixty years until his death in 1109, succeeded in reclaiming Spain from Islam and restoring it to Christianity. The further riches that flowed in from the grateful Spanish resulted in the Cluniac expansion of the old pilgrim roads to Santiago de Compostela, including the Camino Francés that Susie and I followed across the *mesetas*, the high plains of central Spain.

It was largely thanks to the generosity of King Alfonso of Spain that Cluny III was built in all its grandiosity – though it took so long that Abbot Hugues had been dead for years by the time it was finished. But after his death the abbey's fortunes began to decline, overtaken by the changing face of history. The Cistercians appeared on the scene, a cheerless sounding lot: austere, ascetic, and creators of minimalist architecture which was the polar opposite of voluptuous, Benedictine Cluny. As they gained in popularity, the abbey started to fall out of favour and financial donations began drying up just when they were most needed to pay for the building of Cluny III.

From there it was all downhill. The Huguenots repeatedly ransacked the abbey during the Wars of Religion, and eventually the French Revolution finished it off; religious communities were suppressed and in 1791 the last monks were forced to leave.

The abbey was vandalised and abandoned, its flame extinguished forever, and a few years later the church and buildings were sold to local businessmen; the complex was reduced to rubble, the stone demoted to basic building blocks, and the town spread like an octopus over the remains. It wasn't until the twentieth century that any major excavation work was done, and by then the breathtaking abbey church had been so thoroughly dismantled that the locals had forgotten it ever existed.

But as well as the jumbled architectural remains and artefacts, it seems that memories live on in different forms: drawings, paintings, lithographs dotted around France in museums and private collections, some showing the magnificence of Cluny III, and some depicting its destruction: its demolished chapels, its ruined apse gaping at the sky.

The monks had bred horses, the only means of transportation for the abbots and their visitors. The remnants of the abbey's hostelry and stables still survive, and when Napoleon created a branch of the National Stud in Cluny in 1806, the first stallions were installed here, and today thoroughbreds still continue to rub shoulders with the cream of the French heavy horse breeds, descendants perhaps of Napoleon's war horses. I feel I ought to pay the Stud a visit, but really I'm too saturated with impressions of an ecclesiastical jigsaw puzzle not to mention chocolate to be hugely enthusiastic... Peter and I get as far as the gates, but when we find it's not open to the public for another two hours we set off back to Cormatin, overloading our stomachs even more with ripe cherries as we drive along.

But the magnificent moated château at Cormatin does prove to be irresistible, and we wander round the gardens and castle in a bloated sort of way, admiring everything indiscriminately: the jungle of aquilegias in the flowerbeds, the mellow Burgundian stone, the perfectly preserved music room; and the unintentional, intangible oriental rug created by the mosaic of light thrown on the flagstones by sunshine gleaming through a stained glass window. Best of all is the painting showing a heavy mediaeval joke – Temperance with a glass of water in her hand, her feet massively misshapen by gout.

Back at the campsite, Leo's had enough of being pestered by flies and he's ready to go. We sprint off down the Voie Verte next morning and arrive at Cluny in no time at all, but I'm still none the wiser about the Bois Clair tunnel beyond it, and problems start piling up at its entrance. I check the Voie Verte brochure from every angle. At least it shows where the bypass begins … but that can't be right. We're beside the TGV line, and by the time the fifteenth high speed train has hissed by and we're back yet again in a mini-tunnel under the railway, Leo's looking for trouble. There's a signpost saying *cavaliers*, but it leads to a very major road. When a horsy-looking Range Rover comes by I flag it down and the driver tells me someone's moved the sign round, and what I need is a tiny track at right angles to it. It turns out that the entire equestrian bypass has been re-routed through the woods.

The track splits in two. I dither at the junction, but Leo's completely fed up – we've just had an argument about some distant cattle he thinks might be dangerous, and he nips off impatiently along the path that looks cow-free. And it's the right one, a beautiful overgrown trail that clambers over the top of the Bois Clair hill and comes out in a vineyard above the castle of Berzé-le-Chatel. This spectacularly frowning fortress adds further inspiration to my latest plan; usually Peter's worst dread is my starting a conversation with I Have An Idea, but my suggestion a few days ago that we should buy a *corps de ferme* (well, a château like this one would do) and run it as chambres-d'hôte met with no resistance. The only proviso was that he wanted a grass strip, surprisingly not for a driving range but so he could get his pilot's licence and buy a plane. I examined his face for signs of wind-up-the-wife, but he was deadpan. Perhaps the wonderful warmth of our Voie Verte days is getting to him too.

We settle down on the verge outside a wine co-operative as

the sun is easing towards the horizon, leaving Leo fenced in at the end of a vineyard. No flies tonight, so it's supper outside on Bessie's ramp which is strewn with bits of saddlery and plates and clothes and golf clubs and all the mess I haven't had time to sort out. It's so quiet here that I can hear the car approaching from a long way off, a noisy bee disturbing the tranquillity. It pulls up. The occupants are eyeing our belongings.

'How much?'

'Whaddya mean, *how much?*'

'*Vide grenier?*'

'*Vide grenier? Boot sale?* Yes, well, I suppose it does look like jumble, but *non, monsieur, madame, je suis désolée* (sweet smile), these are our personal prized, er, things, and we use them every day and no, nothing's for sale.'

They smile graciously and drive off. What cheek. Anyway, why would we have a boot sale on a grass verge on a deserted country road at ten o'clock at night? It's just as well they didn't home in specifically on horse or golf clubs, or we might have been less than polite.

Leo and I reach the end of the Voie Verte early next day. We're close to Mâcon, and I need to find a quiet bridge over the River Saône. I still don't have a map and the girl in the Voie information office looks at me blankly when I ask for advice, so I try riding south-east-ish and hope we come to the river. I seem to remember that Peter's road map shows a small bridge over the Saône just below Mâcon, near a place called Crêches-something. We cross the seething N6 main road, the TGV line, the autoroute ... the roundabouts get bigger and rounder and here's an unusual one – the middle is full of vines interspersed with street lamps poised in wine glasses eight feet high.

A sign says Crêches-sur-Saône. This absolutely has to be the right place. I turn due east, which means we should reach the river – and we do, though I still can't see it. The road arches up into a hump which I assume becomes a bridge. It has traffic lights, which are turning red. With cars queuing behind us, I vaguely notice a restriction sign indicating no pedestrians – a human stick figure in a red bordered circle. Nothing forbidding horses that I can see and anyway, the lights are now green.

'Come on, Leo, let's go! Trot ... that's it, get a move on ... WHAT? Oh *no*! Fuck! Turn round, quick ... no, can't, it's not wide enough, it's too late now, keep going, trot, trot, don't look down...'

At the top of the hump all is revealed – the bridge is made of metal sheets and the din of Leo's pounding hooves bounces off the water far, far below, as he and I can see all too clearly through the gaps in the tin plates and the tiny safety railings. Keep going, Leo, keep going keep going. And he does. The river's enormously wide, the bridge as skinny as a washing line, what an idiot, of course that's why there are traffic lights, this happened once on the way to Santiago ... why didn't I think of it? And *shit*! – the lights must have gone green the other end, look at all those cars coming towards us.

Leo hurtles on, and on and on, no genteel clippety-clop now but a thunderous fuckety-fuck, fuckety-fuck. We meet the cars. They stop. They can't go on – there must be another forty vehicles behind us, and there isn't room to pass. Leo can just about squeeze by, and now the cars are backing up, trying to reverse off the bridge ... when in extremis, smile charmingly; I glue a grin to my face and try to avoid catching the drivers' eyes, but even so I register that all the female drivers are scowling, and all the male ones are grinning back at me.

'Thank God for that! There's the end of the bridge, well done, Leo, let's get off it, let's get off the road in fact, look, there's a gate...'

We dive through it, disappear into the woods, and there we skulk for half an hour before I dare come out, I'm so convinced all those furious women have phoned the police who'll turn up with their blue lights and hand guns any minute.

But they don't.

9

The Plains of Ain

It turns out that the clanking snake of a bridge was only
supposed to be a temporary one, which is probably why I
had the impression it was made of delicate filigree and might
give way at any moment. The original Pont d'Arciat was a
chunky affair with stone arches, built in 1904 but completely
destroyed by retreating German troops forty years later; its
slender stop-gap successor was installed in 1950, so after
more than five decades you could say it's still doing pretty
well.[1]

Crossing the River Saône has taken us into the next
département, the Ain. Sandwiched between Burgundy and
the mountains of the Haute-Savoie, I know nothing about
this region apart from the fact that a dead duck was found
here earlier this year which caused reports of bird flu to
go panicking round Europe. It did occur to me that some
busybody might tell me I shouldn't be riding a horse around
these parts, but no one's mentioned avian flu at all since we've
been in France.

---

1 A new and permanent Pont d'Arciat was opened in 2010, constructed
by the company that built the spectacular Millau Viaduct. It's twenty-two
feet wide and almost half a mile long, with special lanes for pedestrians and
cyclists – and hopefully for horses too, if any other riders are mad enough to
go that way.

The maps show a starburst of lakes intersected by little roads running inconveniently north and south when I need to travel east, so I have to work my way slowly onwards in convoluted loops, pausing at intervals to try and find somewhere to stay after our unnerving day. Madame at a village *mairie* is disinclined to help, and when we stop at a farm Leo doesn't endear himself to the owners by eating their begonias when I'm not looking. But St James catches up with us again when Peter calls in rather doubtfully at a classy chambre d'hôtes in a château. This is the sixteenth-century Château de Bourdonnel, named after the *bourdon*, or staff, of the Santiago de Compostela pilgrims; it seems we're on a Chemin de St Jacques, and the family are quite happy to accommodate us all. Monsieur's guided tour of their home includes a viewing of a stone scallop shell, the emblem of St James, carved into one of the cavernous fireplaces; normally it's depicted with its ridged convex back to the beholder but this one's turned the other way out, like a welcoming palm in a welcoming house, a shell with more gravitas than the ones that dance across Louis XV rococo mantelpieces. The château itself is quite plain, Georgian in style, massive to my eyes but apparently no match for the one down the road owned by Monsieur and Madame's relatives. That one's so vast it accommodated 2000 members of the family who turned up recently for a reunion.

Madame cooks dinner for us and for another guest staying here tonight, a retired teacher called Jean-Louis who's travelling to his home in the Alps near Val d'Isère. When I tell him we're also going that way he invites us to visit him, and gives me his phone number which I promptly store in my mobile. Encouraged by his friendliness, I raise the subject of bird flu.

'Ah, *la grippe*,' he says. 'Indeed, it was here. A farmer found a wild duck and a swan dead. It was confirmed they had the flu, and the farmer told the authorities that his turkeys had it too. So he shut his birds in and claimed compensation, and no one ever checked his story or whether he had culled them, so once he had his money he let his healthy flock out again and carried on as normal.' Jean-Louis relates this story with a straight face and it's impossible to tell whether or not he's serious, but it seems to have a certain flavour of authenticity.

Rattled by his earlier mention of Val d'Isère, I get out my glacier-packed maps of the Alps after supper and spread them over the bedroom floor, scaring myself stupid with futile efforts to plan an exact route over the mountains when I'm too tired to see straight. In the end I give up and climb into bed, jumping awake when the wind gets up in the night and squeaks the bathroom door eerily to and fro. Wild moonlight floods through our bedroom, illuminating Peter's peacefully sleeping face, but the groans and creaks of the old house protesting at the gale chip away at my sleep, and I dream I'm edging Leo along carved ledges in the Alps where one false step would send us rocketing down a ravine.

The lanes continue to wind round the ponds and lakes of the Ain, still pushing me south when I want to go east. The humidity, the temperature and indeed my temper are all rising.

This place is just a giant swamp full of carp which the practical French catch to eat – no flinging them back in the water as the English do so that the dumb things can be hooked all over again. Not that I care either way at the moment – it's too hot to worry about the fate of fish and I'm more concerned about Leo, who's shaking his head furiously as the flies dive-bomb his ears.

We stop for a break, but I can't sit down on the grass because of the ravenous bugs that sink their fangs in my thighs. And I've got a foul eyestrain headache from trying to make sense of the maps last night, and, and ... *come on, darling, pull yourself together.* What? That sounds like my father lecturing me. A very politically incorrect expression these days, but that's typical of him, and he's right. There's no point whingeing - I'm here because I want to be here, so I have to get on with it. I ease the headache with paracetamol, and the road obligingly turns a corner so we can make some progress in the right direction. Far away on the other side of the plain there are rounded outlines, the foothills of the Jura. Taller, menacing silhouettes are behind them ... but clear off, negative thoughts. At least it might get cooler when we start climbing.

In the middle of nowhere a signpost points to a rural gîte where Peter and I are allowed to park Bessie outside the owner's house while Leo grazes down his garden. I watch as he idles on to the thick grass, but suddenly he's flinging himself on the ground, rolling violently, leaping up, galloping backwards into the hedge, Leo, Leo, what's the matter? I can barely get near him, he's frantic, his tail clamped down, whoa, whoa, what is it?

He's covered in flies. That's nothing new in this region, there used to be malarial mosquitoes here as well, but these are *really* ravenous bugs swarming all over him, crawling under his tail, scuttling sideways, and they're so flat you can't squash them. It takes a big dose of citronella fly spray in unmentionable areas to get rid of them all, by which time he's sweating with distress and attracting every other insect that inhabits the Ain. It turns out these are crab flies, rare in the UK but quite common on the Continent, and fortunately for Leo this is the only time we come across this vile variety of mini vampire.

Monsieur Gîte is as politically incorrect as my father. Or maybe it's just the French way, in Monsieur's case with a refreshing disregard for Health and Safety. Early the next morning two small children are deposited beside Bessie and I see their mother driving away, leaving Monsieur on babysitting duties. The little girl has urchin hair and determined boot-button eyes; she scampers off to greet Leo, grasping the electric fence tape with both hands as she ducks underneath it and ignoring the inevitable shock. She's under his feet and patting his nose by the time I catch up and haul her out, and next minute she's shinning up a tree.

Monsieur meanwhile is simply standing back, smiling indulgently as her four-year-old brother laboriously clambers up beside her, and then they're bouncing about on a branch ten feet off the ground with a sheer drop on to concrete below them. I gaze imploringly at their guardian – *these children are going to fall out of the tree in a minute.* But he's completely unworried. There's going to be a mothers-and-children party here this afternoon by the swimming pool, he tells me conversationally, which makes me wonder if his two early guests will survive that long, and how many unsupervised infants will fall into the pool.

By midday Leo and I have reached the River Ain that bisects its province; we're both completely cooked so we stop on its sandy foreshore, tempted by the broad sweep of water sliding past. I dig my picnic out of a bag, unsaddle him and leave him loose, his tethering rope trailing behind him. He rubs his sweaty face on my shoulder.

'I'm going to have a drink.'

'OK, you do that. Don't go far.'

He wanders into the river and buries his muzzle in the shallows, looking up abruptly when he hears the sound of sandwiches being unwrapped.

'Perhaps I'll have some of your lunch.'

'No you won't. Go and find some grass.'

'Well, in that case I'm just going to ... going to...'

'No! Get up! Leo – no! UP!'

He's buckling at the knees, about to do what all overheated horses do – lie down and have a good roll. But I don't have a brush to clean him up afterwards, and my weight on his back when he's still plastered in wet sand would rasp off his fur coat under the saddle, leaving him raw and unrideable. So I pull him to his feet and surrender most of my lunch by way of distraction before we amble on, the lakes and river gradually receding as we cross what have now become the dustbowl plains of Ain.

Ambronay's a gateway to the Jura, the last village before we set off uphill. It's very appealing with its little St James chapel in a field, but there's no gîte here, no campsite, apparently nowhere to stay. Someone suggests we ask at the police station, but there isn't one of those either. Peter's left Bessie on a wide verge of grass-baked-to-hay just out of town, and for the first time we decide to hell with it, there's no one to ask so we'll just camp here anyway. I feel vaguely guilty about parking for the night without permission, but none of us has the energy to travel further. Back in the town there are no butchers or bakers, but there's a tobacconist who sells ham so that'll do for supper, along with the ubiquitous baked beans.

There's also a Benedictine abbey. I go inside its church, for no better reason than to cool off in the cavernous interior, and find it's an enchanting place with adjoining cloisters – two tiers of stone galleries in a perfect square. I sit down in the choir stalls where the tipped-up seats have wooden gargoyles carved on their undersides, leering in a very unholy way. Even though I have no real empathy with formal religion, the stillness and sense of space here make me pause. My thoughts drift back to home, to Pa to whom I owe at least two letters, to my mother whose God was generally to be found out of doors in the countryside, and then to her brother Wyndham.

Word has just reached us that Wyndham died last week. He was my godfather (which fact he forgot until I was about thirty-five) and he was the last of that generation on Ma's side, his death marking the end of an era. For much of his adult life he lived in the country house where he and my mother spent their childhood, alone in his later years, and defiantly independent well into his nineties. But physically he was getting doddery, and by the time I left to ride to Rome it was becoming obvious that he couldn't continue rattling around in a big old house on his own for ever.

In May he had a fall and chipped his hip. It didn't seem to be that serious, but he was taken to hospital for what was supposed to be a brief stay, and then he slid downhill. Maybe, like my mother, he'd had enough and decided to slip away as she had done, but in his case he managed it before the spectres of dependency and a care home stalked into view.

Wyndham scared me as a child. He loomed over me, tall and lanky, and his biting wit was legendary. When I grew up I learned not to take him seriously, which was as well when forced to partner him at tennis. In his late seventies he could still nip round the grass court in his garden, poaching shots until overcome by creakiness, when he'd suddenly shout 'YOURS!' with no notice whatsoever, when of course I'd miss the ball by miles given that I was an erratic player in the first place. But by then I knew he was all bark and no bite, and would just grin as he loped crossly back to the base line with his distinctive Pink Panther gait.

Ma adored him. Among her papers I found her unpublished autobiography, the descriptions of her childhood peppered with references to Wyndham who was clearly into relentless teasing from an early age. He was addicted to sport and to cricket in particular, organising my ten year old mother into highly unconventional matches:

> Cricket was often the order of the summer days. It was a fiendish version, for two to play, contrived and organised by my brother. Different bushes in the garden were designated 'fielders', a tree stump the wicket. It rankled always to be appointed the opposition, never allowed to be the English side or playing for Kent. In deference to my sex a soft ball was used, but it was still terrifying when Wyndham emulated Cornwallis, then the Kent fast bowler. His run began in the house by the back door. By the time he emerged from the passage and began thundering across the lawn to the crease, this craven batsman had taken cover behind the wicket vowing never to play the game again...

However, she got her own back. During the school holidays Wyndham's best friend Dick often came to stay, and she trailed along behind them endlessly:

> If the boys wished to be rid of me they vanished while I wrestled with the laces of the stout boots we all wore outdoors. And once or twice I managed to have my revenge for being excluded. The most dramatic was the day they made off to look at barn owlets inhabiting derelict buildings at the top of the paddock. These hissing babies were the offspring of the

pair that flitted out as dusk descended, later emitting the bloodcurdling shrieks that woke me trembling in the night. They nested above the broken ceiling of a loft reached only by a vertical ladder. Rightly this was considered too hazardous for me, but with rage in my heart I searched around until the boys' hideout was discovered, and then removed the ladder.

They were imprisoned for several hours before I plucked up the courage to replace it and vainly tried to make a getaway. Retribution was inevitable and they sentenced me to be put to sea on the pond in a tin bath. This was not deep but inevitably I fell in. It was an unpopular episode with the grown-ups when it ended with my being dumped, bawling and festooned with duckweed, into the middle of one of Mother's infrequent tea parties.

For a little while I sit quietly in the empty church, remembering, reflecting on a way of life that's disappearing, an adventurous childhood like Ma's and indeed mine, without a laptop, iPod or Xbox in sight. There wasn't even a television in our family until I was eleven years old, when my parents bought one only because my mother had made a documentary about keeping horses on a shoestring budget. It starred my sisters, me and our hairy ponies, and the TV appeared in our house so we could watch ourselves in our five minutes' slot every week for six weeks.

It's time to go. I put some euros in the church box and light a candle for Wyndham, whose funeral is tomorrow, and then it's back to Bessie via the cemetery tap for some water so Peter and I can cool off our feet in a bucket. I suppose you could say the influence of my upbringing has never left me, and what we're doing now is stripping off the layers of the twenty-first century for a while. The only modern gizmos we have are our mobile phones; I'd rather rely on a wrist compass and maps than a GPS, and I write up my journal by the light of an oil lamp every evening, using an old-fashioned fountain pen.

Ma would certainly approve.

10

Better than Pie-à-*Deux* on the Dump

Half a mile out of Ambronay the world's a different place, filled with shady lanes, crisp air and no flies. I keep to the lower mountains all day, passing through villages dotted around steep meadows where the grass lies cut and swirled in random patterns to dry. Today I don't care that the route I've marked on my map looks like a galloping crazy cardiogram of peaks and troughs, and that there's still no trail directly to the east; the countryside's so wonderful nothing else matters.

Somewhere ahead the River Rhône is flowing fatly down the valley towards the Camargue; we have to cross it and I've pinpointed a little bridge which I hope bears no resemblance to the Pont d'Arciat, but we won't get that far today and I can't be bothered to think about tomorrow. Instead Leo and I spend a harmonious day in the woods, stopping now and then so he can graze and I can look at the view.

Along the way we pass a memorial to Captain Henri Petit, alias Moulin, who created the first training schools for the *Maquis* of the Ain. Originally the *Maquis* were youngsters escaping conscription into forced labour for Germany in World War II, fighting just to remain free, but later they were organised into tightly-knit groups, *maquisards*, the name taken from the word for the scrub that scratched around their native countryside. They became symbols of the whole French Resistance movement, and the Ain *Maquis* were as daring as any – on the orders of Captain Petit, in November 1943 they took over the large town of Oyonnax, away to my north, and laid a wreath at its World War I memorial with an inscription that read *les vainqueurs de demain à ceux de 14-18*: from the conquerors of tomorrow to those of 14-18. They've never been forgotten, and today I ride past numerous reminders of them by way of simple words carved into rocks at the roadside.

In the village of Aranc, perched on one of the cardiogram peaks, I'm directed to Madame Meunier who apparently has a field. Indeed she does, although it has its hazards – for a start, the fencing is made of dead electric tape loosely looped from one post to the next. I know Leo won't try to escape because he'll think it's live, but there's a more worrying hazard than the fence in the form of an old lady in a pinafore and boots. She's walking along just outside the perimeter and she's slashing violently at the weeds with a scythe, close to the legs of the calves in the field with her and alarmingly close to Leo's as well. He's oblivious to anything but the grass, and in the end I decide there's not much I can do except hope that by the morning she's neither cut through the tape and let him out, nor chopped him into mincemeat. She looks like a female version of the Mad Hatter, and in fact I'd say we're definitely through the Looking Glass – when I go back to the lorry the March Hare's crouching underneath the cab, eyeing up Leo's dinner bowl which I've left between the front wheels. Bessie is parked with her bonnet against the church wall right under the clock, hardly an ideal position for a night's rest, but there was nowhere else to put her.

As dusk pours down the mountains, the hayfields behind us stir into life as the village cats go off hunting in sinuous silence. The March Hare abandons the search for stray grains

of horse food and lollops off into the woods, and when Peter
and I climb wearily into bed it's in the certain knowledge that
the clock is going to carry on bonging out every half hour till
the morning.

So it's another sleepless night, not helped by my conviction
that Leo's lying in his field scythed into slices. Needless to say,
when I go to check him in the dull dawn he's still in one piece,
but it's an uneasy start to a day of speeding lorries on the main
road to Hauteville-Lompnes, which we have to take because the
bridlepath is blocked by six strands of barbed wire. The town's
a strange sprawly place and my tired brain won't decipher the
map; we stray first into its vast medical centre and then into
the middle of a great clump of ski lifts. This is surprising as I
had no idea we were that high up the mountain, or indeed up
a mountain at all, but there's a sign showing the altitude here is
around 4000 feet.

Concentrate. Concentrate. I fix my eyes on a path I've
highlighted on what's now the forty-seventh IGN map we've
crossed since leaving Calais; the track's supposed to pass a house
called the Granges Derrière, and indeed it appears exactly
where the chart says it should: isolated, boarded up, standing in
a treeless glade bursting with orchids. But beyond it there's an
anonymous wilderness of unmarked paths spraying out through
the Forêt de Mazières.

'Which one, Leo?'

'This one, this is the one.'

'The one to where? I hope you're right.'

And two minutes later I have to jump off his back to guide
him down a vertiginous track that's eight inches wide. Peter
phones just as I'm creating a horse-friendly route by breaking
a tree trunk in half (with my bare hands, naturally…) and says
there's no available gîte at Hotonnes, which is where we're
supposed to be meeting.

By the time Leo and I have scrambled down the rocks and switched to the road to the village I'm feeling a bit fraught, and Peter gets a black look by way of a welcome when I find he's been sitting there in Bessie for ages and hasn't looked for anywhere else to stay. Unfortunately he still has the same eminently reasonable argument – it's probably more effective for me to haul my tired horse round the houses while I knock on doors than for him to practise his uncertain French on cross-looking natives.

Luckily for Leo and me, two English couples come to our rescue at once, sending us off to a farm next to their gîte. The owner is a little old bloke who isn't exactly expecting callers – he stands in his doorway pissed as a newt with his flies undone and his carpet slippers on, but he's happy to offer us his harvested hayfield where the clover's already sprouting again. Our day improves even more when our English neighbours share out their wine and gin supplies, and when Peter and I reel back to Bessie for another spell of church bells tolling the hour and half hour, we don't hear a thing all night.

Monsieur appears at 7.30 a.m., sober and smart in clean overalls, and points me in the direction of the Rhône via the Col de Richemond which is smothered in cloud. I've been wondering vaguely where in the messy Bessie my stirrup reflectors are hiding, but they turn out not to be needed – on the long haul up to the pass the fog evaporates to reveal a smoky, humid sun. At the *col* I stop to read the words on a monument to members of the *Maquis* killed in 1944, turning Leo round so he can eat a clump of dandelions.

Ting! Ting!

What? Please God that's not right.

Virgin Mobile is welcoming me to Switzerland. My phone comes up with the Swiss service provider.

Christ, where are we, my map reading must be really bad.

Ting! Ting!

Leo is turning again, and here's another text welcoming me back to France and the Orange network. What a relief, for a moment I really thought the Swiss border was in the middle of the dandelions. I carry on as planned down a zigzag track, easy to follow today, and below us the Rhône comes into view, a great grey python winding along the valley.

'Sorry, Leo. It is another one of those metal bridges but it's very short. Look.'

'I don't think I want to go over that really.'

'Come on, it's just the water's a bit close, but it's OK.'

'You sure?'

He looks at it doubtfully, and then he cocks his ears forward and clanks across as the river writhes past just a few feet below. I notice there's a 3.5 ton weight limit, but since Peter is looking reasonably serene when I catch up with him at Challonges, I assume he didn't drive the 7.5 ton Bessie over it.

Tonight's camping spot is at a whiffy location beside the *déchetterie* bins, while Leo revels in the freedom of a field behind the covered market. But St James takes pity on Peter and me and kindly arranges a luxurious supper for us. Our arrival coincides with the presentation of prizes to the winners of the Challonges *vélo* races, and once the hungry cyclists have stuffed themselves with their party food there's still so much left they give it all to us. And there's another treat in store – a lady emptying her rubbish into the bins invites us home to meet her family and use their shower. Her husband has a telescope set up in the sitting room which he says is focused on Mont Blanc, but the clouds have rolled in to obscure the view again, to my relief – I'm only just getting accustomed to the Jura and I don't want to think about the Alps yet.

My method for measuring distances on the maps is a bit haphazard – I use a piece of string cut to a length of four centimetres, the equivalent of a kilometre on the IGN *cartes de randonnée*, and try to squiggle it round the tracks marked on the paper. A miscalculation results in an extra eight kilometres next day, including a couple on the GR65 that's wiggling along from Geneva to Le Puy-en-Velay, at the foot of the Auvergne, from where it evolves into the Via Podiensis, the most frequently trodden of the Chemins de St Jacques to faraway Santiago de Compostela. Peter and I meet at Choisy campsite, which turns out to be at least two kilometres the other side of the village, a further endurance test for Leo after eight hours spent pounding up and down hills; but at least we're here for a couple of days of glorious rest, and this is a stunning location surrounded by mountains with, er, snow on them, I think that is ... maybe better if I just admire the eagles high above us, circling soundlessly on the thermals.

The evening brings a completely unexpected phone call from Justin, the boyfriend of Peter's daughter Kate. He's calling from their home in America. Our hearts skip a beat – this must mean some disaster...

But it doesn't. With wonderful old-fashioned chivalry, he's phoning for Peter's permission to ask Kate to marry him. Peter's touched and delighted, and when Kate calls two days later to say Justin has proposed on bended knee on a beach in the Bahamas and she has (fortunately) said yes, we pull out the stops with all our Bessie food supplies piled into one gigantic omelette, washed down with the bottle of pink champagne from Bouzy we'd been keeping for our arrival in Rome. Somehow Kate's and Justin's news is of much more immediate importance.

Mountains mean temperamental weather. The first night at our relaxing rest-stop brings humidity suffocating as a sponge and clouds of mosquitoes. We tack netting across the open side of Bessie's Luton head and sweat it out in the darkness, but it isn't dark for long. Flashes of white light start searing the horizon, and soon storm after storm rolls up and round and over us, the lorry a little boat in a ravenous ocean of rain crashing on the roof, battering on the windows and driving the Dutch couple next to us out of their tumultuous tent and into their car. I hope Leo's OK, but I'm certainly not going to run across to his enclosure in the warden's garden to check. In the morning I find him lying down in her compost heap, a soft sticky bed that has turned his white coat to the colour and consistency of soot.

Relaxation Day One is spent washing clothes, turning out the lorry to find my stirrup reflectors, and checking out a local golf course.

Day Two is expensively devoted to Bessie.

One of her rear tyres has an oddly raised tread that doesn't look safe, so we drive to a garage outside Annecy to get it changed. Monsieur Wheels is nice, but firm. This tyre, he says, is a different diameter from the rest and it means all four rear tyres will have to be changed and no he can't put two from the rear on the front and use one of the front ones plus a single new one on the back (my suggestion) because the wheels on the front are a different size from the ones on the back. What bollocks. I simply don't believe it – he just wants me to buy a load of new tyres. We hang about waiting while he makes some phone calls at the end of which he quotes me 1600 euros for four Michelins.

We leave.

Monsieur at the lorry tyre shop further down the road confirms our suspicions – of course they're all the same size, Monsieur Wheels is talking rubbish. However, Monsieur Lorry Tyres doesn't happen to have any that fit Bessie and the order will take two days to arrive. She'll have to have two new ones to go on the front and the best front one on the back (my head is spinning by now) but at least the 500 euros he quotes is a lot better than 1600 euros. We drive away gingerly into Annecy so we can have a look at the town, a less exhausting alternative for Peter than four hours of golf.

Annecy is dominated by its lake, nearly ten miles long, fed by rivers and by the exuberant Boubioz spring which belches out nearly 300 feet below the surface. Apparently the water is very pure, but the day is overcast now and the lake's in sombre mood, reflecting the steely sky. As we walk past the boats moored to the jetties, a plaque on a school wall catches our attention. We stare at its inscription and suddenly groups of people wander over to join us, curious to see what we're reading:

> *A la memoire*
> *des élèves Juifs de l'école*
> *arrêtés le 16 novembre 1943*
> *à leur retour de classe*
> *par l'occupant nazi; déportés*
> *et assassinés à Auschwitz.*

And then it gives the names of the Jewish boys and girls, aged between six and eleven, who were dragged from their school to be murdered in a concentration camp. We stand silently with the other tourists for a moment and then we all go our separate ways again to carry on with our sightseeing, the day suddenly colder.

Wednesday, 21st June, Midsummer Day.

On this date four years ago we were with Susie and Apollo in the beautiful little city of Cahors for the *fête de la musique*, which is the French way of celebrating the longest day. This year I set off on a horse who's still grubby from his bed in the compost heap, aiming for the unpromising destination of Dingy-St-Clair.

On the way there we pass the strangest garden I've ever seen. A ghoulish figure catches my eye; I jump out of my skin, thinking it must be the undead owner of the property, but it's only a scarecrow anchored among cypresses crowded with tree houses. Inside each one there's a dim figure sitting or crouching, the whites to his eyes faintly luminous: are they real, these people? But they don't move, so I suppose they're carved out of wood. Some things are moving, though ... a tiny water wheel is turning very slowly, and a miniature helicopter is whistling up and down the garden attached to a wire. What *is* this place? There's a dog sitting motionless in a run. Is it made of wood as well? 'Don't bark,' I say jokingly as Leo and I pass by, and it doesn't. But it does turn its head to look at us with amber eyes, and I notice with a shock that it isn't a dog at all. It's a wolf. The only normal creature here is a boy about ten years old playing quietly outside the house, quite at ease in his crazy surroundings.

Dingy-St-Clair is at the bottom of a little Roman road. Knowing that Peter is ahead of me, I wonder how he's managing to nurse Bessie down a long twisty hill which according to the road sign is only two metres wide, narrower than the lorry. He's looking marginally frazzled by the time I arrive and we decide to have a slap-up Midsummer Day supper at the only restaurant. But it's closed for food, because it's Wednesday. Of course, what else?

Except I thought France only closed on Mondays. The barmaid lends Leo a field, but she can't accommodate the humans and we end up parked beside a tip again. There are some more road signs here, and they're somewhat perplexing. Between the hours of 10 p.m. and 7 a.m., they say, nudism is completely forbidden without special authority. Peter and I are speechless. Who'd want to dance naked in the night on the communal rubbish dump? And for that matter, who would want to celebrate the summer solstice here with a tired shepherd's pie and no wine?

We go to Annecy.

The old town's in joyful mood, its narrow streets full of musicians, the sound bouncing off house walls, rippling through the water on the canals, loud, brazen, a murderous rendition of Whitney Houston's 'I Will Always Love You'. People are leaning over bridge railings at dangerous angles, laughing, drinking, eating. Mmm, eating. We track down two substantial steaks with chips and a green pepper sauce, and I manage to break another filling biting down on the only solid peppercorn among all the soft ones. But it's still worth it, better than pie-*à-deux* on the dump.

Driving back in darkness on a lumpy road, Bessie's headlights glance upwards now and then at those impossibly high jagged shapes I've been ignoring all week – mountains, big ones. The Jura with its velvety trees and rounded contours is falling away behind us, and what I'm looking at now are indisputedly the Alps.

Naked. With teeth.

11

Buttoning Fear in a Pocket

Take a deep breath and set off calmly into the heart of the Alps, where the maps are striped blue with glaciers and brown with contour lines so close you can't stick a pin between them. These are wild maps peppered with charcoal-dotted slopes of scree, with tracks that fade away to nothing, and where hiking routes slither and jack-knife across peaks impossible for a horse.

But we haven't got quite as far as the scariest ones yet. Today is supposed to be an uneventful wander down cart tracks and minor roads beside the River Fier to Thônes, a left turn to St-Jean-de-Sixt, and then a short wiggle along a flattish hiking trail that'll keep me away from the D909 Route Nationale. Tonight's accommodation is already arranged at a horse trekking centre just outside the village of La Clusaz; I used to go skiing there and I was always curious about the Col des Aravis, the road pass above the village which was blocked by snow in winter. I wondered what the view was like from the top, and now I'm going to find out.

I'm about to potter off the rubbish dump at Dingy-St-Clair when a pickup and trailer arrive. Leo swings his head up.

'I can smell horses! New friends, look, look!'

'For God's sake, stand still!'

I'm hopping on one leg, the other in the stirrup as I try to heave myself into the saddle. But no chance – Leo opens his mouth and blasts out a riff of trombone notes that will certainly wake up Peter. There are trampling noises coming from the trailer and two burly blokes leap out of the pickup, let down the ramp and back out a pair of bay horses who glue their nostrils to Leo's for several minutes of ecstatic sniffing and snorting and how-wonderful-to-meet-you.

I'm not so sure.

The bays are brothers, huge part-Arabs with broad chests and long legs. They make Leo look like a pony. Their owners also have broad chests and long legs, and make me look like a dwarf. Bernard and Pierre are out for a *ballade*, that deceptively romantic word for a cross-country horse ride that could mean anything from a relaxing dawdle to a mountaineering session at top speed. They suggest we should all ride together, as they too are going to Thônes. I scan their faces – I think I detect a hint of a challenge here. Of course, I say. How kind.

Leo pirouettes down the road like a circus horse, overcome with excitement at the rare event of riding in company, pouring sweat, snatching at his bridle, the epitome of bad manners. The bays trot purposefully to the riverbank, away from the gravelled track I was planning to follow to a ford that crosses the river to its southern side. The bank is narrow and boggy and paved with rocks, and Bernard and Pierre urge their mounts into smooth rocking-horse canters that take them skimming lightly across the top. Not so Leo, hemmed in behind them in an impatient fury. He thrashes through the mud, plunging and leaping and trying to pass, skinning the insides of both my knees as I struggle to keep a grip on the saddle.

The bays swing abruptly to their right, into the river. It's deep and fast and they gallop upstream on its invisible underwater boulders. There's no ford here – this is the wild torrent draining straight from the mountains of the Aravis through gorges to the Rhône. Leo slips and skids in their wake, the water thrown up in rainbow curtains in the sunlight, soaking his coat and me as well – but he's not to be outdone and I catch his mood and clench my teeth. We'll show them!

Realising we're still right behind them, Pierre and Bernard jink back to the northern bank, follow the path briefly and plunge into the river again with Leo still hot on their heels. This time we do cross over to the south side, and here's the main road, the busy D909. By now I've realised the men are just testing us out, and when they pause to tell me kindly that they're going to gallop up the verge but further on they'll wait for us to catch up, my better judgment is enveloped in a scarlet fog and I give Leo a click of encouragement.

He manages nought to sixty in a split second, smoking past his rivals up the strip of grass beside the road, overtaking cars, lorries, buses … and I'm so busy mentally shouting *so there*! and *just think I'm an old bat on a fat pony, do you?* that I completely fail to notice that actually all the vehicles are slowing down and stopping.

We arrive suddenly at the head of the queue, which is waiting quietly for the lights to turn green at the beginning of a kilometre of roadworks. When they change, the safest thing to do is to let Leo accelerate into a flying trot at the front, proudly leading an army of wheels with a rearguard of two disconsolate horses. Ha! The Charge of the Light Brigade has nothing on us, but perhaps we'd better wait at the other end. I veer into the driveway of a cemetery where members of the Resistance lie entombed, and step on the brakes. Bernard and Pierre don't have a lot to say when they catch up, and we stop so they can rest their horses before turning back to Dingy-St-Clair and home. Leo has caught his breath again, and apart from his need to suck the nearest water trough dry, you'd never know he'd spent most of the morning at a flat-out gallop. As for me, the pounding of my heart is gradually subsiding and I can just about control my breathing. My companions ask me cautiously if I'm tired. Me? No, I say. We do this sort of thing all the time.

The hiking track at St-Jean-de-Sixt falls straight into another torrent. I've have had enough of those for one day so we take to the D909 again, this time at a walk because the verge has vanished and we've hit an Alpine rush hour. La Clusaz looks grey and ordinary without its coat of snow; even though it's a proper farming village, its wooden chalet houses with their pitched roofs are pinched these days between acres of concrete built to accommodate the skiers. At the stables I ask the owner about the Col des Aravis. It's fine, the road is open, she says. I ask her about the bit after that, the picturesque Beaufortain region in the middle of the Alps. Is that OK? She doesn't know, and I haul back my worries to focus on the Aravis for now.

The sun rises on a cloudless day. Leo's on springs, bouncing up towards the pass, still hyped up from yesterday's adventure. There are inviting pedestrian trails alongside the road, and once I've worked out that the ski poles fixed horizontally across the entrances and exits are actually on flexible joints so you can flip them up, we leave the tarmac behind and then climb across country through a wonderland of green slopes and Alpine flowers and cows in leather collars with bells.

At the top of the Col des Aravis, 5000 feet above sea level, there are only two sights that catch my eye. One is a rugged mediaeval chapel, complete with a bell of its own, and the other is the complex of tourist shops, restaurant and car park with a Heineken lorry squeezed in beside the coaches. People queuing for their beefburgers turn round curiously when they hear hooves, and to my surprise they wave and clap and start shouting '*Bravo!*'

Leo's no fool – he recognises friendly faces when he sees them, and he spends a blissful ten minutes hunting through pockets for peppermints, not too pushy, just on the right side of politeness, perhaps you could spare me an Extra Strong? Some chocolate? He works his way through the crowd, and no one can resist him – such a charming horse, and all the way from *England*? How courageous, how beautiful he is.

I feel completely superfluous.

Before leaving the pass I have to make a choice. A dirt road climbs away to the right, up and up by another thousand feet before dropping down to Flumet in the valley to my south. On the map it looks amazing, all sweeping undulations close to the chain of mountains of the Aravis, with Mont Charvin at 8000 feet, and the scary sounding *Trois Aiguilles*, the Three Needles, only slightly lower; it could well be reasonably wide and horse-friendly, but the problem is that it's far longer than the road route.

The easier option seems to be the D909 which has now metamorphosed into a secondary road, hopefully meaning less traffic. This runs downhill all the way, with some elaborate hairpins for the first few miles and then more or less straight alongside the River Arrondine to Flumet. I dither for a bit because the country route is genuinely tempting, but in the end decide it's not fair on Leo to embark on a fifteen-mile scramble just because the scenery's prettier, when he could stroll down the road for ten.

Some stroll.

The horseflies arrive, buzzing packs of them. Leo's solution is to trot and leave them behind, but the descent is far too steep for trotting and there's still no verge. His shoes start to slip on the tarmac despite their tungsten studs so I ease him back to a walk, even though it means the horseflies cruise in grinning with delight and bite us both.

The river materialises to the right of the road, but it seems a long way below us, in fact a very long way ... I'm riding on the right hand side so that no one driving up a hairpin in the opposite direction is suddenly faced with a horse, but it means we're on the outside edge above the drop, and the crash barrier is intermittent and only two feet high. From the height of a horse's back you're looking down for what seems like miles, and indeed the river is growing smaller and smaller until it's just a distant worm. And then it isn't there at all. What's going on? My map doesn't mention a gorge, but that's where the water's gone and the drop is truly perpendicular and oh my God, is that really the bottom down there? A thousand feet down?

I think of Susie and her vertigo, of my impatience with her on the way to Santiago sometimes, but *no*, I remind myself that I personally do not have vertigo and *no*, I'm not going to get off and walk on my own two feet. Leo doesn't like to be led, anyway – he shoves me in the back. But I need to do something to take my mind off the reality that if he shied, one or both of us would go plunging over the edge, no trouble at all.

When witless with anxiety, sing to your horse.

What shall we do with the drunken sailor?
What shall we do with the drunken sailor?
What shall we do with the drunken sailor?
Er-lye in the morning?

But it's no good, I'm going to have to try a rousing hymn.

Um ... and did his feet in ancient times
Walk upon England's mountains green?

When I get to the bit about my spear of burning gold and not ceasing from mental fight, I feel reasonably gritty again and can button fear into a pocket. Leo meanwhile hasn't even glanced in the direction of the gorge; horses don't seem to worry about heights and he just carries on marching down the mountain and cow-kicking occasionally at the flies swarming over his stomach. When we reach Flumet I stop for a detailed scrutiny of the map, and realise from the tiny numbers marking the altitude that we've dropped nearly 3000 feet in ten miles. On reflection, the dirt road might have been easier.

The river has nonchalantly reappeared, and in a fit of chuck-caution-to-the-winds-we-made-it I take a short cut to the start of another long climb – by riding through a mini one-way tunnel from the side that says No Entry. I've almost got away with this flagrant breach of regulations when we come face to face with an old lady standing on the bridge the other side. She waves me down – she doesn't look much like a traffic warden out of uniform (though you never know), and in fact she just wants to tell me that she knows a song about a white horse. We wait in the middle of the road while she sings all twenty-five verses up Leo's nostrils at very close range.

Peter and Bessie are already settled for the night in the public car park at Notre-Dame-de-Bellecombe, stationed between flower beds blazing with geraniums and with fabulous views of jumbled mountains all around. In the late afternoon warmth we dig out our deck chairs and sit in the sun with our books like proper tourists while Leo lazes in a meadow. Like La Clusaz, this old farming village is also focused on the skiing market these days, but the architecture remains sympathetically Alpine, the church an elegant silhouette with its bulb-shaped bell tower and slender spire.

Today's musical theme resumes: first there's the firemen's brass band practising some dismal bugling for a weekend festival, and then at 7 o'clock the church tower springs to life with Beethoven's Ode to Joy, all in bells. By the time its sonorous finale is crashing round the countryside, Peter is grumbling that there'll no doubt be a *reprise* all night on the hour. But there isn't; the only thing to mar a peaceful evening is my effort at DIY tooth repairs – I manage to squirt the entire tube of emergency filling paste into the left hand side of my mouth, cementing up the tooth shattered by the Annecy peppercorn and all the rest as well.

It's a long ride from Notre-Dame-de-Bellecombe to Beaufort, a steady plod up one mountain and down the next as we penetrate further and further into the Alps. From the Beaufortain I intend to cut across the middle of the Tarentaise, and then skirt round the eastern edge of the Vanoise National Park to reach Mont Cenis and the border crossing into Italy. But these are the areas that caused me so much angst last winter – I don't want to stay with the main roads, but some of the cross country trails could still be covered in snow even now at the end of June. Snow or not, they might not be passable with Leo; I have no way of knowing at the moment, but I'll need to find out soon.

There's a particular road I want to avoid. This runs from Bourg-St-Maurice to Val d'Isère; it's a major road that's honeycombed with long tunnels for the last seven miles from Tignes to Val d'Isère, and it's far too dangerous for a horse. Instead I need to cut across behind the Tignes glaciers from Landry using the famous GR5, perhaps the best-known long distance walking route of all. It starts in Hook of Holland and ends in the South of France, and the section relevant to me has the imposing title of *La Grande Traversée des Alpes*. This threads for 400 miles from Geneva to the end of the GR5 at Nice, and my slice of it will be only about twenty miles, but it includes a climb over the Col du Palet at an altitude of 8750 feet, and God knows if it's passable.

But one thing at a time. Today I'm sticking to the minor roads because they're quicker and more direct than the hiking trail of the *Tour du Beaufortin* weaving its way beguilingly across the mountains. I'm acutely aware that patient Peter is running out of books to read and that we still have about 600 miles to go, in other words at least another six weeks of pilgrimage; so no, I'm not going to be distracted by pretty paths ... except this one, cutting across carpets of flowers to, well, I don't know where, but it might be a short cut of some sort so come on, Leo, let's follow it.

Round the corner, his attention is caught by a herd of cows. But my focus is on the horizon beyond them – because there, so clear it seems to be just the other side of the meadow, the massif of Mont Blanc storms into the sky, nearly 16,000 feet high, pinnacle after pinnacle drenched in snow, glittering in the sunshine, so unexpected, so breathtaking, all I can think is *I've ridden all this way, and this is the most amazing thing I've ever seen.* And a pang, a wish my mother could have shared this view. But since she can't (as far as I know), I phone my daughter Clara, hoping she'll be at home; and she is, used to my infrequent calls, only a quick one this time, no jokey hope-you-haven't-burnt-the-house-down-yet preamble that never fails to wind her up – I just want to tell her about this moment, the best one of the journey so far, and one I'll remember all my life.

The short cut in fact loops back to the road, but afterwards I fantasise that maybe St James sent me that way just so I could gaze at the Mont Blanc range. It turns out I could have seen it from the top of the Col des Aravis, but I was so busy smiling at the tourists and puzzling over the map that I never thought to look.

Another corner, another surprise the other side of it – a photographer standing at the roadside with a bride and groom, he in a dark suit, she in a floaty dress as pristine as the snows of Mont Blanc and cut extremely low. They're delighted to see us and it seems we've turned up right on cue: 'Madame, may we photograph your horse with us?' 'No problem,' I say. 'What do you think, Leo?'

'Well, hel*loooo* (striding suavely up to the bride). Mmmmm.'

'*Leo*! What're you doing? That's extremely rude.'

He has buried his nose in her cleavage, snuffling lasciviously... The camera's clicking as I haul him back, and the reason for his over-familiar behaviour is clenched in his teeth – the bride's corsage of white roses. Naturally she's brought them here just for him. I yank them out of his mouth and hand back some tattered stalks, and luckily she sees the funny side. All the same, it would probably be politic to remove Leo before she also notices the green slobber trickling down her dress, so we leave without exchanging addresses – something I later regret, as I'd love to have seen the wedding photos of a greedy horse groping the bride.

A few more corners, and a different sort of surprise – a text from Peter, who doesn't usually contact me during the day. I have a feeling it won't be good news, and it isn't. He's already at Beaufort and has booked us into its campsite for two days – not because we need a break but because Bessie is leaking diesel, not just the odd drop but a steady flow of it. My heart sinks. The lorry's cab doesn't tip which means any technical problems require a contortionist of a mechanic to insert himself into the tiny gap beside the engine. Not surprisingly, mechanics don't like Bessie and produce imaginative reasons why they can't deal with her.

So I have a feeling we could find ourselves staying at Beaufort for a lot longer than a couple of days.

12

On Ma's Retreat
from Reality

Ten days later we're still in Beaufort, waiting for the horsebox
to be mended. If we have to be stranded somewhere then the
middle of the Alps in June is as good a place as any, when the
harsh beauty of the mountains is softened by a deluge of flowers
– but there are reminders of an unforgiving environment: the
other side of the coin from extreme winter is extreme summer.
The sun blazes down on the village, the nights are torn apart by
violent storms, and there are umpteen variations on the theme of
fly: bluebottles, hoverflies, house flies, fruit flies, midges, gnats,
and mosquitoes. Most of all, there are horseflies – grey clegs that
stand on their heads as they gobble indiscriminately into horse
and human skin, and also their hornet-sized monster cousins
with emerald eyes.

Naively, I'd imagined the Alps would be comparatively free of
insects as the cold nights wouldn't suit them. But it isn't very cold
and in fact their numbers have been increasing since Burgundy,
as poor Leo certainly knows. I haven't seen him lying down to
sleep for weeks – he has to doze upright with his legs locked, his
body in neutral and his tail permanently revving. Meanwhile the
mosquitoes pour into Bessie and savage Peter rather than me, to
my selfish relief; but the horseflies prefer female human flesh,

arriving like stealth bombers to attack my legs before I've even noticed, and I'm covered in so many hot itchy lumps that my bulging thighs would be a credit to Superman.

The campsite isn't particularly busy. Its well-behaved occupants pitch their tents neatly and queue quietly with their toothbrushes at the shower block basins, and they're too polite to comment on the new equine camper even though he's surrounded by clouds of buzzing pests that invade their living quarters. Luckily the far end of the site is empty so I can pen him there, with a big tree and a hedge of polygonum fronds to keep him shaded. There are some draft horses nearby for company, grazing in a field with a house in the middle; they follow the shade as it moves round the walls but their donkey companion is far more enterprising – he climbs the steps to the front door and spends his days keeping cool in the porch.

After a couple of days' welcome rest apart from the tormenting insects, Leo is bored and looking for diversions, neighing at his neighbours, deliberately emptying his water bucket and swinging it to and fro in his teeth, and demanding walks round the site so he can crop the grass and poke his nose into people's camper vans.

But we can't leave.

An oil-covered excursion into Bessie's inner workings reveals diesel pouring out of a hole in the outer casing of the fuel pump, an orifice that's machined and obviously there for a purpose. Peter concludes that maybe an interior seal has vanished/split/disintegrated and the hole's there to allow the fuel to escape rather than flood the lorry's innards. Monsieur Avocat (who runs the local garage rather than a law firm) has a cursory look and says the problem is a *joint spi*, a gasket, in the injection pump. Or so he thinks. Either way, with much shrugging he says he can't fix it. We'll have to take the lorry to Albertville, at least ten miles away.

I phone a truck garage there and explain the problem in non-technical French. The mechanic says he can't help and I must contact the Mercedes shop, also in Albertville. First I phone Rufus who normally fixes Bessie in England; sounding lugubriously pessimistic, he says it'll be almost impossible to obtain Bedford parts in the Alps. But when I try Monsieur Mercedes, he tells us to bring the horsebox to him straight away.

We crawl to the town, dribbling a multi-coloured path of diesel; noting the situation, Monsieur says nonetheless that it isn't a problem (much lifting of spirits) – it's a Bosch pump and he can change it, but he needs the regulating instructions for the engine. Back to Rufus, who tells me they're written on the engine itself. Monsieur Mercedes levers himself into the inspection pit where Bessie drips diesel into his eye, which may or may not account for his inability to spot anything written on the engine at all. Therefore (*je suis désolé*) he himself can't deal with it – but he knows a man who can: Monsieur Yves Something, the Bosch dealer down the road.

Yves says it's actually a Lucas pump, but (much falling and rising of spirits) he *can* fix it, though he can't start for a week and it'll take him three or four days. However, he can lend us an old Citroën while repairs are under way, though he has no room in his yard to store Bessie until he's ready to begin work on her. So we chug back to Beaufort again, the hole in the casing plugged with a matchstick, debating what to do. I could set out alone with Leo while we're waiting, but he can't carry enough camping gear and food supplies for both of us for ten days – there simply isn't enough horse to hang the bags on. And there's me to carry as well. I could free up the saddle area for baggage if I walked on my own two feet, but I have no hiking muscles to speak of and probably not enough puff either – it requires a disconcerting amount of physical effort just to cycle the mile into Beaufort village on Minnie the bike.

But at least I can try and find out a bit more about the GR5 route from Landry to Val d'Isère while we're waiting here. After several expensive phone calls to equestrian centres in the area, one proprietor tells me that the path from Landry to the first stop at Tignes is very hard for a horse, whatever the weather. He suggests an alternative route close to Bourg-St-Maurice, reeling off place names and obscure track details that I can hardly hear because the line's so bad, though when I look at the IGN map later, I think I can work it out. I don't want to go anywhere near bustling Bourg but maybe I can keep off the main road altogether, and there's one advantage – it means we can take up Jean-Louis' light-hearted offer, made when we were staying at the Château de Bourdonnel, of a bed for the night at his house in Ste-Foy-Tarentaise on the eastern side of the Beaufortain, not far from Tignes.

Beaufort sits in a valley, the embodiment of a traditional Alpine village, bursting with flowers in window boxes and tubs that drip greenery into the River Doron gliding alongside the main street. The area is famed for its cheese, a kind of tangy Gruyère that varies in flavour according to the time of year it's made and where the cattle have been grazing. The Tarentaise cows that produce the milk are red and rugged, used to a tough existence at high altitude; Peter and I try out chunks of their cheese with bread (averagely tasty), but then we discover *tartiflette* – a puffed up cheese pie with cream and bacon, onions and potatoes. This is completely addictive, so we find excuses to walk to the village for suppers that are far more *gourmand* than *gourmet*, unashamed piggy feasts that we kid ourselves we can digest while waddling back to Bessie whistling Susa marches at a stodgy tempo. In the rain.

These storms. They crack down out of nowhere, out of twilight skies and hushed evenings, the rain spitting and sizzling on roads still hot from the sun, writhing up in swirls of fog from the tarmac. Our next door neighbours arrive back at the site speechless with fright from a drive in the dark when the steam was so dense they couldn't see the hairpin bends skewing down the mountain. Next morning they've recovered enough to consider a game of table tennis before breakfast, and by evening they're playing boules until it's too dark to see; there's no moon tonight and then, imperceptibly, there are no stars.

Tucked up in Bessie sleepily reading a book, I half-hear a little whooshing sound in the distance – and then in a nano-second the wind comes tunnelling down the valley like the TGV, shrieking into the campsite, bending all the trees over, hurling spears of rain as thunder and lightning crack and glitter round the tents and walkways. Torrents spew in through Bessie's sun baked seams, soaking my pillow as I scramble about trying to close the vents. But at least we're more or less sheltered; in the flashlight photography show that's going on outside I can see people diving into their cars for safety and a bloke running around in his underpants, the rain sluicing down his naked back as he struggles to get his tent under control.

After an ear-battering ten minutes the storm goes hurtling off to the next batch of mountain peaks, leaving behind a profound silence. I tiptoe out to check if Leo's still in his enclosure, or indeed still alive, squelching past the ruined tents to find he's still munching stoically, surrounded by a flat jungle of polygonum. Used to living out of doors all year round, he has no concept of danger from the weather, no worries that he might be struck by lightning, and I can only admire his equanimity.

We're running out of things to do; Bessie's living quarters have never been so clean and tidy, every night's squashed mosquito collection meticulously scraped off her ceiling down to the last dismembered leg, every crumb and grass seed brushed off her grubby carpet. I've got bored with trying to cajole my overheated brain into absorbing some Italian grammar from an impenetrable textbook, and Peter is bored both with reading in general and with trying to work out the whereabouts of Megève golf course in particular, if only we could get there. Bessie is now literally immovable – the battery charger's been outwitted by the demands of Frigo the coolbox, and both the batteries are flat. We lug them down to Monsieur Avocat who puts them on fast-charge in his garage and then locks up and goes home for the weekend.

And yet, despite the crazy weather, my days have settled into an easy rhythm, a familiar routine where caring for Leo is the framework. As any horse owner knows, come rain or shine your animal needs to be checked, fed, watered and groomed, his stable mucked out and the dung in his field collected and dumped on a muck heap. And contrary to what ordinary mortals might believe, this mundane work is pleasurable, giving time in the mornings to wake up and ease into the day, and in the evenings to wind down again. At home in Faversham the wild creatures that share Leo's field are so used to seeing me that I've become invisible. The rabbits simply carry on with their annoying rabbity business of digging pot-holes in the pasture, ignoring not only me but also the spring collection of fox cubs yipping and yawning under their noses. On winter nights mysterious eyes gleam from the hedgerows, shining green in the light of my Mad Woman of Faversham poo-identifying head torch, though it's fair to say I must be looking equally eccentric these days in my Alpine dung-collection costume of bikini and rubber gloves.

For decades Ma's life too was centred round caring for her horses. As she grew old she relied more and more on her final pony, The Fiddler, to maintain the structure of her life, and the physical effort of looking after him kept her mind grounded for a long time. She walked the half mile from home to his field every day and then creaked back up the hill again, and sometimes she lined him up beside an upturned water trough so she could scramble into his saddle, and they'd doddle off together for an hour.

Fiddle was also slowing down, most of his illustrious career behind him now after years of hacking, hunting, show jumping, galloping across country and doing dressage with countless riders. He'd instilled confidence in numerous nervous equestrians, young and old, disabled and able-bodied, from my deaf son Oliver (the pony perfectly understanding the orders he was being given by an instructor on the ground, even if Oliver couldn't hear them) to Princess Diana, when for several weeks he lived in luxury at Windsor and then Sandringham, a far cry from his usual two acres of sloping paddock inexpertly fenced by my mother.

As the two of them aged, so Fiddle's work with the Riding for the Disabled Association wound down, and Ma spent more time fussing round him in his field and stable than taking him out for a ride. One morning she was gone for hours, and eventually it occurred to my father that he ought to go and check she was all right. But she wasn't – he found her on the stable floor where she'd fallen over while trying to heave a rug on the pony's back. She couldn't get up, and in typically independent fashion she and Pa decided the best way to deal with the situation was for him to heave her into the dung barrow and wheel her home. By now my father was even creakier than she was and not surprisingly he found this a bit of a challenge, though it didn't occur to him to go and get help. Luckily for both my parents, one of the neighbours spotted them and called an ambulance before Pa did himself an injury as well.

The first I knew of it was via a phone call from the hospital. When I got there, my father was more concerned that Ma was wearing unsuitable underwear, and therefore wasn't in a fit state to be x-rayed, than whether she'd broken anything. In the meantime she was lying prone on a trolley. 'Don't tell your father,' she whispered, 'but I've got my oldest most disreputable knickers on.' 'I won't tell him,' I promised, but his troop commander voice was already booming across the A&E department: 'I SUPPOSE YOU'VE GOT THOSE *AWFUL* PANTS ON WITH A HOLE IN THEM!' 'No I haven't,' she said indignantly, looking him straight in the eye and ignoring what must have been the considerable pain of a broken thigh, as it turned out. To her relief, the doctors decided not to put her leg in plaster but simply to pin her together again, and a few weeks later she was back looking after Fiddle.

And so she continued for several years, but the black tendrils of dementia were gradually crawling through her brain, clouding her memory and her judgment until she was far beyond her intrinsic absentmindedness. It became too obvious for the family to ignore.

We realised then that her pony might be suffering, even though he lived out in a field. Ma refused to let anyone else look after him, but now she probably couldn't remember whether she'd fed him his hay and concentrates or not, although she always insisted that she had. By now in his late twenties, she usually kept him rugged up in deference to his age and so it wasn't apparent what condition he was in. He was uncomplaining, always gentle, always pleased to see us; apart from a certain listlessness that might have been due to his years, we couldn't guess, until one day we saw him without his rug on, that Ma must be convincing herself that she'd fed him when she hadn't.

We pointed out to her that he was too thin, that his coat was harsh and staring, but she couldn't see it. To her, Fiddle was still the fit, glossy horse he had always been, and since he was so well, there was no question of having him put down, what were we thinking of? He was fine, she'd ride him tomorrow, and anyway he was hers. Her responsibility, her decision.

For a short while there was an impasse, and then dementia dragged her down another step on a path of no return. It became clear she wasn't safe; twice while taking a familiar short cut to the field she got hung up on a stile and was discovered upside-down half over it, prickly and defensive because she couldn't work out how it had happened and because she didn't want to bother anybody, even though she was completely stuck. She was extricated and brought home, and for a time afterwards she kept to the road route. But then, smothered in an amorphous cloud of anxiety, she began to get lost.

Leaving Fiddle's field she would turn left instead of right, ending up on the rough track where the metalled lane petered out, heading towards Hythe in a haze. When we found her she'd make light of it, but behind the jokiness she was scared, scared because she'd got in a muddle, made a wrong turn – but it was more than that: the way home wasn't hard-wired into her brain any more, and she didn't know why.

Something had to be done. My father was beside himself with worry as Ma fought to hang on to her independence and self-respect, pushing away offers of help, insisting *I can manage*. But then her confusion began to make her wander aimlessly away from the house, and she had to be persuaded indoors and distracted while her own front door was locked and the key hidden from her. By now she simply wasn't capable of caring for her pony any more and, given his age and increasing frailty, with a mixture of guilt and relief the decision was made to have him put down. I'm not sure she ever really acknowledged that he had disappeared from her life, and she would often insist she'd been out for a ride on him; but without her lifetime's basic routines to rely on, it seemed to me that she deteriorated quickly, her hold on reality broken.

Brain scans, meetings with Social Services, hospital tests followed, and mostly Ma complied amiably enough as we tried to get her help and keep her dignity intact at the same time. Sometimes she seemed to realise all too painfully what was going on, and sometimes she didn't. On one hospital trip I briefly left her sitting in a chair, and when I came back she was stroking something clutched in her hand.

'I found this little pretty on the floor,' she said, 'I don't think it's got a home.' And she showed me what she was holding: an electrical plug she'd pulled out of the wall, its cable snaking away across the floor. 'Poor little thing,' she said, 'poor little hamster.'

Live-in carers came to my parents' home, but it wasn't an ideal solution, particularly not for Pa – at nearly ninety years old, he wasn't physically fit enough to look after my mother who was now going through a phase of believing she couldn't walk any more, but he didn't like strangers looking after her and he didn't like them living in his house, either. One male carer had a very hard time – my father was convinced he was touching up his beloved wife. He wasn't, of course, but it was the last straw and so arrangements were made for Ma to go into a home. And there she retreated into herself, taking refuge in snapshots of her life as she had lived it years ago, sometimes recognising my father and sometimes staring at him and asking, 'where's Tony?' while he tried to hide his devastation that she'd remembered his name but couldn't associate it with the man in front of her.

Years later, as Peter and I are waiting out the days at Beaufort, I still feel bad that in the end a formal care home was the sole realistic option for her, and it's only a small comfort that at least, once she'd settled in, she wasn't stalked by terror any more.

Turning a blind eye to our shrinking funds, we hire a car for three days. The difference in mindset is extraordinary – suddenly a journey that would take me a day by horse takes half an hour, and I have to resist the temptation to go ranging for miles with four wheels instead of four hooves, not exactly in keeping with the spirit of pilgrimage. A search for the golf course sounds OK, though we never do manage to find it, and then a motorised recce of the first bit of my riding route to Tignes seems a sensible idea while we have the opportunity, even though it might be spiritually dubious.

The road across the mountains to the Lac de Roselend rolls through glorious scenery, but it carries too much traffic to be safe for a horse. We enjoy it in the car, though, driving round the northern shore of the artificial lake whose construction in 1960 meant drowning a village for the sake of hydro-electric power. Truncated by a dam, it's nearly half a mile long and deep, deep blue, surrounded by precipitous pastures where the cows have their own portable milking parlour parked nearby, ingeniously created from a flatbed lorry. We can imagine them lining themselves up in the stalls with a sigh of relief, waiting for a download.

Storm-fed streams and rivers come foaming down from the high peaks, and they attract a novel type of wildlife – nudists. The men stride about in the freezing water trying unsuccessfully to look manly, and the women lie flat on the rocks, breasts up like molehills mimicking the mountains. They take no notice of Peter and me discreetly sitting by the car fully clothed while I try to concoct sandwiches out of bread and a swimming-pool of butter – Frigo's still misbehaving, bloody-mindedly switching itself to hot instead of cold when I plug it into the cigarette lighter.

Circling round to Landry, we reach the end of the road where the GR5 picks up the narrow trail across the mountains. At the horse centre there, Monsieur confirms the local opinion that the track to Tignes is extremely difficult, and any thoughts I might have had about risking it regardless are firmly quashed when he says there's still snow at the Col du Palet. He doesn't know if it's a dusting or a metre deep – the Col is miles away and no one's been up there to have a look. My only consolation is that the lady in the Landry tourist office says I'll be able to ride the following stage of the GR5, from Tignes to Val d'Isère, so at least I won't have to worry about the tunnel-infested main road between the two towns. When we carry out a test drive, it's every bit as bad as I thought it would be.

So it's going to be a question of piling essential gear into rucksacks, strapping them to Leo, and getting him and me ten miles up a quiet mountain lane to a campsite next to the Lac de St Guérin with its massive dam, south of Roselend and 2000 feet above Beaufort. From there it looks as though we can carry on climbing on a gravelled track to the pass at Cormet d'Arêches (at an altitude of 7000 feet and stuffed with snow, for all I know, but I'm bound to meet it somewhere) before descending slightly to another site above Bourg-St-Maurice to meet up with Peter in Yves' Citroën. Then it'll be a short ride to Ste-Foy-Tarentaise on the haphazard route I think I worked out following my crackling phone call to an equestrian centre a few days ago. I've finally managed to speak briefly to Jean-Louis to confirm he really meant his invitation; he asked me in a very faint voice (which I hoped was due to the bad line) when we'd be arriving. I hadn't a clue really, but I said some time on Tuesday, not that I can remember which day of the week is which any more.

Anyway, I'm sure I don't need more than a simple plan for what looks like a straightforward cross-country expedition to Jean-Louis's house; it'll take two days and a bit, A to B.

13

A Trail of Disaster

'What's all this?'

Leo's looking round at his flanks, which are almost engulfed by my Faversham market cheapo rucksacks. His ears ping forward.

'My food's in there – I can smell it!'

'Yes, it *is* there and no – you're not having it now. We've got a long way to go first.'

Muddled in with his grain is the heavy portable electric fence and its battery, along with the tent, gas stove, air mattress and everything else I've convinced myself I can't do without. They take up a phenomenal amount of room considering we're only going to be camping for one night. Leo's easing his teeth round a corner of one of the rucksacks and I push his face away; one small tug and the seam will split, dumping everything out. It would have been sensible to attach the bags to the Western saddle with its bigger load-bearing surface, but I keep forgetting to jam the broom handle through its stirrups to turn them out and on a practice ride I found my feet were uncomfortably pigeon-toed. So it's back in the lorry for some more bracing, and I've spent the morning cramming everything on to the lightweight English saddle.

It's a Sunday so the roads should be quiet, and indeed Beaufort is lazily hot and laid back by the time I'm ready to leave, its citizens sleeping off lunch behind closed doors. But the horseflies are awake, and as I make a start on the tight bends towards St Guérin a cloud of them chases after us. In spite of the extra weight he's carrying, Leo accelerates as the pests dive-bomb his neck and stomach, staining him with blood as they slice into his skin. For ten miles he strides uphill as though he's carrying no weight at all, the only sign of his effort the rivers of sweat diluting his blood to a pink wash, and the heat has barely begun to drain out of the day by the time we reach the site at L'Ami, 5000 feet above sea level. There's no one else near us which means I can stretch the electric fencing to create a field that's all of ten square yards, the posts braced with elastic and skewers.

The tent unfolds into a green toadstool on the mountainside and I sit beside it to watch the dusk's slow descent, my stove emitting just a matchstick twinkle as the sun disappears behind a crowd of peaks. For a moment their tops are outlined in a toothy silhouette before they fade into night, and the temperature drops like a stone. In the vastness of twilight the stars come out, the Milky Way unrolling like a carpet in the sky, and when the darkness deepens the moon rushes past from east to west as the earth tilts on its axis, and I've never felt so alone in all my life.

But not lonely. Behind me Leo's quietly chewing the grass, relaxed now that the horseflies have disappeared, and at my feet the stove whispers out a breathy hiss underneath the saucepan-full of baked beans I've decided I need to eat, if only to make sure I keep warm in my tent by means of internal combustion.

Full of food, I lie flat on my back and look up at the sky. Leo too is resting now, his spotted hide a pale ghost coat. The only sound is the far off rushing of a river, while countless million miles above me the planets whirl past silently and I wonder, as I always do, how many other civilisations are out there journeying through infinity.

Time for bed…

Ten minutes after dropping off, I'm wide awake again. That's odd. I seem to be head down a bit, not to mention stifling in a honk of new tent and sweaty saddle and no fresh air. I realise my head is indeed lower than my feet, in fact I'm probably about to toboggan off down the mountain on the air mattress, dragging the tent. So I shift my bed laboriously sideways and then the only thing to stop me rolling off is the non-breathable, man-made fabric of my new sleeping bag to which I'm coldly and clammily stuck. My head aches where Leo whacked me by mistake while swinging round to swat a fly, and I'd probably feel less stuffed up if I opened the tent flap, but it's out of the question – I didn't get round to working out the mechanics of the tightly rolled flysheet, and without its protection I'd be a boiling mass of mosquitoes in seconds.

So it's a few hours of uneasy dozing and by four in the morning, when I can hear Leo galloping about in his enclosure as the horseflies wake up, I'm completely and utterly frozen. So much for the warming properties of a gassy supper. Even the additional layers of coat, jumpers and saddle pad have done nothing by way of extra insulation, and I curse myself for not packing the one thing I really needed – my wimp's hot water bottle.

But it was a brilliant night all the same, not to be missed, even though it'll be midday by the time I defrost.

Outside the tent the mosquitoes have been replaced by black flies. They swarm all over me but there's an effective, if dangerous, way to deal with them – light the stove and stand right over it to drink a disgusting mixture of hot long-life milk and brown sugar, minus any coffee as I forgot to bring that as well as the hot water bottle.

A car is nosing up the lane with a welcome figure in it – Peter-from-Birmingham, an ardent camper and tramper of the Alps who's also been staying at Beaufort. He's come to check I've survived the night and to offer to transport my splitting rucksacks to our next site above the River Isère. As I'm struggling even to get Leo's saddle on him while he dances about fighting off the flies, I'm thankful to hand over most of the baggage. And Peter 2 (or Two or Too) has also volunteered to follow my Peter to Albertville in case Bessie falters to a halt with fuel starvation – which she might, since diesel is now pouring incontinently out of the casing. He gallantly holds my horse in a vice-like grip so I can launch myself into the saddle, and then drives away again to assume horsebox duties.

Leo shoots off up the road and within minutes we're at the St Guérin dam with its fan of buttresses ramming their shoulders against its massive wall, the sheer scale of it reducing the road that runs along the top to a ribbon. Beyond it a lake of motionless water stretches round the corner out of sight, the shoreline dotted with conifers that struggle up the slopes until the last trees give way to bare rock and snow fields far above L'Ami.

We climb away from the dam, higher and higher on stony paths until the gentians growing beside them are pushing their noses out through patches of snow. Now we're 6000 feet up in the peaks, and below us little Fairy Lake, the *Lac des Fées*, shines as blue as the flowers under a cloudless cupola of sky. Leo pauses to take a look, casually resting a hind leg, the flies finally left behind. He's not tempted to go down there for a drink, there's no need; we can stop at any of the waterfalls that come sparkling past every mile or so, and at lunchtime I turn him loose in the sure knowledge he won't lift his nose out of the mass of flowers and grass all around us.

Today's ride is beyond my wildest dreams. The sun has now warmed me through and through, and in a tired haze of happiness we amble across high pastures in a huge empty landscape fringed by mountains. I can't believe I ever felt intimidated by the Alps – today they're at their most seductive, dotted with cows but completely devoid of tourists, hikers, bikers, other horse riders and anyone else at all.

The pass at the Cormet d'Arêche has a sign stating we've now reached an altitude of 7000 feet; from here it's a good nine miles to the Isère, most of it downhill on pebbly tracks that grind away at Leo's worn shoes, but I'm not going to let the next worry – finding a farrier – spoil this wonderful day. We saunter off down the slope, Leo bloated with grass and me by now euphorically light-headed with altitude and fatigue, and just starting to realise that after three more hours of travelling I'm going to be a rag.

St James decides to put a little temptation in my way. Temptation has a capital T and a naked bronze torso, a 4x4 truck and an empty horse-sized trailer. What on earth's he doing here, miles from human habitation?

'I've just brought a cow up the mountain,' he says, 'to put her back with the herd. I'd be happy to give you and your horse a lift, wherever you'd like to go.'

'No,' I say faintly, 'that's really kind of you, but I've ridden here from England and I'm riding for charity and we mustn't cheat and hitch-hike along the way.'

When I tell him our destination is Rome he looks at me as though I'm off my trolley, or else he doesn't believe me. As Leo sidles past on the cart track I smile gratefully at him anyway, and glance enviously at his cow. She's settling down into the grass for an afternoon's rest and serene cud-chewing, her nubbly horns just poking through her ginger fringe. I notice that Monsieur

Temptation looks as though he has horns just like hers, badly concealed in his sun-bleached hair.

Sated with fresh air and exhilaration, we bowl in to Camping Le Bioley to an enthusiastic welcome from the proprietor, who throws her arms wide to demonstrate the breadth and beauty of the views across the valley below. Both the Peters are here, Peter 2 still escorting us and beaming with bonhomie, and my Peter looking thunderous. It turns out that Peter 2 had phoned the campsite in Beaufort after he left me and had been told that my Peter had already set off to Albertville. Unfortunately he was in fact parked beside the road waiting for Peter 2 – who drove straight past, oblivious of the hulking Bessie because he wasn't expecting to see her. My husband had already spent an hour at the roadside, whittling fifty sticks to the precise diameter and circumference of the hole in the casing, and it was probably as well that the first one he inserted remained plugged in for the whole journey.

And he doesn't look particularly enamoured of Yves' little Citroën, either, which is down on its axles and bulging with most of our belongings including a bigger tent, double air mattress and a voluminous duvet. We've never done this kind of camping together before and I just hope it doesn't rain; the tent is several years old and probably leaks, but there isn't room for both of us in mine. Now that Bessie's safely in Albertville we really don't want her back this side of the Col de l'Iseran – it occurred to us even before we left Canterbury that she might struggle to crawl over a pass at 9000 feet. But maybe Yves won't finish the repairs until we're on the other side, and then Peter can bring her round via the longer but flatter route through the Arc valley and villages of the Maurienne.

At least the old tent has big meshed ventilation flaps and is pitched on level ground. It doesn't rain in the night, and after yesterday's long ride I sleep like the dead, waking late in a panic because today's trek is likely to be even further than yesterday's. At 9 a.m. the sun's already blasting down on this south facing slope, and by the time I'm ready to go it's considerably later and hotter – the car isn't nearly so easy to organise as the lorry, and it takes me ages to sort out the food and work out rough directions for Peter to get to Jean-Louis' remote chalet, which I now note with alarm is miles beyond his home village of Ste-Foy-Tarentaise and opposite a truly impressive glacier.

It's a three-hour ride to the outskirts of Bourg-St-Maurice, with Leo and me simmering sweatily all the way. There's a great view of the River Isère bubbling coldly along the valley floor and flowing underneath the bridge towards Landry, a route I reconsider for a fleeting moment since a trip through snow drifts on the GR5 seems suddenly attractive. Less alluring are the ski stations of Les Arcs, brassy carbuncles on the summer landscape. There are golf courses here, but their setting is not exactly attractive – they crisscross the slopes beneath the ski lifts and they wouldn't have tempted Peter even if he'd managed to jam his clubs into the car.

I cross the river just before Bourg-St-Maurice and carry on along its southern bank, keeping to the woodland trails that Monsieur Trekking Centre detailed over the phone a few days ago. There's blissful shade along the edge of the glacier-fed Isère, and I'm thankful not to be on the far side where heavy traffic rumbles on the road to Tignes. A brief stretch of metalled lane leads to a hydro-electric power station and then the trail appears again, threading steeply up through the woods away from the river which retreats rapidly below us, the gentle graduation of its bank metamorphosing into a ravine. I've had my doubts about this part of the cross-country route because on the map it's only just discernible as a broken black line, and the actuality is even worse: the forest has strangled it to the point of obliteration, tangling it with fly-infested weeds and undergrowth. Monsieur has assured me he's ridden it on a horse many times, though, so it must be OK.

But it isn't.

'Leo, this is getting really narrow. Where's the path?'

Now we're scrabbling round tight bends on naked rock, and his paper-thin shoes are slipping all over the place. He's going to lose his footing in a minute, so whoa, steady, just stop for a second and I'll get off.

What track exists is chipped out of the rock face and it's so pinched I have to dismount carefully on to the slope above it. I set off again on foot, puffing round the blind corners with Leo following on a loose rein, fending for himself because I daren't risk my own balance by turning to see how he's doing.

Then suddenly he's right on my heels nudging my shoulder and don't, Leo, don't, DON'T ...

Oh FUCK, no, no ... he's pushed me off the path and I'm falling down the ravine, careering through brambles, picking up speed and ouch, Christ, that hurts...

But thank God or indeed St James, suddenly I see a sapling flying by and manage to grab it and stop, stop, OK, stop panicking too, stupid woman. Shit, that was close.

Leo's peering over the edge. He can't understand what I'm doing down here, and it was fucking lucky I let go of the reins or I'd have dragged him over with me, wretched horse. But I can't blame him really – from his point of view, my shoulder was the best place to rub his face and shift the flies out of his nostrils.

Now I have to get back up there again, which isn't as difficult as it looks as long as I stretch out like Spiderman and try to crawl through the ivy creepers rather than the brambles. It still takes about ten minutes, though, and when I arrive at the top, where at least Leo's had the good sense to wait, I think bugger this, and get on him again. For a second I dwell on what might have happened: as is usual in the mountains, I'm in *un trou*, a communications hole where there's no mobile signal; Peter has no idea where I am (there's never any point in telling him my exact riding route, because I often change my plans mid-journey due to some obstacle or another), and if Leo had gone down with me, we might never have been found. Carrying an emergency whistle is all very well, but there would have been no one to hear it.

But these are the risks you take when you go off on crazy adventures.

A few yards further on the track becomes impossible. I ease myself off Leo's back again and tie him to a bramble with instructions not to move. After five minutes of clambering up the rocks, round more switchbacks and over a precarious *passerelle* – a wobbly apology of a footbridge – I give up. We'll have to go back.

Turning Leo round is a petrifying manoeuvre. There isn't enough room. I climb past him on the slope above and pull his head round towards his tail. He hesitates, puzzled, and I try and push his chest to make him sit back into the bank. His brains click into gear and he leans back, swivels, hops his left foreleg round, swings the other one out over space, and suddenly he's done it and we're facing back the way we came. But for the next mile I hardly breathe with fright as I stumble downhill in front and Leo slips behind me, hairpin after hairpin where one long slide would send him cannoning into me and both of us over the edge. When we reach the hydro-electric station again, we have to backtrack another two miles to get to a lane that will take us eventually across the main road and up to Ste-Foy. There's a stream here we crossed hours ago with a name that graphically translates as the Torrent of Old Piss. It made me laugh at the time, but now it just about says it all.

Christ almighty. I'm almost out of expletives. I don't believe anyone's ridden this way for years, and I tell you what, Leo, that's positively the last time we go off-piste in the Alps.

As for you, Monsieur Useless Instructions, I hope you rot in hell.

14

Pull-Yourself-Together-Woman

One harrumphing horse, one rattled ratty rider.

By the time we get somewhere near Jean-Louis' house we've been travelling for more than nine hours, Leo's famished, and the hungrier he is the skippier he becomes even though he ought to be exhausted. For the last hour he's been eyeballing dangerous rocks, dangerous bicycles and the odd dangerous cow, leaping sideways in mock alarm and pulling my arms out – whereas in my case fatigue has me slumping in the saddle, thought processes grinding to a grumpy standstill.

After our hideous non-existent short cut, the long way round by road is very long indeed – another succession of tight bends up to Villaroger and then the reciprocal set of them all the way down to the bottom of the valley the other side. We cross the Isère and the Route Nationale to find there are even more snaking up to Ste-Foy-Tarentaise. But that's not the end of the story. Jean-Louis' home is at Station de Ste-Foy which, as the crow flies, is about a mile beyond the village – but since it's also more than 2000 feet higher, the shortest route by road and track involves another five miles of switchbacks. Nor is it straightforward; by now I'm very wary of asking for directions, but I do accost the odd hiker and householder, and get all sorts of contradictory advice. In the end I try phoning Peter and to my surprise the mobile produces a ghost of a signal, so he's able to relay step-by-step instructions from Jean-Louis, most of which are muffled by the sounds of partying in the background. This really is the pits – while Leo and I have been toiling up and down mountains all day, and I've taken a heart-stopping trip over a precipice, Peter's had a smooth run in the Citroën and is now happily socialising with a glass or six of wine. Harrumph indeed.

But it's impossible to stay grouchy for long. Jean-Louis seems delighted to see us, and his beautiful old wooden house has a breathtaking view – it faces south-east towards the Pointe de la Foglietta, nearly 10,000 feet high, and behind that a cold glacier gleams at the foot of the Pointe d'Archeboc which is taller still. Various brothers and sisters-in-law of Jean-Louis are here to welcome us as well, and we sit out on the balcony and raise a toast to the storm that comes crashing past. At least Leo and I didn't have that to add to our problems, not that he takes any notice of the din – he's been fenced into a patch of green weeds which may or may not constitute the garden, and he's systematically chomping them down to the roots.

Our host produces an enormous supper of Savoie sausages and polenta, followed by a board stacked with Tarentaise cheeses. I pick up the cheese knife, hovering with indecision at the choice and distracted by a soft tickling in my palm. What's this? It's coming from the knife … the handle, now I come to look at it, isn't a handle at all but a furry leg ending in a cloven hoof. I daren't ask who it used to belong to. Next comes a pineapple cake, drenched in an unpronounceable liqueur and dished up on plates painted with proverbs in the Savoie dialect. Jean-Louis' translation of one of them is mystifying: *I filled my coffer with thank-yous but a mouse died in it.* It doesn't sound exactly uplifting.

The combination of a skinful of wine and a chunk of 100 per cent proof cake means I'm now in danger of keeling over, so I turn down an invitation to play the piano and go off to bed, shortly followed by Peter who's completely unaffected by the large amount of alcohol he's consumed. We cuddle up underneath a blanket which Peter is sure is made of stitched rat skins, though hopefully they're more likely to be goat, and promptly pass out.

At 8 a.m. the irrepressible Jean-Louis is thumping the ivories with a deafening rendition of 'Land of Hope and Glory', just for my husband's benefit. I assure him that Peter is bound to be enjoying it, even though I've just watched him disappear completely under the bed covers at the first chord, stuffing goat or rat fur into his ears. But for the rest of us it's an infectiously cheery morning, and Leo is particularly popular with the family for his hatchet job on the weeds. Sunshine is flooding through the house, and after a breakfast as bountiful as last night's supper I'm ready to tackle another day, one that should take in some properly marked tracks including the GR5 from Tignes to Val d'Isère.

Jean-Louis and his brother Philippe the Priest walk with us for the first hour. They've hiked these paths for years and for me it's pure pleasure not to have to worry about where I'm going; I follow them through woods and mountain meadows, through acres of rhododendrons, carnations and stumpy Alpine pinks, savouring a stroll across the top of the world. The ubiquitous main road meanders along far below and on its other side the glaciers spread out, mile upon mile up to Mont Pourri which at 12,500 feet is the second highest peak in the Massif de la Vanoise, only narrowly beaten by La Grande Casse further to the south-west. The view is utterly awesome.

We're on the outside edge of the Vanoise National Park and its border is so ragged that on the map it looks like a mad piece of jigsaw puzzle. The park was created in the 1960s to protect the local population of *bouquetins*, the Alpine ibex which the locals had been blasting towards extinction since the French discovered the pastime of hunting with guns in the sixteenth century. Presumably the boundary line had to ramble round the mountains and valleys where the survivors were taking cover, and apparently they're thriving these days, though sadly I never see one.

When Jean-Louis and Philippe turn back, I carry on towards a local hiking trail that runs parallel to the main road. Further ahead, fortunately not yet in sight, the park overlooks unlovely Tignes with its high rise hotels and apartments built for the skiers – a discordant mass of geometric shapes which hopefully will become no more than a bad memory once I reach the stretch of GR5 that travels across the uplands to Val d'Isère. That part is also just outside the boundary, and in fact the only time I'll be riding actually in the Vanoise National Park will be when I cross a narrow isthmus of it from the Col de l'Iseran to Bonneval-sur-Arc. This links the main body of the park to a hammer-headed section leaning against the Italian border, back to back with the Gran Paradiso National Park in Piemonte; and somewhere up there in the chaos of blue glaciers is the spot where the River Isère whispers into life.

But before we get anywhere near the Col, Leo's going to need re-shoeing. Much as I love riding on the tracks, their uneven rasping surface is death to horseshoes. Yesterday two nails dropped out and it won't be long before the shoes fall off altogether, probably taking chunks of hoof with them. Ironically, the best surface for Leo at the moment apart from grass is smooth tarmac, not that I have any intention of going near the coach-infested D902 except to cross it again.

Fate decrees otherwise.

We have a gentle descent through forest and past an unusual traditional chalet, four storeys high, with a garden of vegetables in symmetrical rows that look as though they're weeded every day. I'd be surprised if anyone lives in the house, though – the ground and first floor balconies are full of beehives, and every window is prudently closed. Leo and I don't hang about, but I have time to notice when we trot past the length of the garden that it has no flowers in it at all; instead, the owner has planted a red English telephone box at the end of a row of cabbages. I'm still pondering its incongruity as we swing on down to our marked trail – and find it's vanished.

'For God's *sake*, Leo, where's that gone then? It's here, right here on the map.'

Maybe it did exist once, but now the ground's a mass of loose scree and brambles and overgrown forest. It looks depressingly similar to the start of yesterday's impossible track, and now that I'm stuck rather literally between a rock and a hard place, realistically there's only one option and that's the hard place – the road.

We arrive on the tarmac in front of two *paravalanche* tunnels, each open on one side but curtained by waterfalls because the dregs of last night's storm are still draining from the land; to my surprise, Leo takes them in his stride, hammering through at top speed before any traffic appears. Before long there's a quieter lane to take and suddenly the vast edifice of the Tignes dam is smack in front of us, holding back the 600 watery acres of the artificial Lac du Chevril.

Tignes, it turns out, is a collective term for a huge skiing area and five villages, four of them created when the dam was built in 1952 and the resort developed. There was a single village of that name once, but it's at the bottom of the Lac du Chevril. Its furious inhabitants did their best to sabotage the construction of the dam but in the end they were defeated and, to add insult to injury, even though the new lake was supposed to supply hydro-electric power to whole tracts of France, it was never put to use. The nuclear age dawned and technology moved on; now its only purpose is to provide an emergency storage battery for the ski resort if the power fails. But the *Tignards* did score a significant victory, though it took them nearly half a century to achieve it: every decade the lake is drained for maintenance which means the wrecked village briefly reappears, and in the year 2000 they succeeded in celebrating Mass in the dripping remains of their church.

As Leo and I reach the dam, the clouds are building up again. By now I know that the weather in the Alps can go through a ten-day cycle in the summer months; after a few days of high temperatures and sunshine, heavy clouds come sailing over the peaks and then there's an uneasy selection of thunder, lightning, rain, fog, violent squalls and plummeting temperatures before it all cheers up again and the cycle's repeated. Today's storm is the herald of more unsettled weather, which is bad timing for Leo and me since we'll be reaching the highest point of our journey to Rome soon – the Col de l'Iseran.

By the time I arrive at the resort village of Lac de Tignes there's thunder blasting over the mountains and the rain's pounding down. Leo jogs obligingly all round the houses while I try to find the GR5 link which isn't at all obvious, but eventually the path materialises under the chair-lift at the back of the tennis courts.

I take one look at it, and stop.

The track, such as it is, rises steeply up the shale and rocks, as narrow, as crenelated as the dorsal spines on a dinosaur. It's only inches wide and slick with rain; there's a drop on either side that's almost sheer and to ask my horse to go up there is absolutely out of the question.

So that's that.

For the first time since leaving England, I have to fight off an attack of quivering lip. I'm utterly disappointed – having missed out on the wild miles of GR5 from Landry to Tignes because of snow, I've really, really been looking forward to what on my map looks like an easy journey across the Pas de la Tovière to Val d'Isère, and today I was determined we would do it, whatever the weather. But I simply can't ask it of Leo; he's so brave, so obliging that he would certainly try, but I'd never be able to live with making that decision if he slipped and fell and broke a leg, which would be the end of him.

The problem is, what now?

We pull into the shelter of a busy shopping arcade, taking up all the pavement. I really don't know what to do because the main road to Val d'Isère, with its totally enclosed tunnels, is just as dangerous as the teeter up the GR5. Leo would need headlights and a massive reflector strapped to his tail, if I possessed such things, which I don't – I've only got my stirrup reflectors and they're not even on my stirrups at the moment, they're in the Citroën. So I indulge in a spot of self-pity followed by some pull-yourself-together-woman, since I'd probably be arrested if I tried to ride a horse through the tunnels anyway, and then think to look at the map.

There might be a solution here – muddled in with symbols depicting golfers, skiers, hang gliders and the tourist office, there's one of a horse and rider with the words *poney-club* written beside it. The club's about a mile away, past the Lac de Tignes and up the mountain a bit. If I could just find out the phone number …

There's an *Immobilier* in the arcade, an estate agency for those who fancy a square concrete *pied-à-terre* for a few weeks' use a year. That'll do. I climb off Leo, open the glass door and let him poke his nose through first. The agent arrives in a split second, grabs a phone book, scans through it at lightning speed, writes down a number and looks extremely relieved when I back my horse out of his office again.

Patrick at the Pony Club, however, is delighted to see a wandering Appaloosa. He fusses round us and nothing is too much trouble: your horse is claustrophobic? We can put him outside in a field with a pile of hay to keep him happy. You want to get him to Val d'Isère? We have a horsebox, we can transport him there in the morning. I gulp a bit at the price – 100 euros for a seven-mile hitch-hike – but I'm hardly in a position to haggle. So I phone Peter to explain what's happened and he arrives in the car to collect me, inching his way up the narrow road in teeming rain.

What wonderful camping weather, not – it reminds me in a perverse way of my mother's account of a memorable time she had under canvas during a visit to Jordan in the 1960s.

She was a guest of King Hussein, gathering material for a book she was writing about Arab horses, and while out riding with the Bedouin she spent a night in a tent in the desert. '*It was cold*,' she wrote,

> *so cold that I slept fully clothed with the addition of a daughter's reluctantly loaned suede and sheepskin coat, a garment that was meant to be used only 'for best'. Snuggled in this, beneath heavy wraps of camel hair, I was as warm as in any air-conditioned hotel room. The tilley lamp had expired with a sinister hiss, the hurricane lantern threw a dim puddle of light in one corner. From outside, where the sheep and goats lay pressed close against the tents, came the vague sounds of animals stirring in their sleep. A dog was baying, a donkey brayed. Once, when two cats chased each other across my bed, I woke to the soft chatter of invisible women and the wailing of a new-born child.*

It's equally cold at the campsite in Val d'Isère, but there the similarity ends. Peter had put up the tent before coming to fetch me, and by the time we get back it's saturated and so are the bedclothes. I spend the evening fruitlessly trying to dry

1. Peter wonders what on earth he's let himself in for.

2. Archdeacon Patrick blesses us outside Canterbury Cathedral.

3. World War I German graveyard in the St Gobain Forest close to Laon

4. Leo joins Peter and our friends Gerry and Penny for a sociable snuffle at the gin and tonic.

5. The Tree of Jesse, part of a mediaeval fresco in the church at Saint-Seine-l'Abbaye, Côte-d'Or.

6. The farriers putting new shoes on Leo by the roadside near Dijon.

7. Leo looms over me at lunchtime, waiting for his Mars Bar.

8. Rest stop beside the River Ain near Priay.

9. The scary metal bridge over the River Rhône.

10. Leo spots Bessie and Peter catching up with us at La Clusaz in the Alps.

11. Camping in the public car park at the beautiful Alpine village of Notre-Dame-de-Bellecombe.

12. An unexpected view of Mont Blanc; Leo, however, is unimpressed and gazes at the approaching cows instead.

13. Swirling clouds on the road from Val d'Isère to the Col de l'Iseran at 9,000 feet.

14. A pause on the mountain lane to Torriglia, above Genoa, where old villages cling to the hillsides.

15. Leo gloomily checks our bank balance at an ATM in Pietrasanta, Tuscany.

16. Tourists admiring the Basilica of San Domenico, Siena.

17. The ladies in blue in the hamlet of Abbadia a Isola, still an important staging post on the Via Francigena in Tuscany.

18. A Cassia Romana, an original Roman road near Viterbo.

19. Posing in front of St Peter's Basilica, Leo still full of beans after 1400 miles.

20. Pages from my pilgrim passport. The final entry dated 19/08/06 is signed by Don Bruno Vercesi, the priest in charge of dispensing the official Vatican stamp.

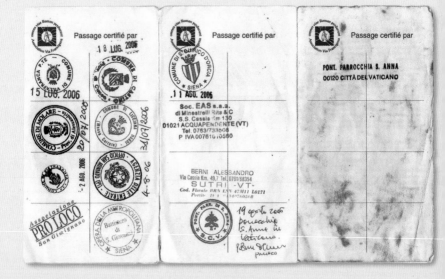

the duvet with the hairdryer, shuddering every time I brush accidentally against the sopping tent walls. The rain stops just as it's bedtime, but we're not lulled romantically to sleep by gentle animal sounds – we're frazzled by the revving and hooting of raucous cars circling the village for hours, and in the end we decide (correctly, as it turns out) that it must be because the French have won their World Cup semi-final match. There's no escaping football, even here.

Despite the racket, however, Peter eventually falls asleep in a sog of damp duvet feathers while I remain annoyingly awake for hours, my brain in overdrive with Worry One, which is the absolute impossibility of finding a local farrier, and Worry Two, which is what to do about Leo and me both cheating by taking a lift from Tignes to Val d'Isère. Ultimately I decide there's not much I can do about the farrier as I've already tracked down and phoned several and they're all unavailable, so Leo's just going to have to keep his shoes on until we're over the Col de l'Iseran.

But I keep chewing away at Worry Two. There's no alternative to a lift for Leo, but it's different for me. Never mind the disapproval of St James, Susie and indeed possibly the Alzheimer's Society if I miss out a chunk of pilgrimage – more to the point, I just know that God will send some lightning my way if I don't stick to the rules. So I decide to load Leo into the horsebox tomorrow at the pony club and then walk back here on my own feet.

When our expedition was still at the planning stage, I'd toyed with the idea of taking time off at Tignes so I could go skiing on a glacier, but now that I'm here I'm not remotely tempted to drag my achy self off for something so frivolous. Instead, my over-active mind is filled to the brim with guilt that Leo's going to miss out on a scenic trek on the GR5.

But that's anthropomorphic nonsense and it's high time I switched off my brain and went to sleep, because my horse isn't going to give a toss about a breezy canter on the most spectacular hiking track in France. What he'd prefer is what he's actually going to get – a day's rest and a non-stop feast on the long grass up the mountainside behind us.

15

An Atmospheric Sea of Cloud

I can hear Leo's accusatory voice in my mind while I'm walking across the Pas de la Tovière – *what do you mean, I'm better off scraping up the grass in this tiny enclosure?* It turns out he'd have been in horsy paradise here with me because the meadows are teeming with flirtatious fillies. And for exactly the same reason, I'm thankful he's travelled to Val d'Isère in a truck. My spotted Don Juan isn't good at multi-tasking – he'd only have room in his head for lascivious thoughts, and none for where he was putting his feet on the track.

Peter Two has caught up with us again, and he and I walk from Tignes to Val d'Isère together, or rather we toddle along at a reasonable pace once we've climbed the stegosaurus path from the tennis courts, with much puffing and cursing on my part. It is indeed no place to bring a horse wearing smooth metal shoes – even my riding boots are skidding all over the place despite having been re-soled with tractor treads. Peter does a bit better than me in his proper hiking footgear, clomping doggedly along while I struggle up the hairpins and send cascades of pebbles hurtling down the drop on either side. Trying not to be outdone, I attempt to leap nonchalantly from one steep stony step to another, but the reality is that I'm going to have a heart attack if I don't sit down soon. It's fully a mile before the trail levels out, and then suddenly we're on top of the plateau with a soft wind blowing the clouds away.

To my relief, Peter is in need of a rest just as much as me, so we stop to admire the mountains parading off towards Mont Blanc in the north and the Italian border in the south. They rear up on either side in their cold granite austerity, the floral carpet of the Pas de la Tovière tacked to the rocky floor between them and patterned with rhododendrons, stonecrop and big trumpet gentians.

There's wildlife here, and life that's not so wild: the horses. They're piebald and dappled grey and chestnut; pregnant mares, skittish adolescents, foals full of curiosity. They're equine pickpockets in search of peppermints, and Peter Two retires to a safe distance so he can take some photos. I get my camera out to take a shot of a personable brown and white skewbald baby, but it's impossible – all I can see is the pink blur of his nose pressed against the lens. They've been turned loose up here to graze the summer pastures, and whoever owns them knows they'll never attempt to take themselves down the rock staircase into Tignes; the only restraining fence they need is the electric one that zigzags through the forest on the Val d'Isère side. Peter and I duck carefully underneath it because there's no insulated gate handle, no opening at all that we can see, and that's another reason to be glad Leo isn't here – I'd have had fun trying to lift the wire so he and I could pass under it without getting electrocuted, or indeed without letting forty horses through to follow my suave Pied Piper back to Val d'Isère.

Of the real wildlife, the first creatures to appear are marmots, bumbling around in the sunshine outside their burrows. They're at least two feet long and look more like gormless guinea-pigs than cherished members of the squirrel family. They sit up in surprise when they see us, and then they start whistling – and I realise the sound I've been hearing all over the Alps, which I thought was the mewing of hawks, must have been invisible marmots sounding the alarm as Leo and I trespassed across their territory.

All the same, there *are* hawks wheeling on the thermals overhead, and one of them is huge, bigger than a buzzard, bigger than an eagle ... I'm hoping it might be a rare bearded vulture, *Gypaetus barbatus* of the ten-foot wingspan, black moustaches and fluffy culottes – a species reintroduced into the Alps in the 1980s after the last wild one was shot at the beginning of that century. It was the final victim of a shocking reputation – the birds were hunted because the locals believed they stole live lambs and babies. But it wasn't true. What bearded vultures like best are marrow bones from creatures definitely already dead, though apparently they do have one unnerving habit – they soar to an enormous height carrying the larger bones and then drop them on to the rocks below to crack them open, which means I can add another worry to my list: that Leo and I might get knocked out by a flying leg of lamb somewhere between here and Italy.

It turns out to be a fantastic walk across the high plateau and down through the woods into Val d'Isère, sunshine all the way to the site before the clouds roll in again; I just have time to wrap Leo in his mac before waves of icy rain come sluicing down, settling into a deadening deluge that carries on all afternoon. My Peter takes refuge in sleep, while I divide my time between trying to keep our belongings away from the worst bits of dripping tent, and reading a book by Jean-Louis called *Sainte-Foy-Tarentaise*. He's kindly given me a copy, with an interesting inscription in English: '*To*

Mefo whom I was happy to meet at Bourdonnel with all good wishes for lots of rich experiments and discoveries all along her way to Rome.'

The book's written in French, of course, which calls for some serious concentration on my part, but it's a lot better than spending the afternoon peering at the fog that's now blotting out the landscape and wondering if I'm going to get over the Col de l'Iseran tomorrow. The story of the Tarentaise valley unexpectedly gives me a chance to catch up on my religious education, which has been more or less dormant without my sister to frogmarch me into a church every few miles.

First, though, there's the long-ago presence of the Romans to ponder, and Hannibal's crossing of the Alps with his elephants in 218 BC. The inevitable question is asked: which way did they go? Jean-Louis speculates they might have used the Petit-Saint-Bernard pass, not far from here, and that maybe the inhabitants of Ste-Foy saw them in the distance as they trundled by – but I'm not convinced, since everything else I've read points to them struggling over the Col de la Traversette, a lot further south.

Christianity arrived in this area 600 years later, possibly brought here by St James - but a different St James from the one familiar to me. This was St Jacques de Tarentaise, an Assyrian pagan who converted to Christianity, and unfortunately my French won't stretch to working out how he ended up in the Alps.

I do learn that I passed through the village of Les Boisses on the way to Lac de Tignes completely oblivious to the presence of its St Jacques de Tarentaise church, built in 1952 and an apologetic replica of the one rotting at the bottom of the Lac du Chevril; and I didn't notice the ruined Chapel of St Jacques either, perched spikily above us in the Clou valley. Beady-eyed

Susie would have seen both and been off her horse Apollo in seconds, camera in hand.

Really I should be scouring this book for mention of St Peter and St Paul since I hope I'm on the genuine secondary route of the Via Francigena, but the problem is that I'm such an entrenched Santiago de Compostela pilgrim that any mention of St James grabs my attention first, even if he turns out to be another saint with the same name.

And Ste Foy too has an important Santiago connection. She was a young girl from Agen in Aquitaine, a Christian convert in the fourth century who refused to sacrifice to the pagan gods and was executed by the local Roman governor. Not that he was much good at it – according to my literal translation of Jean-Louis' words, the governor tried to roast her on a grill but the fire refused to light, so he had her decapitated instead. After her martyrdom she began to perform miracles in her home town, and Jean-Louis smoothly explains that in 866, some 500 years later, her mortal remains were transferred to the abbey at Conques, which became a major pilgrim halt on the path from Le-Puy-en-Velay to Santiago after Ste Foy arrived.

He doesn't mention something that I find out much later. The relics are there not because of a civilised arrangement between Agen and Conques but due to a disgraceful sequence of crimes: conspiracy, fraud and theft. The monks at Conques realised that to have a virgin martyr in their abbey would boost its status no end, so they hatched a plot to steal her. One of them infiltrated the monastery at Agen and waited for ten years for the opportunity to whip the saint away and bring her back to Conques, where her relics were incarcerated in a grandiose statue. She remains there to this day, painted gold and plastered in jewels.

Conques is on the list of important places for Leo and me to visit one day, since Susie's and my route to Santiago didn't go that way. Its abbey is described as one of the most perfect examples of Romanesque architecture in Europe, and I look forward to finding out for myself whether the enamelled eyes of the pilfered saint really look as uneasy as they do in the only photo I've seen of her. But her expression isn't surprising, given that the statue's head is much too big for the body – apparently it belonged to a Roman emperor before Ste Foy's skull was posted into it.

Her namesake village in the Alps has its church, of course, although not the original one; Jean-Louis isn't sure when the first one was built, although there's a written record of it in the twelfth century. Over the years it's been repeatedly demolished, rebuilt, re-consecrated, patched and repaired after a succession of wars, revolutions, and landslides that threatened to send it sledging off down the slopes. Needless to say I haven't noticed the most recent version of this church either, having passed through the village at the end of a very long day with my brain at a standstill, but there's a photo in his book of its sumptuously restored gold tabernacle, dominated by a statue of the risen Christ who's attended by ten saints, among them St James the Great and, I'm relieved to note, St Peter and St Paul as well.

Even Thomas Becket is here in the book and in the collective memory of the people of the Tarentaise. He wrote a hymn dedicated to the Virgin Mary called 'Gaude Flore Virginali', and a copy of it was brought back here by his friend St Pierre of Tarentaise. It remains very popular with the local congregations, and Jean-Louis has set out the words in full, both in Latin and in expansive, flowery French.

More succinct is the short prayer recorded at the end of the book in the patois of the Savoie and in French. According to my stumbling translation into English, the last three lines go something like this:

May the Good God preserve our house, our livestock
From fire, inundations, sudden death,
And from all unpleasant encounters. Please.

I think I should adopt this prayer. It could easily be applied to
Peter, Leo, Bessie, the tent and me.

In the night, rain. In the morning, more rain. I decide to
leave anyway or we could be here for days, but the clouds are
squatting in the valley and it isn't safe to embark on a blind
expedition up the steep convolutions of the GR5. So it's a
tarmac trip once again, following the looping bends of the road
with Peter driving ahead in the Citroën with its headlights on,
in case some boy racer fails to see us. This time I do dig out my
stirrup reflectors, along with a neon yellow browband for Leo
and a luminous belt for me.

Once we leave the valley the rain stops but the fog remains,
billowing to and fro across the mountains. One minute all I can
see are swishing curtains of cloud, so spooky that I wouldn't be
surprised if we arrived suddenly at Dracula's front door, and
the next second they sweep back to unveil the distant toy town
silhouette of Val d'Isère.

For three hours we wind up and up towards the Col, Leo
on springs after his day's rest, striding easily up the 3500 feet
of the l'Iseran ascent, not sweating or puffing, calm in the fog,
and looking about him inquisitively when it whirls away to
reveal snow and rock and desolation in every direction. I stop
cursing that the sun's not out and instead become enchanted
by this atmospheric sea of cloud that lifts and spins and

swallows up the road again; sometimes the Citroën's tail lights are fuzzy pinpricks ahead of us, and sometimes it's just Leo and me following what was once a mule track trodden by invaders and smugglers, travellers and pilgrims for hundreds of years.

We arrive at the top to find both Peters waiting there, and Peter Two takes pictures of us in front of what must be one of the most photographed signposts in the Alps: *COL DE L'ISERAN*, it says, *ALTITUDE : 2770m*, which is well over 9000 feet. To the right it points back towards Val d'Isère, more than ten miles behind us now, and to the left to Bonneval-sur-Arc, about nine miles down the other side of the mountain, 3000 feet lower, and our destination for the night.

First, though, there's a wonderful pit-stop at a hot chocolate café, where Leo rests in the lee of its wall with his rug on while the rest of us pile in to the warmth for ten minutes. When we come out again the fog's still flumped on the road, the visibility so bad that it isn't until long afterwards, when I'm admiring Peter Two's photographs, that I notice the ghostly presence of the Chapelle Notre-Dame-de-Toute-Prudence in the background, its roof tiles splattered with snow.

The clouds pack themselves back into distant corners of the sky as I begin the long descent to the valley of the River Arc; it's still a grey day, but now I can see all the way down six loops of road at once, across bare rock and snow patches, and then across acres of gentians and azaleas as we drop below the snow line. Leo and I play Spot The Marmot now I know what to look for when I hear whistling, and while I'm picking out their podgy outlines he gazes briefly in their direction before turning his attention to the grass at the roadside. There's not much traffic around, which is lucky as most of the drivers who pass us stop to have a chat in the middle of the road, but two coaches do shoot past, pulling out at the last minute to avoid my horse but shaving the Citroën so close that Peter is forced to shove its nose against the side of the mountain.

And then I can see the outline of beautiful Bonnèval-sur-Arc below a final bend, marking the end of an extraordinary ride at easily the highest altitude that Leo and I have ever travelled together. The village turns out to have everything that tired, hungry pilgrims-and-horse could wish for: a ready-fenced field with grass and hay, a comfortable hostel, a restaurant that serves *tartiflette*, and a helpful lady who tracks down a farrier who can put new shoes on Leo tomorrow. Unfortunately he doesn't have a mobile forge which means we'll have a long hack to his workshop at Termignon, way beyond our turn-off at Lanslebourg towards Mont Cenis, and then several miles back again; but at least I won't have to worry any more that Leo's shoes are going to drop off in the road.

Peter and I manage to claim adjacent beds in the hostel below a window that creaks open when I shove it hard, but by the time I get back to the dormitory after a fruitless search for a nightie in the car, the light's out and someone's shut it again. There are about ten comatose bodies packed in a small space and I daren't make a noise cranking it open, let alone think of shining a torch so I can rustle about writing up my journal. So it's off to the brightly lit shower room for a freezing few minutes with a pen and paper, followed by a cautious tiptoe in the direction of what I hope is my bed (or else someone's going to get a horrible shock) for what I know will be a snoring night of honky humanity.

But if it is, I won't hear it. My head's still filled with impressions of our journey which has been the antithesis of a picture-postcard-Alpine-day; instead, I've ridden through a restless, shifting landscape of mist and cloud and spectral shapes, as eerie and primeval as it must have been when the first Romans picked their way over the pass.

16

Teetering on the Border at Mont Cenis

Bonneval in the early morning is a place of blinding colour, from the vivid grass of the Arc valley floor to the blue glaciers gleaming thousands of feet up on either side. When I turn to look back at the village, the sun's rays are lancing down on the church spire, on the houses with their fish-scale roof tiles, on the clear waters of the river lazing along; and suddenly I'm filled with a sense of nostalgia and of time rushing past. It's 8th July and in a couple of days' time we'll be leaving France behind. For the last month our world's been filled with mountains, but it won't be long before they fade into memory.

Italy... I haven't really thought about it; I've been totally preoccupied for weeks with the highs and lows of our Alpine days, most of them as variable as the weather. My feeble efforts to teach myself Italian came to a halt when I decided a raid on my teenage recollection of Latin words would do instead, plus some English ones with an *a* or *o* tacked on the end. At least I seem to have more empathy with the Italian language than I did with Spanish on our last pilgrimage, when the only expression I really got to grips with was a rough translation of *I have an electric fence I'd like to put up in your field*.

But I think the question of language might be the only aspect of this journey that's easier than the last one.

What certainly isn't straightforward is the route ahead with its confusing ragbag of out-of-date maps. When Susie and I rode to Santiago, all we had to do once we were in Spain was to follow the yellow arrows of the Camino Francés. Life's not going to be that simple in Italy. The path of the Via Francigena hasn't been easy to track in France either, even before I switched to its secondary route at Châlons-en-Champagne, and I haven't seen any official VF yellow-walking-pilgrim waymarks since leaving Canterbury. But it could be that I'm going to have the opposite problem once I re-join the Via at Pontremoli: far too many signs, an *embarras de richesses*, given that the internet told me (so it must be true) that the Via's been expanded into multiple tracks, away from its original path (now mostly buried under the motorways) in an effort to end the problem of flattened pilgrims. I dare say I'll come across every single version of it, each with its own individual signposting system.

Today Leo and I go very slowly and carefully down the main road to Termignon, avoiding all gravel, stones and risks of depositing a tyre-puncturing shoe nails-up on the tarmac, and with plenty of time to admire the glaciers as we go. It's like picking our way along the bottom of a tray of gigantic ice cubes. Peter is due to drive down this scenic route on his way to collect the mended Bessie, but he hasn't passed us by the time we turn off what's now the very major N6 to go and find the blacksmith's house.

Patrick tuts over Leo's hooves but doesn't utter the horrible word *impossible*; he hammers on some thick and heavy French shoes, says he can't get my English tungsten studs to fit them but *ça va*, Leo will be fine, and then lets slip that he isn't a qualified farrier at all, he just shoes his own horses. Well, too bad not to mention too late now; I'm hugely grateful he agreed to help us, and Leo is indeed fine. Our return journey to Lanslebourg on the pretty track of the Chemin du Petit Bonheur takes half the time it took to plod to Termignon.

By the time I get to the village, Peter Two (still loyally keeping track of us in case we need assistance) has already found a field for Leo, courtesy of a local landowner who turns out to be well qualified to join my Monsieur Macho List. When I thank him for his kindness he extends it further, insisting on showing me the whereabouts of the back route up through the woods to the Mont Cenis pass. As this takes in the part of the Chemin du Petit Bonheur I've just ridden along, I know very well where it is, but Monsieur's taking no chances. We go bouncing off in his 4X4 for an hour's drive, at the end of which I've given up trying to convince him that I'm not just a clueless female who can't read a map. Reduced to weary silence, all I want to do is collapse into bed after today's long ride – my proper bed, oh bliss, since Peter has returned with Bessie, the horsebox with the most comfortable mattress in the world on her parcel shelf.

Monsieur Macho warns me I must stay on the backwoods track all the way to the top because on a Sunday (in other words, tomorrow) the Mont Cenis main road is filled with speeding Italian motorbikes swarming over from the Susa side. His brow furrowed with worry, he reveals that five of them were killed last year.

Peter's face brightens considerably.

'Perhaps I'll be able to knock off a few of them on the way,' he says, 'if I depressurise Porta Potti on a hairpin bend.'

Since he last did this by accident at Beaufort with spectacular results, I'm concerned the mortality rate will indeed be high. But Monsieur Macho's expression smoothes into benevolence again – either he doesn't understand English, or he thinks it would be no bad thing.

At least there are no motorbikes skidding down from the pass as Leo and I turn south on the forest trails towards the Italian border, but there are plenty of hikers struggling up through the woods and sometimes bicyclists as well, sweating along looking miserable. I can't resist singing out now and again *c'est moins difficile à cheval!* as Leo overtakes them, but unsurprisingly no one wants to hear it's easier by horse, and they all look completely unamused. Anyway, the cyclists will get their own back when we're over the top and they can scoot by without pedalling at all, while Leo has to slow right down in case he slips.

We climb and climb, and now I can barely see Lanslebourg straggling along beside the River Arc; the track goes over a bridge, and then suddenly we pop out on to the N6 where there isn't a lethal motorbike in sight or even the odd squashed Italian left behind by my murderous husband and Bessie. In fact the traffic's quite light apart from a rally of Deux Chevaux cars with lawnmower engines and drivers who think it's a great joke to point out that they have two horses each whereas I have only one.

We're almost at the Col du Mont Cenis itself, first passing its chapel with a lonely bell outlined against the sky, ready to guide travellers lost in fog or snow between France and Italy. Its presence reminds me of another chapel at a high border pass, the Puerto de Ibañeta in the western Pyrenees. It was erected on the ruins of the original one built by Charlemagne after he travelled that way from France to Spain some 1200 years ago, intent on invasion, and Susie and I saw it on our way to Santiago. And in fact for me there's a connection between that pass and Mont Cenis, since Charlemagne and his army also marched into Italy the way I'm riding now, on their way to cut across Piemonte and attack the Lombards further to the east.

Napoleon was another invader who rode over the Col du Mont Cenis, and he too has links with the Puerto de Ibañeta due to his own occupation of Spain – he crossed it using an old Roman trail which then became known as the *Route de Napoléon*. It's a high level path still followed by some of the St James pilgrims, far more interesting than the road route but steep and prone to foul weather, and stories continue to filter back of modern day pilgrims who've got lost there and died of hypothermia, out of earshot of the Ibañeta chapel's bell. Needless to say, Susie and I stuck to the road.

It was Napoleon who upgraded and improved the Mont Cenis track, repairing and enlarging the original hospice that had been built on the Col in the ninth century to shelter exhausted travellers. But that refuge and its neighbouring section of his road no longer exist. As Leo and I move on towards Italy, the enormous artificial Lac du Mont Cenis fills my vision; another dammed lake, as it were, with history drowning in the bottom of it – in this instance, both the hospice and a piece of Napoleon's road, submerged when the French electricity giant, EDF, built a 400-foot high *barrage* of compacted earth and boulders capable of holding back more than three million cubic metres of water.

Apparently Napoleon had intended to construct a pyramid at Mont Cenis to commemorate his Egyptian campaign. For whatever reason, he never got round to it, but EDF did – and in an endearingly whimsical gesture, the company built one on his behalf at the old frontier on the eastern side of the lake, and it's home to a museum tracing the history of the pass since Roman times.

Anxious to keep off the Route Nationale, I steer Leo round the lake's western flank, and on the other side of the 1500 acres of water I can see the pyramid, from this distance just a mini two-dimensional triangle on the far shore. I can also see Bessie, a toy truck pounding along the main road. The lane I'm on becomes an uneven track that Leo copes with very well in his new shoes, but now there's another equine anxiety to bother me – if we move faster than a walk, he starts coughing.

A few months before we left England his breathing suddenly became very noisy and his whinny turned into a squeak. Investigation meant an endoscopy which the unsedated Leo endured with perfectly good humour, inspecting the inside of his throat with interest on a computer screen. This revealed a deformed soft palate that had somehow flipped over backwards. The vet said it was due to a birth defect, but it was impossible to say why it had started misbehaving in a horse then twelve years old. However, he assured me it wouldn't compromise our pilgrimage and that basically Leo could live with it – though I wasn't sure I could; I had visions of riding a snoring horse to Rome. The palate somersaulted back a month later and life became quieter, but now I'm wondering if the same thing's happened again. Or whether it's the altitude. Or an allergy to the hay he ate when he stayed overnight at Tignes. Or some other reason that hasn't occurred to me yet.

The trouble is, when horses cough they do it violently, and that's not all they do – they also fart explosively. Which can be embarrassing for the rider (if not for the horse) when there's an equine fan club around – and there are several of those here this afternoon.

We seem to be on the tourist route: the lake's shores are dotted with picnickers with vast quantities of food and wine, loose dogs and even cross-looking cats on leads. Everyone wants to pat Leo but they risk getting sprayed with regurgitated grass by one end or blasted into the water by the other. I try to answer endless questions of the what's-an-English-horse-doing-here variety as quickly as possible, in what's now a necessary mixture of French and gibberish Italian, and attempt to keep on the move. The western path is so convoluted that it takes forever to reach the ancient fort squatting at the southern end of the lake, but luckily by then most of the day-trippers are more concerned about getting home in time to watch the World Cup final than trying to pat a noisy horse. I ride away through a queue of overheating cars and owners, and a chorus of angry hooting.

Far away in the windswept landscape a large rectangle comes into view. As we get nearer, it morphs into a building that looks as though the architect relied on his box of Lego for inspiration, adding rows of windows and sticking capital letters on one end that spell out the words HOTEL MALAMOT. Not the prettiest place in the world, but it looks as though we'll be stopping here for the night because next to it there's a considerably smaller rectangle – the stationary Bessie, with Peter slumped peacefully in the driver's seat with a book.

The hotel doesn't seem to have any guests, but the proprietor doesn't mind when I ask him rather guiltily if we can just spend the night in his garden. We fence in a portion of grass and flowers for Leo, and park Bessie beside the outdoor table ready for an *al fresco* supper. But it's far too cold to eat outside. Although the Mont Cenis pass is now behind us, we're still at an altitude of well over 6000 feet and Peter Two, who's about to leave us to drive back towards the Vanoise and carry on with his holiday, takes a final photo of Peter and me – two frozen people zipped into anoraks, snuggling up to Bessie's bonnet out of the wind. In the background, Leo is alternately troughing, coughing and farting in his paddock, oblivious to the cold.

My evening is spent struggling with the charts and trying to work out how I can get Leo and me to Susa tomorrow without using the N6. The distance is only about sixteen miles but I can see that the altitude at Susa is just 1650 feet, so it's going to be downhill all the way from here and then some, if the tight bends that curl to and fro across the map are anything to go by. There's a faint trail linking the main road with a parallel minor one at Moncenisio, just over the border, but Peter Two went on a mission to find it earlier in the day and reported back that it doesn't exist.

Monsieur Malamot, however, is full of optimism. There *is* another way, he says – a *sentier des moines*, a monks' footpath. He wiggles his finger across my chart and says I can't miss it. I hope he's right, as otherwise I can see us being steamrollered by tourist coaches or indeed by Bessie hurtling down the mountain. I wonder if my Peter is feeling apprehensive about his own journey tomorrow, given that we can see from here that we're poised at the top of a helter-skelter he can't avoid. But if he is, he's not letting on, and maybe it's better not to ask.

Tomorrow will be my first night in Italy with Leo but not, as it happens, my first one there with a horse. Aged twenty-one, I spent five weeks in the country with 120 of them, having impetuously responded to an advertisement in *The Times* for someone to work with an American rodeo travelling in Europe. Two or three weeks were spent in Rome during which time I saw plenty of cowboys, native Americans, broncs, saddle horses, carriage horses, stage coaches, Brahma bulls and the rodeo clown's chimpanzee, and nothing whatsoever of the city.

After Rome, the whole outfit moved north to Turin before rumbling on to Zurich and finally collapsing in financial ruin in Rouen. My memories of Turin are still very clear, of stately buildings and elegant streets – or at least they were elegant until seventy saddle horses had paraded round them leaving a trail of crots. The noise of 280 iron shod hooves was absolutely deafening as the over-excited animals danced and shied, and every evening I struggled to control my fizzing horse with one hand and an eight-foot flag pole shoved down my boot with the other.

Our road to Rome will pass close to Turin when we cross the flat expanse of the Po river valley. I don't expect to have quite such a lively couple of weeks in the area as I did with the rodeo (at least, I hope not) but you never know – the gut feeling has stayed with me that Italy is going to be a very, very different experience from France.

17

Benvenuti in Italia

Here goes.

The first batch of switchbacks turns out to be a doddle – from the height of Leo's back I can see round every corner as it drops away below us, and we don't meet a single coach as we wind from left to right and back again. The road is edged with bollards like blunt crocodile teeth by way of a crash barrier, with plenty of room between them for out of control cyclists and horses to plunge through the gaps, but Leo walks carefully down to a straight stretch where the map shows a green dotted line bisecting the N6. I suppose this means we're crossing the border, but in reality there's nothing to show for it except a sign saying the N6 has now become the SS25, and there's no one asking for equine importation papers or veterinary health certificates, in fact no one here at all.

Just beyond a shuttered building which may or may not have been the customs shed years ago, there's an unusual sight to welcome us to Italy: the mouth of a tunnel curled like a concrete caterpillar along the side of the road. I stop to peer doubtfully into the darkness.

What is it? There's a sign board nailed up at the entrance, its faint writing spelling out the word Fell, it looks like, and something else ... get a bit closer, Leo. *Fell?* That doesn't sound Italian. Or French ... Fell Railway. I haven't a clue what that might be, what's an English railway tunnel doing here? The name's perplexing – we're in something a bit more extreme than fell country, given that we've just dropped 500 feet in a mile of bends that were more like kirby grips than hairpins.

But later I do find out, and the name doesn't relate to the terrain but to an engineer called John Barraclough Fell who patented a super-safe mountain railway system in 1863. He added a raised central rail to the track, which was gripped so firmly on either side by extra horizontal wheels attached to the train that it couldn't capsize, even on the tightest turns. His ingenious scheme caught the attention of the French authorities, and this led to a commission to build a railway line over the Mont Cenis pass.

The adapted track opened in 1867 and the system was extremely successful, the trains snaking safely to and fro and plunging through covered avalanche galleries all the way to Susa; but technology was marching on and it was just a short-term solution while the Fréjus tunnel was under construction. Three and a half years later the line was closed and the story of the Fell Railway at Mont Cenis was consigned to the history books, though the complete system itself was shipped to Brazil where it was used for almost 100 years. All that remains at Mont Cenis is the odd section of tunnel like the one I'm staring at now, while simultaneously trying to work out where and when we're going to get away from this road.

It turns out to be quite obvious. A bit further on there's a small signpost flicking its arrow to the left, exactly where Monsieur said the monks' *sentier* would be, and in seconds we're on to a track so tortuous that I have to dismount and let Leo follow me, hoping he doesn't shove me down some ravine again. We come out of the woods on to the top of a wall which we have to walk along for several minutes, and it's another of those unavoidable situations where all I can do is carry on in front and not look behind me to see how Leo's doing. But he's fine, pottering along in my footsteps until I find a spot where we can jump down on to a lane and carry on towards the village of Novalesa dozing in the valley.

It occurs to me that I must be back on one of the many paths of the Via Francigena that crossed the Alps during the Middle Ages, in fact possibly the exact one marked on my official VF map. If so, I believe it drops down through the hamlet of Grangia, passes through Susa and then goes on to Turin, but there's no way of knowing if I'm right or wrong: there are no signposts at all, let alone any showing the VF pilgrim on his way to Rome.

Oh well. I'm too relieved just to have escaped from the main road to care. Lunch is a relaxed affair in a field, propped against a tree; the sun isn't too hot and all's so well with the world that I don't even tell Leo off for stealing my Mars Bar. When we get going again I manage to navigate successfully through Grangia and bypass the busiest part of Susa, relying on the last of the French IGN maps which has had an Italian one vaguely superimposed on it south of the dotted line, a map so old it doesn't even show the *autostrada* that unexpectedly flies over our heads on a clacking viaduct.

We cross the Dora Riparia river flowing through the town, and beyond it a hill climbs away towards the Colle delle Finestre, the final Alpine pass before we swap the mountains for the flat plains of the River Po. But that's for tomorrow. For now, I need to find a place to stay, and I'm suddenly overcome with fatigue at the thought of having to put my halting Italian into practice. I turn into a lane that is promisingly dotted with houses and big gardens, and the residents listen patiently to my stumbling request for pasture before replying helpfully in French that no, there's nowhere here suitable for a horse – I need the equestrian centre back down the hill at somewhere unpronounceable.

Peter catches up with me just as I'm trying to make sense of the directions offered by a stunning lady in a bikini. We set off back to Susa again but we never do find any stables. My husband looks exhausted, almost too exhausted to have appreciated Signora Bikini's charms, and we grind to a halt and ponder what to do next. It turns out that, unlike me, Peter didn't spend his lunchtime lazing under a tree; he was struggling to keep Bessie under control round thirty-seven hairpin bends as she roared down the main road from Mont Cenis to Susa.

He describes his journey in graphic detail: Bessie gathering speed even in second gear, the continual need to step on the brakes; nowhere to pull in, nowhere for the traffic piled up behind him to pass; a smell of burning invading his nostrils, and the realisation when finally he steered her into the town that the brakes were on fire.

The locals drinking coffee in the square stopped to observe the mad Englishman manoeuvring his smoking lorry into two small parking spaces. They watched with interest as he bundled our towels over the wheels, cursing the wind siffling down the river valley that was doing its best to coax the smoke into flame. No one moved. After fifteen minutes, five of Bessie's six wheels had been subdued, but the one under the driver's seat was still glowing rebelliously and Peter sat down on a wall, wondering what he should do now. The locals continued to gaze at him expectantly.

But help was at hand – a Lancia pulled up and the driver walked over to look at Bessie's number plate.

'Gee, mate, you from England?'

The accent was broad Aussie. Peter admitted that he was indeed English.

'Your brake drums alight?'

Peter agreed they were.

'Jeez,' said his new friend, 'same thing happened to me driving a lorry down out of the Blue Mountains outside Sydney.'

Peter enquired what happened next.

'Well, mate,' said Mr Laconic reassuringly, 'I didn't have any fucking brakes for a week.'

And with that he strolled off.

No one else stirred in the square. They were waiting to see what the Englishman would do next. Silently he climbed back inside Bessie and extracted one last towel, dragged it underneath the chassis and draped it over the inside surface of the smouldering tyre. Then he too sat down to see what would happen. A full thirty minutes later the final wisp of smoke dissolved in the breeze, to the disappointment of the general audience and to my husband's profound relief, and he departed to the nearest bar for a gallon or six of whatever was on offer.

By the time I come to look at the wheels several hours later, six molten caps fused on to the valves are the only remaining evidence of the near-conflagration – and fortunately for us, the fucking brakes are still working.

The immediate answer to our present problem seems to be some more liquid refreshment from the bar we're now hovering beside: water for Leo and something more substantial for Peter and me. St James is draped over a chair inside, disguised as a helpful Italian customer who offers us an orchard full of alfalfa for the night. His field turns out to be in the same lane I rode down earlier, and the French residents together with Signora Bikini are very pleased to see us back again.

The rich alfalfa has an unfortunate effect on Leo. For some reason it makes his cough even worse, and each hacking harrumph is accompanied by a rear end explosion. House windows are flung open. Accusatory looks are beamed at Peter. Trying to cook the supper, I start to laugh, and then we're both so tired we can't stop. Our meal's completely wrecked as we get more and more childish, falling about and inventing disgusting newspaper captions: Horse Sphincter Spotted in Space, No Sign of the Horse; Iran accuses the United States of Firing First; Susa Evacuated (As It Were)...

It's amazing how fatigue sparks puerile humour. I ought to be worrying about the last and probably the most testing of all our very long climbs through the Alps tomorrow, but instead we're still giggling when we go to bed. Even then, The Hills Are Alive with the Sound of ... oh *NO*, that's enough, don't start me off again.

Noisily refuelled, Leo makes nothing of clopping up to our third high pass in five days, and we reach it in less than four hours. We're able to keep to the shaded side of the mountain, following a single track road that was beautifully metalled last year for the Tour d'Italie race which came this way for the first time. But then the new road surface ends abruptly, as though the authorities suddenly ran out of funds, and we're picking our way across rock and loose stones.

At the top of the pass Leo and I both run out of steam. We're in the brassy sunshine now, looking over the ridge at the view to the south, and it's boiling hot. There's a random yellow digger up here, its driver on his lunch break with a newspaper propped on the dashboard, and he obligingly takes our photo beside the Colle delle Finestre signpost so I can record that today we climbed up to 2178 metres, or 7461 feet. When I see the photo later, we both look shattered and I've lost so much weight that my clothes are hanging off me like a scarecrow – but at least it's sort of downhill from here to Rome, or so I'd like to believe.

My first attempt to read a messy Italian map is a complete failure; it looks as though it's telling me to follow a proper road and I end up riding four miles towards the ski resort of Sestriere, completely in the wrong direction, before I realise my mistake and turn back. Peter, who's driving Bessie to the village of Fenestrelle by an extremely long route since there's no question of taking her over the mountain pass, would have been very surprised if he'd come across me heading towards him. As it is, I'm not at all sure how or where we're going to meet because this map is pretty useless even when I seem to be deciphering it correctly: it's to a smaller scale than the French IGN ones, loudly coloured and as crude as a prehistoric cave painting.

But St James turns up again, this time in the form of the loquacious Agostino on a BMW motorbike. He points across the hillside towards the currently invisible St Agnelli (which remains permanently invisible on my map) and allows me to continue on my way only after he's given me a potted history, fortunately in English, of his failed marriage to a lady who now lives in New York with their two grown-up daughters. They all get on wonderfully well these days, he says, and he himself organises motorbike rallies and reunions, and his machine is his passport to freedom, and now that he comes to notice we're carrying scallop shells then actually it must be me that's St James, a divine messenger directing him towards Santiago de Compostela and liberation. At which point he kisses my hand (not easy when wearing a face-scrunching helmet) and accelerates off in the general direction of Spain.

I carry on along a dirt track towards St Agnelli, turn a corner and find I'm in a thank-God-Susie-isn't-here situation: the trail's now clinging to the bare mountainside and there's a ravine to my right with no barriers. On the other side of it I think I can see the old village of Fenestrelle stuck to the rock face, and it's quite obvious that Peter and Bessie will never get up there.

But it turns out that what I'm looking at isn't Fenestrelle at all – instead, it's the biggest Alpine fortification in Europe, a series of forts linked by 4000 steps that climb up the mountainside for nearly two miles. It looks like the Great Wall of China, and it's obviously pretty old. I find out later that the first foundations were laid in 1728, and the intention was that it would scupper any French plans there might have been to invade Turin; however, given that it took 122 years to complete, it was probably just as well for the Italians that no prospective French conquerors had invasion by that route in mind. Maybe its mere colossal presence was deterrent enough.

Anyway, just as I'm concluding that whatever it is I'm looking at, Peter's not going to be there, he texts me to say he's found accommodation for us all at Chambons, a village in the valley of the River Chisone and one that's actually marked on my map. Not that the chart bothers to delineate the large number of bends we have to wind round to get there. As Leo picks his way down, the beautiful meadows of Piemonte open out to either side, a feast for my eyes and indeed for his, but they're incongruously scarred by what I assume is St Agnelli: a couple of modern blocks described on my map as a *Centro Educazione*. There are lots of children about, but the buildings are cold and forbidding and one of them displays a sinister sign saying *Laboratorio*. My overtired imagination shies away from thinking about what might go on there. Far more attractive are the three Fenestrelle forts which we pass one by one, haunting symbols of battles never fought; all massive stone walls and pillars, barracks and ramparts, their towers crowned by hats of summer grass.

I can see Peter, a dot on the plain, but by the time I meet up with the life-sized version of him in Chambons it's 7 p.m. and we've been climbing up or scrambling down the mountains for ten hours. When Leo puts his head down to graze, he goes into paroxysms of coughing. I'm still puzzling over the cause – when we're walking it tends not to bother him so much; it's only when I try trotting or else when he's at rest with his neck extended to eat that he lets rip regularly at both ends. Anyway, he seems to be well in himself, happy as ever to munch on grass, my sandwiches or whatever's available, so I'm hoping the cough will right itself in time. If it doesn't, it's going to take a long time to get to Rome if all we can do is pootle along at a walk.

Peter has chanced on a B&B run by an English couple, Kent and Michelle, who are kindness personified despite their busy evening, caused not so much by the number of guests staying but the number of animals belonging to their English neighbour that have escaped. They're looking after them while she and her husband are on holiday, but seven horses and one foal have left their village field in pursuit of greener grass, and rounding them all up is very time consuming. At least the neighbour's sheep and long-legged donkeys have stayed put in their mountain pasture with its richer grazing. They're moved from place to place up there during the summer, the donkeys tagging along with the sheep because they're on lamb-carrying duties. The ram lives with the ewes all year round, resulting in a succession of wobbly lambs which are then transported to their next billet by packing them four to a pannier slung each side of every donkey's back.

Leo has been fenced in on communal land with the solid Bessie to provide shade, and while Kent's trying to catch the horses, Michelle makes sure that Peter and I are comfortably installed in their sixteenth-century house. Nothing's too much trouble; even though we've appeared unannounced, she provides an impromptu supper, and offers to put our filthy clothes in her washing machine tomorrow. This prompts an immediate and unanimous decision to stay for two nights and have a bit of a rest, our first in nearly a fortnight.

And it's just as well we do, because the days following Chambons mangle together into the most tiring, demoralising, mosquito-ridden, stinking hot and humid episode of the whole pilgrimage.

18

Across the Po to Bra

Chambons, Italy
10th July 2006

Dearest Pa,
Sorry about the gap in the letter writing – all energies have been concentrated on getting us over the Jura mountains and then over the Alps! – which we've done, and now we're in a village not very far from Turin ...

My conscience tells me this is a feeble excuse for my silence. I haven't sent him a letter since the middle of June, in spite of all my promises before we left that I'd stay in touch. So I make this a six-page missive, tell him I'll write again soon, and finish with an airy exclamation of *and now a day off, before we set off for the boiling heat of the Po plains!* never thinking for a moment how uncomfortably true this will turn out to be.

My father was in the Po valley during World War II, in circumstances far more testing than we could ever dream of facing. Seconded from the Royal Artillery into the Hampshire Brigade, he was posted to Italy in 1944. All through that autumn the Brigade took part in savage fighting on the eastern end of the Gothic Line which stretched from the Mediterranean coast below La Spezia in the west to the Adriatic coast below Rimini. Pa was with one of the three battalions that made slow and painful progress northwards, inching their way past Rimini to cross the Rubicon and then move on beyond Ravenna. The weather was unspeakable and the list of casualties long; by December, when the Brigade was relieved, more than 1200 of its members had been wounded or killed.

During the spring of 1945 the final ferocious campaign that led to the first major surrender by the Germans was fought across the Po valley. But my father's battalions missed it. Instead they were sent to Greece at the beginning of the year to disarm the communist guerrillas, and there, far from being plunged into more conflict, they had a rapturous reception. An old newspaper cutting of Pa's makes interesting reading:

> *The soldiers were welcomed with enthusiasm everywhere … the hospitality of the Greek people was formidable. They gave generously from their meagre supplies to entertain the British soldiers. Their national drinks, retsina and ouzo, were offered with embarrassing generosity, and it became necessary in the interests of international relations for the men to acquire both a taste and a head for these powerful drinks as soon as possible…*

The communists and royalists reached political agreement before long but it still took some time for the British Army to round up stray communist groups, and it wasn't until the beginning of April that the Hampshires were shipped back to Taranto in southern Italy. They prepared themselves very quickly for combat again and set off for Forlimpopoli, 300 miles away to the north, and by 1st May they were ready for battle.

But it was a battle they were never called upon to fight.

Another of Pa's hoarded press cuttings records what happened next:

> *… the day after the Brigade arrived at Forlimpopoli came the greatest news of all, the announcement by Field-Marshal*

Alexander of the surrender of the German armies in Italy and southern Austria. Then came VE Day, and that night the sky was magnificently illuminated by the whole of 46th Division's tracer ammunition. It was indeed fitting that it should be in Italy, amid the scene of some of their toughest battles, that the Hampshire Brigade celebrated the victory for which they had fought so resolutely.

A couple of weeks later my mother sent Pa an intense, ecstatic letter:

Dear love dear love, the bean fields are in bloom again – there is a wind that is blowing their sweet scent across the lanes and into my heart, and though I prayed God that the next time that they bloomed your hand would be lying in mine, yet they bring me happiness and contentment – for I know past all doubt or uncertainty that I shall not smell that honeyed breeze in loneliness again. This year you will come home to me.

And so he did – eventually. He wasn't demobbed until the autumn, which meant Ma was on tenterhooks for months since she had only the vaguest idea of his whereabouts while he was moved around, caught up in the messy aftermath of war. In September my sisters Penny and Susie, then six and four years old, watched curiously as a stranger in khaki walked through their garden. They didn't have a clue who he was – neither they nor my mother had seen him for three years.

The Po river is the longest in Italy, its source a trickle on the flank of Mount Viso in the Alps near Sestriere. From there it writhes for 400 miles to its web of deltas in the east before emptying out into the Adriatic Sea below Venice. My father crossed it on his way home after the war was over, though he was never as far to the north-west as we are now.

I'd wondered whether my pilgrim path would travel along any of his wartime routes, but the answer was no – though he did go to Rome. The city was captured by the US forces in June 1944, and among Pa's memorabilia there are two very surprising leaflets which show that, while on leave there at the end of that year, he went to the ballet and the opera. Amid all the mayhem of war, the arts lived on.

The valley of the Po spreads out over almost 18,000 square miles. These days much of it is dedicated to horticulture, to tapestries of soya beans, wheat, corn, sugar beet, grapes, olives and rice, all bordered by irrigation dykes. If I was going to follow the whole of the secondary route of the Via Francigena from Susa, I'd be riding eastwards from Turin almost half way across the gigantic river plain to join the primary route at Pavia before doubling back towards Pontremoli and continuing to Rome. It was fortunate that when planning the pilgrimage I'd decided it wasn't worth riding round two sides of a triangle when I could go straight down the third one from Susa to Pontremoli. At more than 100 miles, this short cut looked remarkably long, but travelling via Piacenza would almost have doubled the distance – which, as it turns out, would have meant another week or two of melting by the roadside, cooling irrigation channels or not.

At the B&B in Chambons, Michelle is as good as her word and our clean clothes are soon hanging from her balcony rail to dry, indistinguishable from all the other washing flapping from other rails above the street. Kent puzzles with me over my map and sketches in a track alongside the River Chisone which I can follow for a few miles to the town of Perosa Argentina, switching there to a minor road to our next stop at San Secondo di Pinerolo.

By then I'll have progressed to a large scale map, in fact so large that Turin is sprawled over most of it, complete with diagrams of Fiat factories and a large blue wiggle inscribed *FIUME PO* pouring out of its southern side. I think I'll be able to keep well away from the city, though, and at least my planned route looks vaguely rural, liberally embellished as it is with symbols of ruined castles and a lot of orange bicycles in bubbles, pedalling along what I hope are country lanes. This map, at twenty-five years old, is one of the most contemporary ones I have in my Italian collection.

But our riding day is ruined by Leo's worst *bêtes noires* – horseflies, yet again. The Italian types are the colour of marmalade with alien green eyes, and the minute we set off down Kent's track they come pouring out of the woods and drive my poor horse so mad that we have to return to the main road, where at least the slipstream of passing traffic shoots them back into the sky. Even so, Leo clatters through the centre of Perosa Argentina like a demented camel, kicking constantly at his stomach, and one of the flies bites a chunk out of my thigh as well for good measure.

A few miles further on we reach the end of my map and I find I've forgotten to bring the next one with more of the bubble bicycles. But it probably wouldn't have helped, because the road is inexplicably closed and I keep on getting diverted on to a new one that wouldn't be on the map at all. However, according to the compass I seem to be riding in the right direction, and just as I'm getting to grips with the next problem – nowhere to stay – I chance across a sign saying *Agriturismo*, a new one on me, which turns out to be the Italian version of *Camping à la Ferme*.

Flavio is charm personified and politely listens to my stumbling request for a pitch for the night for one lorry, two people and one horse who has his own portable enclosure. He waits till I've finished before telling me in perfect English that he has room for us all, including a field that's already electrically fenced. His farm is delightful apart from the swarms of insects that engulf Leo despite my best efforts with the fly spray. But tepid rain comes to the rescue, glugging and slapping at Bessie's roof all night long, and sheet lightning sears the outlines of the mountains while Leo wallows in a warm bath that washes the mosquitoes off his skin and into the mud.

By morning the rain has sludged off, leaving behind a suffocating sticky day for us to get lost in. The bicycle bubble map turns out to be useless, omitting several roads altogether along with every single road number, but I know we must be making progress because the peaks that have filled the skyline for weeks are subsiding into distant humps as the furnace of the Po plain sucks us in.

We mosey along flat lanes with no horizon. The mountains are now out of sight which makes it difficult to get any sense of distance or perspective, even from the height of Leo's back, because we're claustrophobically hemmed in by fields of sweetcorn as tall as saplings. For eight long hours we sweat our way vaguely south-eastwards, with me getting more and more dispirited. We're in a maze of maize, but I'm far beyond appreciating any play on words. And getting thirstier and thirstier, the water bottle drained long ago, though Leo's doing all right – irrigation channels tinkle along beside the road, and every now and then he pauses to dip his face in right up to the ears.

Just as I'm beginning to eye them up as well, even though I know it would be stupid to take such a risk, a farm materialises beside us and Signora Agricoltrice sizes up the situation instantly. I don't have to say a word; silently she hands me a glass and a litre jug of frosty cold water from her fridge, followed by a refill. I'm almost tempted to ask her if she'd like to have some visitors for the night, but I don't because I can see there's no pasture anywhere. The farmhouse is entirely surrounded by corn.

Peter and I meet at a crossroads on the far edge of the miles of maize, but this evening there's no convenient Agriturismo anywhere around, no houses, nothing except a garage that's closed. We have no water, either, because unfortunately he forgot to refill our ten-litre jerry can, and my latest woe is yesterday's horsefly bite on my thigh which is now alarmingly swollen and itchy. By this stage I'd quite like to indulge in a spot of Poor Us – but there's no point and no time. We have to find somewhere to camp.

A wood. We're beside a wood, and next to it there's a cut hayfield. I've no idea who owns either of them, but we're past bothering to find out. Peter eases Bessie down a track into the middle of regimented lines of poplar trees, where she's more or less concealed, and I sneak round the field with the electric tape and fence off a strip for Leo. Not much grass, but truncated hay stalks will do.

Water. We walk up the road to the garage hoping to find a tap. After a fruitless hunt across the forecourt, we're just sneaking round the back when two *carabinieri* suddenly appear. Peter guiltily waves the can at them and their puzzled expressions clear to sympathy: 'Signor, Signora, there's a tap here, a *rubinetto*.' And indeed there is, right beside the car wash. They help us fill up, and show no curiosity as to where we've come from and why we have this enormous water container with us which we then lug off down the road on foot.

The day doesn't cool down at all; stuck to our clammy mattress at midnight, I become aware there's a nasty honk of decay pervading Bessie. It's obviously coming from my horsefly-chewed leg which looks as though I've inflated it with the bicycle pump – great, I suppose I'm getting gangrene now. And that'll mean we can't continue… I debate whether amputation would be better than having to carry on in this stifling humidity but decide probably not, on balance. And in the morning, to judge by the greasy film of grey ash that's coating the lorry, the trees and my horse, the smell's probably coming from some burning dung heap rather than my disintegrating thigh, which has returned to normal size overnight.

It's impossible to groom the oily Leo, and since he's drunk most of the water, I have one flannel-full to try and get the filth off my face, and a bit more in a bottle to fend off dehydration. I decide not to wake up Peter with the news that I've left him about two mouthfuls plus enough to dampen his toothbrush, and he's still asleep when Leo and I tiptoe away down the road. At least he knows where we're hoping to meet at the end of the day – outside a little town with the memorable name of Bra.

After our gloomy start, things brighten up considerably. I decide early on to make a stand against grumbling, which takes a lot of effort, but the fact is we've still got a long way to go and 400 miles of unavoidable heat accompanied by avoidable grumpiness is hardly going to promote harmony of the marital kind, or indeed with my uncomplaining horse. Next I decide on Riding Plan B for the time being, which is not to look for tracks at all but to stay with medium-sized roads from town to town – refilling my water bottle as I go. Unlike France, there are no verges here, but at least there's a wide expanse of tarmac and not much traffic; a tiny breeze plays along with us, accelerating to a welcome rush of air every time a car passes. The corn fields spread out on either side, washed by the tempting sprinklers that throw their rain in a ceaseless arc, and it isn't long before we cross the Po river, just a lazy dribble here beneath a little bridge. Beyond it there's a sign that shows we're moving into the province of Cuneo.

On the outskirts of Bra, Peter and I chance on an equestrian centre and manage to persuade the owners, Walter and Valeria, to take us in for the night even though they're packed out with horses and riders. There's a residential training course in progress for students learning how to communicate with their mounts using Natural Horsemanship. I don't know much about this kind of training except that the aim seems to be to inspire mutual respect between animal and owner, using the kind of body language horses use with each other. This should then result in the horse happily co-operating with its human's wishes rather than getting bloody-minded and deciding it's the one who should be Pack Leader.

Leo and I are about to learn a bit more.

When I've finished hosing all the grime from last night's smouldering muck heap off him, Walter asks if my now pristine Appaloosa can take part in the training. It seems churlish to refuse even though my poor horse is tired after slogging along the roads all day, so we go into the covered school where various students appear to be trying to teach their reluctant animals how to do party tricks. Or at least that's what it looks like to me. Their horses are tall, thin-skinned types, probably with perfect pedigrees, and most are prancing about and being extremely uncooperative when asked to push their way through curtains strung on a pole, or to stand with all four feet on the kind of upturned tub designed for circus elephants. The week's course is nearly at an end, and I'm not convinced the horses at any rate have learned much so far; those that aren't skipping about are standing looking mulish with all their hooves planted firmly on the ground.

A student takes Leo from me and I stand back. I don't know what to expect, but it certainly isn't what happens next: she advances into his personal space and starts shaking his lead rope violently just under his chin. Leo flings up his head in alarm and tries to back away, his thought bubble transparent: *what are you doing? What have I done wrong?*

As for me, I'm filled with instant, murderous rage. I can't explain it properly in Italian, but the girl understands very well when I just shout NO! at her. She stops, looking confused, but not nearly as confused as my horse – as far as he's concerned, he's being dominated and told off, and he has no idea why.

The student attempts to explain the principle to me, and I do try to understand what she's saying (something about letting the horse know from the outset he must respect her), but I feel like a mother who's just seen her baby smacked by a stranger in the street, and that's enough of Natural Horsemanship for me. If only I spoke reasonable Italian I could point out to Signorina Bossy Boots that Leo's gentle demeanour and body language are obvious to anyone: he respects people anyway, and always does his best to please. His manners are (mostly) impeccable, and even when he's stealing my Mars Bar he does it with charm and finesse, no grimaces, no ears-back intimidation … perhaps best not to mention the greedy side of his personality, but I don't have the words to describe it anyway. So I just take him back and that's that, as far as I'm concerned.

Walter, however, has noticed what's going on. He speaks sharply to the student and asks me politely if he may take over. I give him the rope with some reluctance, but Walter is quiet and unhurried, realising instantly that Leo is an amenable chap who just needs things to be explained to him. Once again, his thoughts are transparent, but this time he's relaxed, and fully focused on what Walter would like him to do.

'You want me to follow you, off the lead? No problem, I'll follow you. Turn left? Turn right? Stop? That's easy.'

'You want me to walk up to these curtains? OK. Shall I push my nose through? Walk through them? Of course.'

And finally: 'You want me to pick up my hoof and put it on this tub? Both my front feet? And now … a back foot? Both hind feet? OK, no problem.'

And there he is, balanced with all four hooves crowded together on the top of the tub, beaming.

Leo Is A Star.

Walter's very surprised. In halting English, he tells me my horse has achieved more in ten minutes than some of the resident ones have in five days. I suspect the fact that mine has weathered more unusual situations in the last two and a half months than most horses do in a lifetime has something to do with it, but I accept Walter's accolade on his behalf with a grace worthy of Leo himself – and an uncharitable satisfaction that my tough little spotted friend has a lot more intelligence than all the fizzy thoroughbreds put together.

Valeria finds spaces for Peter, me and about thirty other people at the table for a supper of pizza and wine. It's a friendly, noisy meal, but when the conversation afterwards becomes full-on horsy, not surprisingly Peter goes off to bed with his book. I decide to stay, fuelled by a lethal liquorice liqueur that Walter digs out of a cupboard, followed by all the riding centre's horse photographs and videos going back at least two decades. More alcohol is produced, and hours later I stagger off to Bessie just as everyone else is tuning up with Italian love songs.

Tomorrow will probably be another unpredictable day when anything could happen, though I do know I've got at least twenty miles to ride while Peter diverts to a golf course for some light relief from horses. We could both do with a good sleep, but it doesn't happen; the night's another tossing and turning one, punctuated by exclamations of got-you-you-little-bugger as another mosquito is pulverised by a flying sock, and by crescendos of communal singing in the background.

19

And a Premature Trip to Purgatory

My horse has such good manners ... not.

Just south of Bra, I come across a track that might or might not go somewhere useful and decide to take a break from Plan B. A smiley man is walking past it, and I manage to ask him (by the simple method of pointing to the east and uttering the words '*Grinzane Cavour?*' with my eyebrows raised) whether it might lead to this particular village, which is where Peter and I are supposed to be meeting this evening.

'*Sì!*' he says enthusiastically, and moves forward to pat Leo. In his other hand he has a bunch of dandelion leaves which could be for the family rabbit, or indeed the family lunch for all I know, but they get no further than Mr Greedy who vacuums them delicately into his mouth and munches appreciatively.

'Thank you SO much, I knew they were for me.'

The man looks astonished and then he bursts out laughing, giving Leo a compliment I'm beginning to hear quite often – *che bello cavallino!* what a beautiful little horse! – before we go our separate ways in a mutual spirit of *benevolenza*.

The track lasts all of a mile before it re-joins a road we have to trudge along for hours, crossing the River Tanaro near Pollenzo where two ornate towers still rise above the ruins of the original bridge built for a long-dead king. Beyond it the Sunday drivers seem to be out in force, most of them racing each other. They squeeze past us at top speed, and it isn't long before I get fed up and stick my foot out into the road when I see them coming, in the hope they'll notice my stirrup reflector and slow down.

This gesture results in the high point of today's ride, which is to wreck a competition between a Ferrari Dino and a Porsche Boxster which come streaking towards me, the Ferrari in front closing in on a Fiat Panda ahead of it, and the Boxster intent on overtaking both of them. The Panda is sedately approaching Leo and me, and in the end neither of the other drivers quite has the nerve to pull past it and risk splattering a horse and rider all over the road (thank God) so they have to slow right down. I debate giving them both the finger, but decide a stony look will do. They glare back at me, their race ruined.

Little hills are starting to pimple the Po plain. Even at the top of them it's still baking hot, but at least they make a change from the flat scenery of the last couple of days. They're striped with tidy rows of vines as far as the eye can see, not a tendril out of place, all lovingly nurtured to uphold the reputation of the Barolo wines which are made from the Nebbiolo grape and considered to be some of the best in Italy. My route doesn't take me into Barolo itself but it does pass through or close to other well-known wine villages: Cherasco, where Peter's playing golf today, Verduno, Roddi, Gallo, tonight's destination of Grinzane Cavour and tomorrow's first village, Diano d'Alba. Passing revered vineyards without pausing is easy for me since I'm too hot to be tempted by alcohol; the villages are just useful watering holes, and by the time I get to Grinzane both Leo and I are nicely hydrated, courtesy of a succession of bemused barmen who must be more used to upending a wine bottle than putting a plastic one and a bucket under the water tap. It turns out that Peter certainly intended to buy a bottle or two to add to the stash in Bessie, but the prices were so prohibitive that in the end he wasn't tempted either.

The camper van park in the village seems an appropriate place for an overnight stop; Bessie might be an unusually large example of a camper but that's what she is these days, and Peter and I don't feel the need to ask anyone's permission to squeeze her in. There's no one else staying here anyway, and there's even a square of grass for Leo. Our only problem is Porta Potti. Nasty humours have been wafting into our sleeping quarters for the last week (in addition to those attributable to smoking muck heaps and/or my gangrenous leg) and now they're so bad we're going to be sleeping outside on the grass with Leo tonight if we don't do something about it. There's no convenient campsite with bog-emptying facilities anywhere near here, and the only alternative is to cart it to the public loo.

Smuggling Porta Potti into the loo building isn't easy, in spite of my efforts to disguise its presence with all the water buckets. Once inside I leave Peter to deal with it, looking green, while I stare nonchalantly at Grinzane's beautiful castle on the hill.

Oh no, please no … don't come over here. An old chap's emerging from the house opposite and he's heading in my direction. Oh God. He's going to sit on the bench under the open lavatory window … what? You want me to come over? He's beckoning me to sit beside him, and there's the most awful stench pouring out above his head, I can smell it from here. I stretch my mouth into something that must look more like a grimace than a smile and go over, trying to explain that all we're doing is getting some water for our horse…

Signor isn't fooled. He lifts his nose and takes a long, deliberate sniff. I debate trying to tell him Peter's not very well (which he probably isn't, by now), but the old man's already informing me that the water from the tap below the castle comes straight out of the *terra* and is a lot better quality than the water in the *servizi*. I'm sure that's true, but please just go away, I can't think of any pidgin Italian small talk while I'm waiting for my husband. After a very long ten minutes Peter staggers out with Porta Potti under his arm, and Signor eyes him up suspiciously before marching back to his house.

We sneak back queasily to Bessie. Somehow our supper of pasta with spinach and ricotta has lost its attraction. And our night in the fumigated lorry is no better – after sleepless hours listening to equine coughing interspersed with barking from a neighbouring dog who thinks we shouldn't be here, I saddle up early and leave, already drenched in sweat from the humidity huffing over the hills at seven in the morning.

Unfortunately the dog's not the only one to think we shouldn't be here – a municipal policeman with a gun turns up to turf Peter out of bed soon after I've gone. When my weary husband points to the sign spelling out that this parking area is for camper vans, the officer ostentatiously hitches up his holster and orders him to leave within the hour.

We reckon the disapproving Signor Lavatory must have reported us. He probably spent the night worrying about the effects of a pungent stink on Nebbiolo grapes.

Trying to find my way across country from Diano d'Alba is impossible. I cast round in circles like a clueless hound, searching for the scent of a track that's on this map somewhere, or should be, and wearing Leo out in the process. In the end I give up and ride straight down the main road, which isn't straight at all but wiggles round the hills. At least the mad Sunday drivers have turned into more sensible Monday ones, and everyone slows down when they see a horse. In fact one HGV driver stops altogether and I assume it's because he wants to come out with a *bello cavallino* remark, but it isn't – he appears to be lost. And you're asking *me* the way, dear Signor? I'm afraid I've no idea – this map I'm trying to read is of the planet Jupiter.

By the time I get to Castino many hours later, Peter's already there. He parked in the village square to wait for me but found himself moved on for the second time today, on this occasion because Bessie was blocking a funeral cortège trying to get to the church. However, Alex the English builder, working on a house in the square, noticed the lorry's number plates and came to his rescue.

It turns out he was brought up in a hamlet twenty miles from where we live in Faversham, and in a very welcome gesture of neighbourliness he offers us a Bessie space for the night next to his house outside Castino. His friends Dario and Bearn have a field that Leo can use which is so full of grass I don't bother shutting the gate while I go and fetch some water, but to my surprise he comes to find me as soon as I'm out of sight, like a faithful Labrador with separation anxiety. He trots up to me coughing dismally; he still seems to be in very good spirits as we travel along but I don't feel I can ask him to move faster than a walk, and I decide I'm going to have to phone the vet in England soon and ask for advice.

No need to cook dinner tonight: Dario and Bearn invite us to their house along with Alex and his dog Alfie who's the product of a lustful liaison between a Spinone gundog and an Italian bloodhound, a romance that has endowed Alfie with a long bloodhound nose with a Spinone moustache and beard at the end of it. Alex rescued him from the dogs' home at nearby Alba. Apparently Italians like to buy puppies but tend to abandon or conveniently lose them once they become adults, or tie them up on short chains and leave them out of doors, relegated from family pets to guard dogs.

In this area of Piemonte, however, there's one highly prized type of dog – the truffle hound. Black truffles grow round here, and the hunters rely on their dogs to find them. This has caused some hideous fungus wars as the hunters try to keep their whereabouts a secret from each other and, according to Alex, it's another no-win situation for Italian canines – the hunters poison each other's hounds. Last year, he says, one particular villain killed fourteen of them. Although there's an official breed of truffle hound called a Lagotto Romagnolo, any obliging dog with a keen sense of smell can be trained for the job, and it's probably just as well for Alfie that his parentage has resulted in a preference on his part for hunting meat rather than veg.

The next day dawns with a roar of approaching machinery. Bessie's squashed in to the verge beside a nut orchard and I have visions of us being moved on again by its owner, the fat farmer who's now homing in on us on his Lamborghini tractor. Hazelnuts are also big business in this area, promoted by orchards-full of Euro cash, but they're a long term project; it takes seven years for the young trees to reach maturity and start cropping in commercial quantities. Judging by the size of Signor Farmer, he's been sitting around on his own nuts raking in the euros for at least that length of time, but that's probably just a prickly and unjustified assumption on my part because after the Signor Lavatory experience I've already concluded he's going to be hostile. Which he isn't – he looks quizzically at the lorry which the tractor certainly can't squeeze past, and gives me a cheery smile before turning round and rumbling off down the lane again.

It's another cloudless day on sizzling roads as we travel down the tight bends from Castino, the only minutes of coolness spent listening to Leo's echoing hoofbeats as we pass through the shade of a gallery carved out of the cliff face. Then we're back in the frying pan of the Po river plain, the road following one of its endless tributaries, and at Monastero I cross over the water and join Peter in a field of dust which is all that remains of a harvested alfalfa crop. We've all had enough by now, but we'll have to carry on, there's obviously nowhere to stay around here … except possibly on this piece of desert.

Would that be all right, Signora? A worried-looking woman has appeared, all kindness and concern, and she's sure it won't be a problem if we camp in the field, and here's some water for your horse ... anything else? I'd like to suggest some alfalfa, but wherever the crop may be stored, it's nowhere near here. There isn't a barn in sight. However, Leo's used to making do; I collect up some straggly bits of greenery still flopping round the field's edges, and he's quite content with that.

As dusk falls, I scrawl wearily in my journal:

P and I think we've spent our time in purgatory and should get to heaven direct. Purgatory is mainly the mosquitoes – as I write this, P is trying to swat them with his pants. There are hordes – all over us, all over Leo, in his ears, up his nose ... purgatory is also the boiling heat, the breathless humidity, the slog on the main roads with the fumes and traffic, and it's purgatory too for my endlessly willing but coughing horse...

And after another night of listening to him rasping and farting into the darkness, I do phone Chris the vet. Explaining the problem is extremely easy – all I need do is hold my phone next to Leo, first at one end and then the other. Fortunately, Chris doesn't think the situation is serious, or indeed anything to do with Leo's deformed soft palate. It's more likely to be an allergy, triggered by mouldy spores in the hay he ate at Tignes, and perpetuated by the wholesale dust of our days on the plain. When we get into the mountains of the Apennines it'll probably get better, and he reassures me that whatever's caused the lurgy, it won't stop us getting to Rome.

At the moment I can't even begin to focus on the thought of Rome, or indeed on anything beyond today's journey, another eight hours of crawling along a river valley, still on the road because I haven't the energy to fight with the map about its inaccuracies on the subject of tracks. And even if Leo wasn't coughing, I couldn't ask him to trot; most of the roads still have no grass verges, and pounding along the hard metalled surface would jar his legs into lameness. Today's map is full of the pretty symbols etched in red that indicate castles, but I can't be bothered to scan the horizon for any of them, however dramatic they may be: Morsasco, Prasco, Trisobbio, Cremolino and finally Molare, on the edge of another river which is no doubt another sodding tributary of the sodding Po. It's here that we call a halt.

Somewhere in my saddlebag there's a tourist leaflet describing all the beautiful villages of Alessandria province and I expect Molare too is stuffed with attractions, but at the moment I'm more preoccupied with the tacky state of my riding trousers, so stiff with salt from Leo's sweaty coat they could walk round on their own without me inside them. And Peter's no better off, trapped as he is in the oven of Bessie's cab; when he catches up with me, he's glued to the driving seat by his shorts.

We're directed to the banks of the river where there's room to park and even something that resembles proper grass for Leo, which cheers him up no end; but as for Peter and me, any good intentions to stay positive and not be grumpy have vanished. We agree this is the dreariest evening we've had so far. As the sun slumps below the treeline we dab our mosquito-bitten feet with TCP and I heave out the camera to record this nadir moment, epitomised by a photo of Peter standing with the damp washing-up bowl in his hand, its yellow plastic crusted over with the black scum that came off his face when he scrubbed it.

Mouldering here in the valley, the mountains of the Apennines seem light years away.

20

Putting on the Kettle for a Cup of Nude Tea

If I'd bothered to check Peter's Michelin road atlas as well as my large- scale *Carta dei Sentieri e dei Rifugi*, which has us simmering forever on the Po plain, I'd have seen that in fact we're homing in fast on the mountains again. My not-exactly-pilgrim-route will soon veer towards the Apennines, the backbone of Italy: 870 miles of lumpy vertebrae at right angles to the French Alps.

They hop across to Sicily and tail off around explosive Mount Etna, which at almost 11,000 feet is considerably taller than the highest peak in the chain on the mainland. That one is Corno Grande, a long way to the east of Rome and definitely not on my route. I believe the mountain closest to us at the moment is Mount Tobbio, poking up just 3500 feet in the Parco Naturale delle Capanne di Marcarolo, but I've no idea how far away it is.

My first stop today is supposed to be in the town of Ovada, pinched between the Orba and Stura rivers and famous for its ruby wine, apparently best accompanied by the local *taglierini* pasta in truffle sauce – which would make a welcome change from tinned-whatever's-in-our-cupboard, but which isn't likely to feature on the Bistro Bessie menu. I have a leaflet about Ovada showing a photo of a restored mediaeval fresco of St George and the dragon; it caught my eye because St George's expressive horse is frowning furiously at the dragon, and I'd like to see it. But when I ride into the town I decide not to investigate it after all, nor even try to get a stamp from the *municipio* for my pilgrim passport – the leaflet promises 'Ovada is a quiet little town...' but it isn't, it's full of HGVs roaring through and it would be madness to stop here.

So we carry on towards the smaller villages of Lerma and Mornese, both decorated on my map with castle symbols which I ignore as well, because all Leo and I are interested in is the next garage we pass which has a cold water tap. A mechanic there tells me that what I've been riding along for days is the worst of a long sultry Po corridor and it doesn't end until I reach the Apennines, which I'm expecting to take weeks since I haven't checked the bigger picture.

But it doesn't. When I leave the flat main road and switch to a lane that should eventually get us to Voltaggio, Leo starts to walk uphill and the air lifts out of its soggy torpor into something lighter, ethereal almost, blowing the cobwebs out of my brain so I can think clearly again. And then we're out into true countryside, the road the best since leaving the Alps, shaded by trees and winding up to an open ridge where a breeze swirls Leo's mane away from his sweat-sticky neck.

I can't believe the transformation. It's taken just an hour or so to reach a different world, one where low peaks ramble away in front of my nose and the arc of blue that frames them has just one odd-shaped cloud in it, like a person running across the sky.

We settle down for a lunch break, Leo dozing under a tree and me gawping at the incredible view. And also wondering, as usual, where we're going to stay tonight. We won't get as far as Voltaggio, and the miles of forested slopes ahead are completely unspoilt by any sign of human habitation. At this point I realise I must already be gazing at the Capanne di Marcarolo national park since I remember reading that it consists of around 20,000 acres of wilderness occupied by all of forty people. Maybe we could just set up camp anywhere ... though Peter's got to find us first.

Further down the road a stone statue of a French soldier stands waving a flag at the empty landscape. He's commemorating the considerable presence of the *Maquis* here in World War II but apart from him, I pass no one and nothing for miles until I round a corner and come face to face with a sign advertising an equestrian centre and B&B combined. In this lonesome spot, St James has come to the rescue with tailor-made lodgings, and I phone Peter to tell him of our incredible luck – not that I can give him precise directions because I don't know where we are.

By the time I can hear the lorry coming up the hill I've realised that the sign is very old and there haven't been any horses here for years; but at least there's a house, maybe it's a rural gîte that's still in use. I can't quite make it out but the owners welcome us anyway, on condition we eat with the family that evening, I think they say. Leo turns up his nose at ten empty stables and settles into a paddock instead, and Peter has to manoeuvre Bessie on to a flat piece of land ready for a cooler night's sleep in her than we've had for weeks, given that it looks as though the house has reverted from a gîte to a private home.

Or so we think. But that's not quite the case: when we turn up for supper, two cars come chugging up the driveway and we find that the family run a gourmet restaurant here in this far-flung corner of Alessandria. Sitting outside on the patio as the daylight sinks away, we start working our way through a beautiful meal of cold roast beef, strawberries and local wine against a backdrop of inky mountains, deciding the tallest of them must be Mount Tobbio, identifiable by the pinprick star thrown by a lamp at the chapel of Our Lady of Caravaggio on its peak.

The only sounds are the murmurings and munchings of the other al fresco diners – and then an unusual crescendo of purring.

Juliana, our hosts' little daughter, is putting two kittens on our table. She knows we must like animals – why else would we have a pet horse? – so she places them carefully beside our now empty plates. We have in fact been defeated by the enormous amount of meat piled on them, but it seemed such a shame to waste any of it that I've slithered four slices into a napkin to sneak into the lorry for tomorrow night's supper. We only just escape detection later when the family dog follows us back to Bessie, sniffing at my bulging pocket.

Thank you, St James, for shelter and wonderful food; for a gulp of cold air and one bug-free night for us and for Leo, who stands like a statue with his nose to the breeze and his usually fly-swishing tail as still as the rest of him. Pity we can't stay here for a week.

The descent to Voltaggio next day takes longer than I expect because my optimistic map has ironed out most of the bends, and the reality consists of a lane that restlessly crosses and re-crosses the River Morsone, using bridges with signs warning that they're not much more than two metres wide. I have a feeling they're narrower than Bessie. Peter's behind me somewhere and when I see a notice by a set of broken bridge railings emphasising the word PERICULOSO, I wonder whether I should phone him. But I can't because there's no mobile signal, and anyway there's no other road he can follow.

The final dogleg into Voltaggio goes via the river at a point where it's been dammed into a pool full of swimmers. There's no signpost to Busalla, the next village, but the lady I accost with a halting request for directions speaks English and it turns out she's on maternity leave from her work as a paediatrician in London. We're busy discussing our respective life histories when Peter appears looking thoroughly stressed and is relieved to be told that the road gets wider once he's closer to Busalla.

Leo and I set off again, trailing behind Bessie this time, the heat building to furnace level as we come down from the mountains on another melting road, and when we get to Busalla I find it's not a village at all, it's a big industrial town right in the bottom of the valley of the River Scrivia which, needless to say, is another tributary of the Po. It's a hideous place, filled with railway sidings and queues of lorries, and I pass a clock in the choking street that shows the temperature has now reached 46°C. I've never been in such heat in my life and I'm sure Leo hasn't either; we've sweated all our sweat away and now we're both so desiccated we probably look like a couple of old pieces of biltong.

Peter phones from further down the road. Bessie has chosen this moment to develop an air pressure leak and he asks me to check out Busalla's industrial estate for a garage. Who to ask? I'm hesitating outside a shop when Valentina passes by, all cool blue jeans and bright orange T-shirt, mad about horses and anxious to help. She too speaks English. There's no garage here to assist you, she says, but there's one a couple of kilometres down the road; and off she goes to rescue Peter while Leo and I plough on through the town's foul traffic and diesel fumes, and negotiate our way round a vehicle transporter that's stopped in the middle of the road because one of its cars has fallen off.

By the time I find the garage, a small mechanic has already squeezed himself in beside Bessie's engine and is fixing the leak; he welds up the oil pipe brackets too while he's about it, and all for 30 euros with a smile and an invitation to help ourselves to water. Many gallons later, horse and humans have revived, and Valentina has now pointed us in the direction of a tiny set of livery stables at nearby Savignone whose proprietor she has charmed into squeezing us all in for a night. Tomorrow we need to find somewhere to stop for a couple of days, and I scour the map for symbols that might be more helpful than the castle ones. We haven't had a break for nearly a fortnight; all our clothes and bedclothes are filthy, and I need to find a *lavanderia a gettoni* which according to my dictionary is the proper translation of launderette. The map helpfully provides a drawing of a red tepee, presumably indicating a campsite which surely, surely must have a washing machine, and better still it's only a short ride away.

The site at Montoggio turns out to be a bit like a mini-Butlin's for large families, and it straggles down the edge of another breathe-in-Bessie lane in a long line of chalets and caravans and shelters and huts of every description, all squashed in with about an inch of space between them. It's really too small to accommodate a lorry, but that gives us an excuse to position ourselves in the far corner of the car park with Leo beside us, well away from the pandemonium of dozens of schoolchildren on holiday.

Unfortunately my hunt for a *lavanderia a gettoni* is completely fruitless; the only *gettoni* we're given are for extracting hot water out of showers that shut down altogether if you're not quick, as Peter discovers when he's still coated in soap. So my afternoon is spent grimly washing the sheet, duvet cover and clothes all by hand, plus the more disgusting bits of Bessie, to the accompaniment of Leo coughing violently into the dust and Peter noisily turning the leaves of his book. This leaves me muttering grouchily about having to do all the work, but there's no point in getting even more overheated by grumbling at my husband – he's switched right off, so far out of his comfort zone that I'm sure he wishes he wasn't here at all.

At least the view's amazing. We're poised well above the village which is yet another one quivering in a damp river valley, but beyond it there are mountains crowding the horizon. Afternoon storm clouds are building up around them but it's as well they're not coming this way – an icy drenching would be bliss, but if the washing doesn't get dry we'll be turning this campsite into a *campeggio da nudista* (or whatever's the appropriate phrase in Italian) because we won't have any clean clothes left to wear.

Rest Day Two is spent almost relaxing, at least for the three hours that I manage to escape into my own book. Then it's back to the thorny subject of navigation once again. I'm almost off the edge of my last chart in the Sentieri and Rifugi series with its cheerful red symbols on a green background, and my three different maps of the roads and tracks ahead are exactly that: different. From each other. In the end I choose a military chart dating from 1981; it's severely monochrome apart from its roads which are all bright orange, but I can just make out a dotted cart track traced across the mountains to the town of Torriglia, about fifteen miles away, which should be a fair day's ride. This means I can avoid the road which shows up on Peter's atlas as a very major one weaving across the Scrivia valley. By the time I've highlighted my cart track in Day-Glo yellow, I've convinced myself it looks crystal clear and positively inviting.

And it is.

It's really quiet on the mountain lane, mostly upgraded now from a cart track to a metalled surface that carries no traffic at all. Somewhere below me there's another river trickling along, but I can't see it through the forest that clothes every hump and hillock in a green fur coat, and we're too high up to be bothered by its humidity. Now and again the view opens out to reveal whole villages hanging on the slopes above another valley, another ravine; old stone buildings and pointed church spires in a landscape that can't have changed in hundreds of years.

At the junction with the main road a mile or so beyond Torriglia, I stop to look at the map and wonder whether we should double back to the town or whether it's worth carrying on a bit further towards Montebruno. We've made very good time ... what shall we do, Leo? We've been travelling in dappled sunshine for hours, but it seems to be dimming suddenly and I twist round in the saddle to look behind me. Oh ... trouble. Could be a lot of trouble. Silent clouds are pouring blackly across the sky towards us, boiling and writhing and rearing up into tower blocks; by now I know very well what a cumulonimbus cloud looks like, and this is an army of them.

'Rats, Leo. That's a storm. Coming up.'

I never thought about the chances of getting caught in bad weather when I was wondering whether to take the high level track, but I should have done because there've been afternoon storms in these mountains on both days we spent in Montoggio. Well, I need to give it a thought now, it's going to catch up with us.

'We'd better make for Torriglia ... whoa, Leo, I need to phone Peter and tell him what we're doing.'

I've just put the phone back in my pocket when suddenly some supernal sluice gate bursts open, rain and hail in a solid sheet, the ice bouncing and hissing on the overheated road; there's hardly time to struggle into my not-so-waterproof jacket, no time to drag on my reasonably-waterproof trousers, no time to cover up the sheepskin on the saddle. And then I hear a strange click and the air quivers, the hair rises on the back of my neck as I half-realise what this means ... *Christ!* A white flash, another, lightning bolts smacking into the ground just yards away, too close, much too close, must get off Leo, all this metal on the saddle – God, thunder now, this is *earsplitting*.

My angelic horse stands calmly while I jump down. We can't carry on, it's right overhead … shelter. What shelter? I try pulling him into an alcove in the wall that runs down the edge of the road, but it's hopeless, there's thunder and lightning everywhere and the road's a river.

Leo doesn't blink an eye. He waits to see what I want him to do, and in the explosion of noise and blinding light I decide there's no point stopping, we're as likely to be hit here as anywhere else so we might as well carry on, and if this is our day to be struck by lightning, then this is our day to be struck by lightning and there's not much I can do about it.

We walk side by side down towards Torriglia, wading through the torrent that's turning my riding boots into twin paddling pools. A police car shoots past us up the hill without stopping, blue lights flashing, a bow wave foaming off its front wheels as though it's a motor boat.

By the time I spot a bus garage at the bottom of the hill I'm totally soaked and Leo is so wet his pink skin is showing through his hide. But this *is* proper shelter.

'Come on Leo, we'll stop here, it's getting worse and worse.'

'I don't want to stop. I want to go on!'

'No! We're going to wait here. Stop fidgeting! Oh, great. Trust you.'

Mr Impatient is dropping crots right inside the garage and when a bus turns up a few minutes later, he turns broadside on across the entrance and has the most copious pee he's had for days, his eyes closed with relief. The bus driver looks stunned, not to mention anxious to drive into what is clearly his depot, but there's no way I can explain to him in Italian that you can't budge a pissing horse – it stretches its legs wide so it doesn't splash its fetlocks, and it won't move until it's finished.

In fact, there doesn't seem any point in trying to say anything at all, so I just give the driver an apologetic wave when I can finally shift Leo away from the manure mountain and personal flood he's created on the otherwise dry garage floor, and we move out again into the deluge.

Down the street, past the bank, past the church, can't see much, I need windscreen wipers for my eyeballs, but finally here's the municipal car park and here, thank God, are the blurry outlines of Bessie and Peter. As the rain thumps down and the thunder cracks, I tie Leo to the lorry, snatch off his saddle and bridle and dump them underneath it, scramble in through the groom's door, shed my dripping clothes all over the floor and then, to Peter's amusement, do the only thing possible in the circumstances. Put the kettle on for a cup of nude tea.

21

A Night in the Middle of a Roundabout

This rollercoaster pilgrim life is turning out to be even more unpredictable in Italy than it was in France. Yes, sometimes it's frustrating (can't make sense of the maps/can't speak the language), sometimes it's dangerous (I don't want to get caught in a thunderstorm like that again), and mostly it's exhausting; but I can't say boredom has featured much on the emotional menu so far.

Life would be easier if I did manage to make the time to learn how to speak Italian properly. In between dealing with the unexpected, and when not so knackered that all I want to do is sleep or read something mindless, I do try. *Non capisco* (I don't understand) is certainly etched on my brain because I use it so frequently, but there's no point in trying to remember *la pista è segnata?* – is the track well-marked? – when the answer's inevitably going to be No.

It doesn't help that my phrase book is so full of imaginative information that I get distracted every time I open it. It deals with dramatic situations you'd never think of normally, from complaining that your accommodation is rat-infested (*infestato da topi*) to moaning at the hairdresser: *non dovevo mai permettertele di toccarmi!* – I should never have let you near me! A visit to the dentist because you have a broken tooth (*un dente rotto*, which sounds more like

211

a bad case of decay) can end in disaster – you're warned to listen out for the exclamation of *torni qui che non ho finite!* – come back, I haven't finished! – which makes you think you might stick with the shattered tooth rather than risk a drill through your lip.

There's even a riveting section on sex in the book – who would have thought that addressing your loved one as *ciccino mio* (my little fleshy thing) would be considered a term of endearment? It also tells you how to say fuck off – *vaffanculo!* – which is more than the foreign phrase books of my teenage years ever did; it would have been useful to know how to say it back then, but I don't suppose I'll need it now, given my fifty-seven years and the unhelpful wrinkles added to my face by the sun.

Not surprisingly, there isn't much in it that's specific to horses, but I've cobbled together the expression for electric fence – *recinto elettrico* – and those words together with a finger pointing at waste ground/small patch of stubble/someone's garden and, occasionally, a proper field, have been enough to find somewhere to put Leo for the night. And of course I know the word for horse or even what I imagine means little horse, because so many people continue to look at him and exclaim *che bello cavallino!* while said beautiful *cavallino* is inserting his muzzle through an open car window and begging for peppermints.

This evening in Torriglia we don't need to unravel our electric fencing owing to another dose of the unexpected. While wading down the road earlier it never crossed my mind there might be an equestrian centre here, but when the storm finally goes rollicking off and I've found some dry clothes, I look over the car park wall and see there's a set of stables down in the dip below it. My holy sister Susie would say this is no coincidence. I'm not sure about that, but I continue to have a strong sense of something or someone keeping an eye on us and, whimsically or not, I still like to think the someone is St James.

The people at the centre know all about Santiago de Compostela and San Giacomo, and show me a Compostela certificate belonging to a horse rider who travelled there from Torriglia in 2002, arriving a month before Susie and I did. They're not so clued up about their own Via Francigena, probably because we're nowhere near it at the moment, but they're intrigued to hear we're on some kind of short cut to Pontremoli to find it again, and of course we can stay at the stables for the night; my pilgrim horse can go in this field…

My ungrateful pilgrim horse doesn't approve of his lodgings, an enclosure of steep stony terraces, and he trots restlessly up and down the highest one and refuses to come down for any food. In the end I catch him again and shut him in a stable with a heap of hay, claustrophobia or no claustrophobia, while Peter parks Bessie in the middle of the yard since she's too big to tuck in a corner. He opens the driver's door and climbs out of the cab into bedlam.

A rabble of barkalots come charging across the yard and rush up the lorry ramp headed by the odious Roly, a Jack Russell terrier who keeps rummaging round in the back and seizing our belongings, growling angrily when I try to grab them back. But even he is seen off by the most possessive animal in the yard – a pygmy goat. It's strikingly coloured with a white shirt and dun breeches, and it thinks it's a horse. All the proper equines are neighing their greetings at Leo, and they're a polyglot lot: two Bardiggiano ponies from Piacenza, some Criollos from Argentina, an Appaloosa/Irish cob cross, an Arab, an American Quarter Horse – and the goat. It lives with the Quarter Horse and attacks any dog that comes too close to its friend. Roly's teeth are no match for its horns, and it insists on trotting along beside the horse every time the owner goes riding, while the dogs hang back well out of butting range.

Peter and I are absorbed seamlessly into the horsy community. It's difficult to tell how many people actually live here on site, but at supper time the long table under the trees is packed with hungry humanity, and over another aromatic meal we all try to work out (amid much chart waving and gesticulation) which way I should ride tomorrow.

There's no direct route to Pontremoli. On the main road it's probably only about forty miles beyond Torriglia, but for Leo and me, working our way somehow over the hills and mountains, it's going to be a lot further and it'll probably take another three or four days to get there.

The lovely Marco, who owns the centre, insists we should all three of us travel via Barbagelata, a village with a name that sounds like prickly ice-cream. Eventually I find it on the military chart, but minus a road to reach it unless I ride two sides of a triangle and go through distant Montebruno. Peter's map is no better. Marco's solution is to pack Peter, me and Gabrielo-he-speak-English into his car with a yapping dog in the boot, and drive us up the mountain at around midnight to show Peter the invisible turning where he can leave the main road, rather than risk missing it and having to drive most of the way to Piacenza with nowhere to turn round. Even in the dark Peter can see the turn-off involves a very tight hairpin bend, and meanwhile I've noted that we've driven through two covered galleries and a tunnel that's at least half a mile long.

Peter says he can manage the bend in Bessie. I say I can't manage the tunnel on Leo. No problem, say Marco-and-Gabrielo, you can take the old road. Which isn't on my map, but I gather that all I have to do after actually finding it is to follow the signs, red to turn right, white to turn left and yellow to go straight on.

OK … but it's a bit late in the evening to assimilate these directions and by the morning I still haven't, due to a deafening night of neighing, munching, coughing, farting and door-kicking horses who think breakfast should be served before dawn.

Leo's popping out of his skin with suppressed energy after his incarceration in a stable, and we make very good time as far as the old crossroads to Barbagelata which is much more obvious in daylight, thundering through the two covered galleries and diverting off the Piacenza road before we have to tackle the long tunnel. Now it's miles of cart track and watching out for Marco's signs, which turn out to consist of coloured horseshoes painted on the track's rough surface; yellow's no problem, but the red and white ones usually appear some distance beyond the relevant turning, and on one occasion I pass a real yellow horseshoe nailed to a tree.

We climb and climb until we're travelling along a ridge at about 4000 feet, but it's not the panoramic view that catches my eye, it's the black cloud bank rolling up behind us. At the very highest point, needless to say, thunder starts clattering overhead and the only cover consists of scrubby vegetation at rabbit height. It takes just one big crack and a bolt of lightning very close by to have me leaping off Leo and into all my proper wet weather gear, including my rubber boots which I assume will save me from electrocution and a premature reunion with my mother (wherever she may be).

But it's like trying to waddle along in a portable sauna. The rain pelts down, cascading off the impermeable surface of my full length mac, but I'm so soaked with sweat and condensation from the inside out that we haven't even reached the far edge of the storm before I peel off my suffocating wetsuit, and heave myself like a floppy filleted fish on to Leo's back again.

On the other side of the hills the countryside is softer and dotted with empty fields, all of which I eye up automatically as potential horse enclosures; in tiny Barbagelata Peter and I meet up and wend our way slowly on through other hamlets as the sky clears and the shadows lengthen. In the distance the village of Cabanne looks promising, big enough to have a church and maybe a place to camp as well.

It turns out that its most prominent feature is a bar with a luscious piece of pasture outside it, all proper grass and wild alfalfa, a real horse treat. I manage to engage the attention of the owner just as he finishes a tense game of cards with three customers and before he embarks on a two-hour boules competition. He waves Peter and Bessie genially into the car park and points Leo, me and the electric fence towards the grass.

We settle down for a relaxed ending to what I've now remembered is an auspicious date: 25th July, St James' Day. On this day in 2002 we were in the middle of the Spanish city of Burgos with Susie and Apollo, rowdily celebrating the saint's birthday with crowds of other pilgrims. Today in 2006 we're completely off any beaten track and there are no pilgrims at all – but the evening turns out to be almost as noisy as Burgos because all the villagers arrive to check out Bessie, Leo, the fence, Peter and me in minute detail, while pretending that what they're really here for is a drink at the *albergo*. Periodically Signor interrupts his game of boules to come and ask us repeatedly where we were yesterday and where we're going tomorrow, presumably so he can update the customers. We tell him we've come from Torriglia, but tomorrow's a bit of a mystery; the road is dotted with numerous villages that might or might not have some communal land where we could stay, all with names that sing across the map: Brignole, Isolarotonda, Rezzoaglio, Cornaletto (could be another ice cream village), Allegrezze; and Santo Stéfano d'Aveto, the most musical name of all. After that one there's a long haul over the uninhabited Passo del Tomarlo with nowhere to stop, so it'll have to be Santo Stéfano, if not before.

Anyway, Signor, please go back to your boules … it's getting dark and I need to do a recce with my trowel tonight just in case the bar is closed tomorrow morning…

No chance. First the owner of an Arab horse wants to tell me all about it (I manage a knowledgeable *si, si capisco* by way of response when he says the word *cavallo*, so he launches into a torrent of unintelligible high speed Italian) and then I bump into a priest from Nigeria who also wants to engage me in lengthy conversation, this time in English. He's very animated in his description of his usual life in a seminary which has a philosophy fuckulty and a geological fuckulty, I think he says, and I gather he's in Cabanne on a working holiday, preaching at the church here and looking after five other parishes as well while the local priest takes a proper holiday somewhere else. By the time he's finished detailing all the local churches and I've wished him good night, it's so dark that an exploratory trip into the undergrowth is out of the question. At least he didn't ask me why I've got a trowel in my hand.

Back at the *albergo* the bar has closed but all the locals are still congregating round Bessie, apparently discussing her merits (or faults) very loudly, while Peter's crossing his legs and looking desperate. No one is in a hurry to go home, so we have a bit of a fidgety night waiting for an opportune moment to nip out of the lorry under cover of darkness.

There's more than one way to get to Santo Stéfano, as I discover when I arrive at a crossroads next morning. I puzzle over the military chart for ages wondering whether to take the high orange road or the low orange road, and of course choose the wrong one. This adds an extra three miles to our journey (not at all obvious on the map) and an additional hour which is full of growling thunder and the odd flash of lightning. But no rain, at least not till I meet Peter at Santo Stéfano and can take cover in Bessie for lunch and a debate as to whether we should look here for somewhere to stay, or carry on after all. In spite of riding the long way round, it's still only early afternoon and today's thunderstorm is grouching off into the distance again. Maybe the sun will come out, maybe St James will find us another horsy place, maybe we should just go on and see what happens.

For the next five miles it's all uphill to the Tomarlo pass with Bessie chuffing along in front. Peter waits at the top for Leo and me to catch up for a photocall beside the sign that shows the altitude here is nearly 5000 feet, while Monte Tomarlo behind us is 1000 feet higher still. At the pass there's nothing except a great view and an enormous roundabout where the road divides: north to Piacenza, south on a vague rambling route towards Rapallo and the coast, and east to Bedonia which is where we want to go. But that's much too far away to reach today, sooo...

We could stay here. Right in the middle of this roundabout.

Switching into equine pilgrim mode, you can see it isn't so much a civil engineer's creation for safer motoring as a perfect circular field, a green oasis surrounded by tarmac. There's plenty of grass and clover in it for Leo, wild strawberries and raspberries for Peter and me, level off-road parking for Bessie, trees for shade ... no water, that's the only thing. Or maybe there is – alongside us on the roundabout, the ruins of an old house stare rooflessly at the sky, surely it must have had a water supply. I go and investigate what might be the remains of a cistern, and find there's a dripping pipe poking through the mountainside into the bottom of it. When I wedge Leo's bucket underneath, it fills up in ten minutes.

Thank you again, St James.

It's a night of extraordinary stillness in this lonely place. No cars pass by, no pattering herds of sheep or goats, no gossiping locals; even the breeze drops away to nothing, and as the temperature falls Peter and I are able to cuddle up instead of trying to keep cool on opposite sides of the mattress. If he wasn't here I might be daunted by the isolation, I suppose, but together we're cocooned by the mountain's silence as we drift down through folds of sleep, cosied by a night so unexpectedly special that its images sink deep into the thick layers of memory, never to be forgotten.

22

A Night in the Bottom of a Cauldron

After our soul-restoring night of quietude, the next day is a pig. A second storm follows on from the usual daily one at lunchtime – but it's a storm of a different kind.

Leo and I leave Tomarlo in comfortable harmony which lasts for miles as we clop down the mountain and bypass busy Bedonia, this time striking it lucky with the hit-and-miss orange roads and chancing on one that's just a lane. This is my third military chart with a title beginning with the letter B (from Bargagli to Bedonia and now to Borgo Val di Taro), and I'm just cheering myself with the thought that the next map after this will get us to Pontremoli when the lane divides into two roads and I choose the wrong one again. On the chart they look identical, but the one I've taken widens rapidly and fills up with heavy lorries. What's more, there's an expanse of water moving slowly alongside it, and I realise that Val di Taro quite possibly means Valley of the Taro river – in other words, another basin of escalating heat.

I'm trying to keep Leo pressed right in to the side, away from the traffic, when the thunder starts up and then the rain arrives. There's no opportunity to drag on my sauna trousers so we have an hour of spray and splashing from countless wheels, at the end of which our legs are soaked and I'm praying that Peter, ahead of us in Bertorella (another B village, you could say), has found us somewhere to stay. No airy mountain pass for us tonight – we're back in the bottom of a cauldron, steaming with sweat and exhaust fumes.

From the heights to the depths, all too literally. Tonight the only available space for us is on a garage forecourt where Leo can nose around in the tired blades of grass on its fringes, right beside the busy bridge that crosses the Taro. The rain hasn't cleared the air, and a smudgy sun peers through the haze rising from the road and the river. Peter, who is almost speechless with discomfort, manages one sentence which unfortunately is to the effect that he'd like his suppers cooked earlier in the evening than I've so far managed. My response to that is to suggest that perhaps he'd like to lend a hand with the preparation. The result is some angry bickering which eventually subsides into mutinous silence, something I hate – I'd always rather try to resolve an argument and move on, but tonight we can't; it means dredging up tact and consideration, and we just don't have the energy.

Given our unusual situation – two people, horse and fractious lorry well over 1000 miles from England on a journey that's not exactly comfortable at the moment – the question of who does or doesn't shirk the domestic chores back in Faversham, never mind here in Italy, is a nit-picking irrelevance. But in fact, of course, our comprehensive spat has nothing to do with that – it's simply an overspill of tiredness after three months on the road.

The HGVs grind over the bridge all night and my brain goes into overdrive, a treadmill of guilt and misery tramping round inside my head. Guilt that somehow I must have made Peter feel he had to come on this pilgrimage with me, even though I tried to convince him he really did have a choice – I could have gone alone with Leo and a pack horse, and maybe I should have done. And misery because he's miserable, and whereas I've been thinking we were united in adversity, now I'm wondering if he's just been gritting his teeth and hating the whole expedition.

It's easy to see why the days are hard for Leo and me, given our constant exposure to whatever the weather chucks at us and the long, long hours of trekking; but Bessie's no breeze either, with her bulky body and wandering steering wheel, and Peter's lost a lot of weight since we left England due to the stress of driving her. He's also finished most of the books he brought with him, and he seems to be too tired and enervated to bother with any sightseeing, or even to play golf; he just spends hour after boring hour waiting for me to complete my twenty miles a day at a snail's pace and catch up with him.

But at least neither of us has suggested we should pack it in and go home.

The night drags by in slow motion as I wriggle to and fro with my husband an inert heap beside me. I've no idea whether he's asleep or not but for me it's out of the question; in the end I reach for a torch and the nearest book, which turns out to be an unfortunate choice – a sad little story about a young vicar who doesn't realise he's dying. After half an hour of depressing reading and wakeful flies ricocheting off my nose, I give up.

But my overactive imagination doesn't – it latches on to the subject of death and I start wondering if my mother is somehow able to follow Peter's and my journey to Rome from wherever she is, even though I don't really think she can be anywhere at all. And then, as sometimes happens in insomniac moments, I stop remembering her as she used to be before her wits departed, and conjure up images of how she became when Alzheimer's engulfed her.

A bittersweet memory floats into my head: an afternoon in the summer before she died, an outing from the care home to our house in Faversham with my father. We've had lunch, all of us sitting at the kitchen table, Ma smiling and eating and talking a little. The sun's shining and we're in the warm conservatory afterwards, my parents side by side on the sofa, my mother leaning back against Pa's chest. We're listening to her most favourite piece of music, Beethoven's violin concerto in D, and suddenly she stretches out her arms to conduct it, completely focused, following its cadences and rhythms to perfection.

For an hour she's wrapped up in contentment, almost restored to her old self – but then we have to take her back, bewildered, not understanding, sure she should be going to what used to be her own home to cook Pa's supper. But I know, we all know, that a few moments after we've gone she'll be all right, in a sense, because she won't remember where she's been; it's heart-wrenching but true that in the care home the residents seem to descend to the lowest common denominator, and in no time at all Ma will be right there with all of them, as mad as the maddest.

That's enough. I need to concentrate on making various resolutions since sleep is still not on the agenda: get up earlier, leave earlier, stop earlier, feed Peter earlier and go to bed earlier. Then maybe we'll both recover our equilibrium.

Leo and I are on our way soon after dawn, but my stop-earlier resolution may fail because we still can't go faster than a walk. Our days continue to be punctuated by doleful coughing, and trotting still wouldn't be possible anyway because I continue to have no option but to stay with Plan B, the metalled road. A brief effort yesterday to follow a dirt track ended at somebody's house within half a mile, and I'm not going to risk prolonging today's ride by diverting on to more trails to nowhere. It seems a long time ago that we were able to whistle down through Burgundy on the wonderful Voie Verte, covering our twenty miles in five hours. At the moment, it's taking eight hours to ride the same distance.

Peter's atlas has shown that the main road switches to the south bank of the river after Bertorella, so I stay on the north side even though it means a ride through the town of Borgo Val di Taro to cross the only bridge for miles. Borgo's quite a big place and by the time I've wormed my way through it to the crossing, the police are just closing it for roadworks and no, Signora, you can't go this way. Well, where am I supposed to get over the river, then? The snotty officer's still wearing a hatchet expression that probably mirrors mine when I notice something I'm certainly not expecting – a Via Francigena direction sign where the bridge begins, a red arrow decorated with the yellow walking pilgrim. This is more than perplexing since as far as I know we're nowhere near the Via, but I point out the sign to the officer and add a complicated pantomime indicating pilgrims, Leo, and the St James scallop shell hanging from his bridle. The shell has nothing to do with St Peter, St Paul or the Via Francigena, but the officer is now so confused that he takes the line of least resistance, which is to allow me over with the pedestrians. The policeman on the other side is completely charming, and holds up all the traffic so we can cross the main road and escape to the hills, well away from the procession of lorries hauling gravel into the town.

Now there are signs everywhere telling me I'm following the Via Francigena. I still don't understand how this has come about since I know the official Via approaches Pontremoli from a completely different direction, but perhaps this is a branch line, so I show willing by photographing the church at San Vincenzo in case it turns out to be culturally significant. Behind me in the distance there are people walking – probably just hikers, but maybe they're pilgrims, the first I've seen if so, and they make me nostalgic for the camaraderie of the Camino to Santiago with its evenings of multi-lingual chat in the *refugios*.

At a T-junction the signs point back to the main road, blistered and bubbling but thankfully deserted. Leo climbs slowly over the Passo del Brattello and we share my lunch in the shade of a church in another B village the other side, Bratto this time, a suitably cross-sounding name. Then it's all downhill for miles and miles, the soles of my boots slurping through tar as sticky as treacle when I get off to give Leo's back a rest. I wonder how Peter's getting on in Bessie's scalding cab, and decide it might be politic to find a gîte tonight.

In the hamlet of Grondola someone summons English Angela from the Agriturismo up the road. She tells me this is the hottest summer for 100 years and the insect population has trebled this season, not the most welcome news, but Leo is ecstatic when she lets him into her field because it has a cow byre in it, dark and cold as a cellar. He has no trouble in forgetting he's claustrophobic and installing himself inside for the rest of the day, waiting for night to fall and the flies to disappear before he comes out to graze.

And for Peter and me there is indeed a gîte; it's an expensive luxury and the bed's like a board, but it has a high-pressure shower which cheers us both up so much that we can almost

– if not quite – look back on last night's disagreement and see how ridiculous it was.

The final stretch of the road to Pontremoli runs through a long tunnel I can't avoid; worse, it has traffic lights and roadworks. By now I know the how-not-to-spook-your-horse routine inside out, but it's still not easy to stick to it. The trick is to remain physically relaxed however apprehensive you may be, because a horse picks up instantly on its rider's body language. Any uneasy shift in weight, any tension, and your mount will think there must be something to be frightened about and start looking for trouble. But it's literally a very fine balancing act, because you can't be so laid back that you're going to fly off and end up dumped in the road if your horse decides to shy anyway.

As Leo and I enter the tunnel there's a sudden terrible din behind us, but the cause is Peter and Bessie rattling through at the same time, with no other vehicles behind them, and Leo is so pleased to recognise his own lorry it doesn't occur to him to be scared. Peter passes us heading for Villafranca, which I still hope to reach this afternoon rather than tonight so there's a chance to carry out the feed-spouse-earlier resolution.

Pontremoli reveals itself as a little city rather than a town, packed wall to wall with tourists in its old streets. Its name means Trembling Bridge and, having been travelling downhill since the Passo del Brattello yesterday, it's no surprise to see it spans yet another river in a valley, this time the Magra which idles its way through Villafranca, Aulla and Sarzana to roll out into the Ligurian Sea between La Spezia and Carrara. I'm back on the 'proper' Via Francigena now, and it too goes to all those baking places.

I'm also back on the picturesque Topofrancigena official maps with their multi-coloured starred tracks. It'll take a while to get used to the layout again, following the Via from the bottom of each chart to the top which still seems back to front to me, with south instead of north at the head of the page. However, it's gratifying to see I've come straight in at page 21 on the Italian set of daily maps thanks to my short cut, leaving only another twenty-two pages to navigate. Just 300 miles to Rome, which still sounds like a trip to infinity, but at least we've got into the next region – Tuscany, with its rolling hills and romantic reputation. I'm right at the northern tip, and the path of the Via runs through the area's provinces for nearly 200 miles. I hope it's as fabulous as the guide books would like you to believe, and if it's just a bit cooler than what we've experienced in Italy so far, that might be enough to stop us all moaning.

I don't get the chance to see much of Pontremoli and its fabled churches. The press of people means there's no question even of getting my pilgrim passport stamped, so I work my way through the middle without stopping and emerge on to what's described on the Topo map as an alternative route towards Villafranca, delineated with black stars. I don't see a single VF sign the whole way but at least it's a quiet road, the only sound the clank of Leo's shoes and the squeak of his dehydrated hooves shifting against their inner surface.

The final batch of today's stars dance along to a bridge over the Magra which is alarming. The railings hang away at right angles, broken and rusted where some long ago (and probably deceased) motorist must have skidded through them and plunged forty feet into the virtually waterless gravel bed below. Villafranca's on the other side, as is its campsite where Peter has managed to organise the overspill car park into a horse field. The only vehicle in it is a derelict lorry, and Leo wastes no time in stationing himself with his head inside the doorless cab to keep cool.

I have indeed managed to arrive here by the late afternoon, but it's only because I haven't done the full quota of twenty miles today. Oily raindrops start globbing down but once again they don't clear the air; they just get sucked into the humidity dripping from the hedges that coats us all in a film of sweat every time we move. I do manage to produce supper early, but the law of unintended consequences prevents me from sorting out tomorrow's route plan afterwards, something I'd usually do before eating, because by the time we finish our meal and clear up it's too dark to see a bloody thing. Planning with my disparate maps is so complicated and the print so small that trying to work out the path of the Via Francigena in anything less than broad daylight is hopeless.

OK, that's it, I'm giving up. We'll have to take a day off tomorrow and I'll have another go at it then, and at least there's a washing machine here so I can grab the opportunity to get all our stuff properly clean. But that doesn't happen either, because I overload the machine next day and it sighs to a terminal standstill mid-cycle, so it's a case of hand-scrubbed bedclothes that are still damp even before Peter and I insert our sticky selves between the sheets.

As for the Via Francigena, in daylight it's clear from the next few daily charts that a chunk of the authentic route is buried under the Via Aurelia, the main road. Topo suggests a number of alternative lanes and tracks but mostly they're not detailed enough for me to risk following them, and they don't resemble anything marked on the local maps. I decide to miss out the mess of busy roads around Sarzana, for a start, and focus on reaching Carrara without getting tangled up en route with the holidaymakers clogging the coast in the height of the tourist season.

It probably means another slow trek inland over the mountains, but I persuade myself it's pointless worrying about the myriad pathways of the Via. I might as well take advantage of the cliché that *all roads lead to Rome*, and adopt a Via Francigena of my own.

23

Saddle Sore

'OK, Leo, how are we going to get over that lot?'

'That lot' are mountains, a wall of them; a shock after the flat land around the Magra river. They're smack in front of us, they look impenetrable, and we need to go that way. These are the Apuan Alps, part of the Apennine chain, and although the tallest of them is Monte Pisanino which at 6500 feet isn't that high, I suppose, the rampart ahead looks so forbidding that I pull up and just stare.

I thought I'd done quite well so far today; for all my ideas about a personal pilgrimage route, in fact I've managed to follow the Topo map for miles, from Villafranca to the crowded streets of Aulla. But on the other side of that town the red dotted route (recommended) merged with the green starred route (excursion) and looked as though it might ferret through a long tunnel, so I switched to another series of black stars instead (definitely obscure) which wibbled over the page unaccompanied by any kind of track. In the circumstances it's probably not surprising I'm now stumped. The only trail I can see is so undefined it would be stupid to try following it.

I don't know exactly where we are, but at least this is a proper lane and it seems best to stay on it even though it's not going in quite the right direction. It comes to a dead end in an anonymous hamlet, but a woman leaning over her balcony rail dispenses directions: left at the first house, Signora, and then straight on to Ponzanello which has a *castello*. For which read: over the rocks and up the mountain.

It's incredibly steep but Leo powers his way to the top without stopping, loosening his already clacking shoes even more as he scrabbles over the rough surface of what can't really be described as a path. A ruined castle comes into view on the skyline; Ponzanello is one of the many villages dotted round the province of Massa and Carrara that are dominated by a fortress built to discourage invaders, but impressive as it is, at the moment I'm more interested in the mundane – there's a roadside tap here, such a miracle of chilled relief it doesn't cross my mind it might not be *acqua potabile*. Leo and I glug it down anyway, and climb laboriously over the top of the hill to find a total surprise on the other side.

A chunk of the horizon isn't lumpy with mountains at all, not even fuzzy with forest trees; instead, the smooth expanse of the Mediterranean stretches westwards, glinting in the sunshine as it surges gently in towards the Gulf of La Spezia and then rolls back to a misty fusion with the sky. I don't know why I wasn't expecting to see it given that we're not far from Carrara, which is almost on the coast, but it makes me catch my breath with as much astonishment as I did many weeks ago when I came round a corner and found I was staring at Mont Blanc. Today's panorama seems to be another such marker, an underscoring of the long distance we've travelled – this time the whole way from one sea to another, from the grey Channel to the blue Med.

The road to Fosdinovo is easy to follow – with no distracting tracks on either side, it wiggles along as part of my private Via Francigena running inland parallel to the coastline. It too has a fortress – the magnificent Castello di Malaspina, turreted, crenelated and so solidly planted that it simply shrugged off a monstrous earthquake in the 1920s. It has been in the Malaspina family for the last 700 years and a luxurious B&B has now been created inside; it would be great to spend the night there, but I expect it's beyond pilgrim pockets and anyway, Leo's not likely to be welcome in its hanging gardens. So I stop at the village bar to see if I can find something a bit more humble.

Signora Pub Proprietaria contacts her son, handing the phone to me so he can tell me himself in fluent French that Peter and I can put Bessie at his farm and Leo can lodge with his goats in their paddock. He gives me directions but when I get there I wonder if I've misheard them; the silently smiling Signor who arrives to greet us doesn't speak French or even Italian as far as I can tell, and this isn't a farm but a very small smallholding with an even smaller yard full of goats. It is indeed a lot more humble than Malaspina Castle.

But we're grateful to find anywhere at all, and I realise we must be in the right place when Signor gives me an electronic gate pass and leaves us to it. Later on another man arrives to feed his colony of rabbits in the shed beside Bessie; he doesn't speak French either, and the identity of Signora's son remains a mystery forever.

I count eighteen goats in the yard but Leo ignores them all, even an impressively rugged and territorial Billy Goat Gruff which luckily has had its horns lopped off. In his good-natured way my horse allows them to eat his hay until in the end I stuff it into a net and hang it up out of the goats' reach, and take the opportunity to check him over thoroughly while he's chewing. Running my hands over his coat to check for sores, I come across a patch on his back that's completely raw. Shit. It must have been rubbed by the edge of the saddle as it shifted on the climb to Ponzanello. Sores like this are the long distance rider's nemesis – they can spell the premature end of an expedition in the blink of an eye, and I have visions of Leo in luxury in the lorry while I puff along on Minnie the bike for weeks while his back heals. In fact I'm so hopeless on two wheels I'd probably be walking, pushing Minnie all through the summer, all through the autumn...

Today is 1st August, and originally I'd thought we'd almost be in Rome by now, not still 250 miles to the north. And even though I factored in some extra time for mishaps, I didn't reckon on a break of ten days while Bessie was being repaired in Albertville. I probably won't be able to make that time up now, even if Leo's fine – it's impossible to rush when every day's an endurance test of hard roads, indecipherable tracks, and long pauses while I puzzle over the maps.

But on the plus side, Leo isn't coughing anymore; I've no idea why not, since our days are still as dusty, still as hot as they ever were, but it's a great relief (for all of us) that he's stopped trumpeting at both ends. And also on the plus side, now I come to think of it, I can finally try riding him in the big Western saddle, which spreads its weight more evenly and securely over a horse's back. It'll be better for him, and its braced stirrups must have baked into a more congenial position for my feet by now. So, comforted by this thought, I fall into bed for the hottest, stickiest night of all, enriched by the stink of the goats' deep litter which I've transported into Bessie in the treads of my riding boots, and deafened by the sound of twenty rabbits in the shed next door furiously digging their way to Australia.

To my relief the Western saddle applies no pressure to Leo's sore patch and is quite comfortable for me, even though it has no squashy knee rolls to support tired legs. Its tooled leather is very attractive and ornate, and it has numerous brass D rings and plaited tassels and tags for attaching far more baggage than I need for carrying Leo's and my daily supplies.

However, we've only been travelling for half an hour when I acquire an extra and unusual piece of luggage – an owl. It must have been hit by a car, because it's sitting by the side of the road in a state of shock when I pass by. I stop to pick it up, and it looks at me crossly with gleaming yellow eyes; it's small and spherical (a Little Owl, in fact) and it's very appealing. It's not at all interested in a comfortable ride in a saddle bag – it wants to perch on my hand, and it wraps its long predator talons uncomfortably round my thumb and sways to and fro in time with Leo's stride. I'm very, very tempted to let it join the expedition permanently, but I can imagine Peter's reaction if he had to drive Bessie with an owl balancing beside his ear, its claws digging into his shoulder. It probably wouldn't help our nightly knock-on-doors search for accommodation either, since owls mean bad luck in Italy. So regretfully I place it on the top of a bank well away from the road, and hope it gets over its trauma and flies away.

Mountains streaked in snow start to fill the landscape on the way to Carrara, an odd sight at the height of summer; it takes me several seconds to realise that of course it's not snow, it's *marble*, that's what Carrara's famous for. Away to the left the peaks rise up, each higher than the last with Mount Pisanino the furthest away, most of them savaged and ravaged by quarries and diggers hacking away at their glittering hearts.

I must be really dozy today – flatbed trucks loaded with great chunks of the stuff keep passing us, but I haven't been clocking what they're carrying, I've been too busy sticking up a finger at the drivers who think it's funny to hoot when they're right up Leo's tail. The traffic's bad because we seem to have strayed on to a main road into the town, and it gets worse the other side of it – once through Massa I realise we've inadvertently joined the Via Aurelia, the worst road of all.

But we're not on it for long. The Topo map reassuringly shows that the Via Francigena turns off to the left – no doubt I'm actually on the original Via but I can see why it's been diverted: the railway line comes easing in alongside the Aurelia, leaving pilgrims to shrink away from trains as well as lorries. It's a relief to follow the quieter Via Casone that winds through the foothills to Strettoia and then down to Ripa, which is far enough for today; it's an unpromisingly crowded little town but there must be someone here who likes horses … yes, he'll do, a builder in fluorescent shorts who is unwisely admiring Leo.

He's easily bamboozled into taking me on a round of all his friends' houses to try and find a patch of grass; we're inspected at length and at very close quarters but it turns out that no one can help, and eventually Signor shrugs apologetically and speeds off into the distance, leaving me beside a house which I notice has an empty field right next to it. An elderly couple open the door, twinkling a welcome: Signora, *che bello cavallino*, of course you may stay, your husband and lorry too, right here beside our home.

So we plant ourselves on their driveway before we realise the field doesn't belong to them and they're assuming that Leo will cosy up in Bessie with Peter and me. But our hosts are unfazed: *non c'è problema*, they say, the horse can go in our garden. I have my doubts about this as their lawn is as smooth as a bowling green, but they carry on smiling benignly while Leo tears up the grass by the roots. Then they retire into their house and don't come out again, which is just as well because by late evening there's not much of their garden left. I feel really bad, so under cover of darkness I sneak into the proper field next door with the kitchen scissors, and snip every alfalfa plant down to ground level until there's a whole pile of it to give to a very hungry horse. By now I'm so riddled with guilt that when a helicopter flies overhead I know beyond a doubt it's the Alfalfa Police, but at least Signor and his wife can't see or indeed hear what I'm doing; they've got *Star Trek* turned up full volume on their telly and they don't turn it off and go to bed until one o'clock in the morning. Riding along to Pietrasanta the next day, I wonder how long it'll be before their lawn recovers.

Now we're on a long and unlovely road passing marble factories and surrounded by trucks that smother us in clouds of dust as they rumble by. There are rocks and blocks and sheets of marble everywhere, stacked and layered and chucked in corners of the yards, some quarried locally, some imported stone in rainbow colours. The most vivid of all is a discarded offcut in wavy stripes of cerulean blue and white; I think of trying to persuade the factory owner to part with it, but it's far too big and heavy to manhandle into Bessie and cart back to England via Rome. And any wishful thoughts of buying some on our return home vanish when I later discover that it's rare Azul Macauba marble from Brazil, and its price is stratospheric.

Pietrasanta is a mediaeval town that gobbled up its neighbouring villages some centuries ago, and now it straggles through suburbs to the central square. Here I look around for somewhere to tie Leo in the pedestrian precinct so I can go and explore the cathedral of San Martino, which to my eyes is an intriguing mixture of stunningly graceful and stunningly ugly. Its façade is clothed in pale marble complete with an exquisite rose window, but its angular bell tower next door looks like a factory chimney. It is nearly 100 feet high and built of plain bricks, and apparently it was also supposed to be coated in marble slabs but no one got round to doing the work. I believe the cathedral is packed with mediaeval paintings, sculptures and a stone spiral staircase, but there's no chance to take a look because there's no convenient horse hitching post here. The best I can manage is a quick check round the exterior while Leo stands unattended outside the bank, gloomily examining the cashpoint buttons in the wall and hopefully not checking how much money isn't in our account.

We set off again down a traffic-free street where he attracts a lot of attention from the pedestrians, not because of his good looks but because his loose shoes are clanking so loudly that everyone feels obliged to turn round and point this out to me. I know, *I know*... I could hardly be unaware of it, but I just have to hope they'll stay on a while longer because I haven't a clue where to find a farrier around here. I haven't even seen another horse for weeks.

The Via Francigena tootles along on a long and boring route for mile after tedious mile with nothing much to look at; I could turn off on to an excursion trail but it would extend the day, and I absolutely don't want to do that – the Western saddle is starting to take its toll on my seat bones and I'm getting stiffer and stiffer as the hours drag on. I manage to bypass crowded Camaiore and then the road starts to climb; some cyclists pant by standing up on their pedals, their padded green Lycra bottoms sticking up in the air like chimpanzees – normally I'd think their luminous suits look ridiculous, but today I'm just jealous. Traditional Western saddles don't have sprung seats as English ones do, and unless you're naturally well-padded (which I'm not) or have a sheepskin on the saddle that's six inches thick (which I don't) then on very long rides it's you who can get saddle sore rather than the horse. And I am.

At the top of the hill a determined lady plants herself in front of Leo, convinced he must be for hire. By now I'm on my own feet, walking along like John Wayne with bandy legs, and I can understand her mistake: my riderless horse looks magnificent in his beautiful saddle and she probably thinks she can leap on him and go galloping off into the sunset. It's difficult to explain in Italian that he's mine, he's not for rent, that we've come from England and we're staying together all the way to Rome no matter what; she's completely mystified and eventually wanders away looking disappointed while we go trudging off into the distance.

One good thing about today however is that for once I know where we're staying tonight: at San Martino In Freddana, just short of Lucca. We have friends who own a holiday home near there, and although we can't stay in it because it's at the top of a steep lane so narrow that it's an impossibility for Bessie, they've persuaded friends of theirs in the village below to put us up, or possibly to put up with us.

The River Freddana appears, burbling alongside the Via Francigena on the road that leads to Lucca. It isn't far to Dee and Vincenzo's house which is as well since I've gingerly remounted to keep myself out of the way of the cars. By the time we arrive I feel as though I've skinned my bum, which turns out not to be the case, but there's bad news when I unsaddle Leo. The original sore on his back is no worse, but four more have appeared today: two hairless patches under the saddle itself, and two raw places where the wide Western cinch has caught the loose folds of skin behind his armpits.

This means I can't use the saddle again, and I'm genuinely sorry because I do like it and I'd decided to persevere by putting a layer of foam on top of it and sitting on that. Its girth never rubbed Leo when I was trying it out in England, but then the flat marshes around Faversham weren't exactly testing. And I can't use the narrower English girth because it has completely different fastenings.

So that's that. I'll have to put Leo's own saddle back on him and hope it doesn't cause any more damage; otherwise I really will be digging out Minnie (who since her last airing in Beaufort has taken to jumping out of gear at every revolution of her wheels) and setting off on a leg-spinning wobble down the roads to Rome.

24

The Delights and Dangers of Lucca

For one disconnected night we can abandon our identities as pilgrims on a mission. As Dee and Vincenzo welcome us into their family it's almost as though we're simply on holiday, and over a wonderful supper filled with wine, laughter and conversation that's entirely in English, I realise there's something else boosting our morale: it's *cool* outside, almost chilly in fact. We haven't felt this comfortable in a valley since we were in France.

In the morning the temperature's still at least 10°C lower than it was this time yesterday, and the wind blows Leo and me along towards Lucca and keeps the flies away. The Via Francigena is mindlessly easy to follow – it stays with the Freddana all the way to the river's junction with the wider Serchio that curves round Lucca on the northern side, and then it goes over the bridge near Monte San Quirico and into the city. And city it certainly is – the largest place we've visited since Canterbury.

I work my way through the suburbs to the mediaeval Porta Santa Maria and then plunge into a jumble of streets for which I have no map. Topofrancigena says I have to get across to the eastern side and leave through the Porta Elisa; I've no idea how to get there, but there's one way to find out – take Leo up on to the wall that runs right round the historic centre of Lucca, and hope for a bird's eye view across to the other side. So we climb the steps to the walkway high above the old town, and he's only too happy to graze in the picnic area while I work out where to go from here.

You can see this was once a Roman settlement because it's built on a rectangular grid system, and as it expanded over the centuries wider rings of fortified walls were created. The final version under our feet now was finished in the seventeenth century, and it circles for two and a half miles. You can walk all the way round, or cruise on a skateboard, or pedal your bike. I don't know whether anyone's ridden along it on a horse, but I hope Leo and I are making history as we amble round towards a ramp down to street level near the Porta Elisa.

On the way there I get a wonderful view of a beautiful little city within a city, full of churches, towers, piazzas, columns, monuments and numerous eye-catching buildings; I would need to spend several days here to get to grips with it all, but unfortunately I don't have even a few hours. It's also debatable whether sightseeing with a horse peering over my shoulder would be exactly practical, so I just make a note that Peter and I should come back one of these years and take our time to wander.

I know there's another San Martino Cathedral here, this one housing what is probably the main reason that Lucca is an important stop on the Via Francigena: apparently it contains a life-sized image of Christ on a wooden crucifix, carved in dark cedar and known as the Holy Face, the *Volto Santo*, its expression sad and resigned. Its origins are the stuff of ancient legend and mystery, and involve a miracle or two; on a more prosaic note, it's said that this statue is actually a thirteenth-century copy of the eleventh-century original, which had so many bits chipped off it and pocketed by mediaeval pilgrims that it had to be replaced. Anyway, it's still a good reason for a festival every year on 13th September, an atmospheric procession by candlelight that celebrates not only religion but the city's heritage of music and opera as well.

The Porta Elisa turns out to be the gateway to an afternoon of hell-on-wheels. There's no quiet way to leave Lucca by any of its numerous historical gates that I can see; strictly I suppose we should be going out through the Porta San Pietro for the sake of pilgrim authenticity, but the road beyond it leads in the wrong direction. Ours is the only gate that isn't named after a saint; instead it commemorates Elisa Bonaparte Baciocchi, the arts-loving sister of Napoleon and one time Duchess of Lucca who commissioned it 200 years ago.

And it's an unholy exit, leading to the strident Via Romana and miles of misery. Once or twice Topo diverts us on to quieter back streets, but in the end I can't escape the main thoroughfare into Porcari which is packed with heavy traffic travelling too close and too fast. There's no verge and often no hard shoulder, and after Porcari the road is simply lethal. My bombproof horse plods on stoically until a lorry roars past with empty cable reels rattling and bouncing on its flatbed trailer; it startles him into jumping forward in alarm and I realise that if he leaps sideways next time, we're going to get run over.

'Easy, Leo, easy, I'll get off, that's it, just follow right behind me.'

I slide down his side and wrench off one of the stirrup reflectors to hang on the end of my dressage whip, sticking it out sideways to keep the traffic away. Leo's nose is glued to the back of my neck as he walks on my heels while the HGVs hurtle by so close they shave the tip of the whip. It's as if the drivers haven't seen us, or they think a horse is an emotionless machine, or else they just don't care.

Fuck *off!* Keep your sodding distance! God, this is just as scary as falling down a ravine in the Alps…

We march on for what seems like miles before the Via Francigena goes tripping off on a red-starred recommended route towards Altopascio. I remount and for a couple of miles have time to try and get my breath back, relax my leg muscles and force the fear under control so I don't communicate it to my horse. Calm down, stupid woman ... oh no, we're going to have to go back on that road to get under the motorway.

'Whoa, Leo, I'll get off again, don't worry, we'll be OK.'

But it's a close thing.

The road has an intersection with traffic lights on it, right underneath the motorway from Pisa.

'Please, please Leo, don't do your red lights fidget, you'll back into a lorry or something...'

'I want to *keep going* ... what's that noise?'

He looks up, and so do I – the *autostrada* above us is shaking as the vehicles go crashing past, the racket amplified by the tunnel we're waiting to go through. The lights are still red. Leo gathers himself up, ready to explode with impatience, and that prompts me to do what I should have done in the first place – loosen my instinctive iron grip on his bridle and let the reins hang in a casual loop instead. Of course it's a risk because there's nothing to stop him dancing about, but it works – the tension drains out of him, and he lowers his head with a sigh.

'Oh all right then.'

And he stands perfectly still until the lights change, when for once the multitude of drivers actually twig there's a horse in their midst and keep a respectful distance while we go through the tunnel and off down a lane the other side.

That's it, I'm not going much further today, it's been exhausting.

I abandon the pathway of the Via Francigena in favour of the straight little roads to the town of Galleno – it's not that far beyond Altopascio, but it's far enough. If my sense of humour hadn't conked out I might have tried to carry on to Fucecchio, since the name sounds like an appropriate expletive for this afternoon's horrible journey, but it's getting late and it's time we stopped.

'*Mi scusi, signori...*' The group of blokes loitering in a street turn as one and regard Leo and me sympathetically as we do our old, tired and pathetic double act. When I mention the Via Francigena, they show me the proper pilgrims' *sentiero* close to the way I rode on the lanes, but I'd have got stuck if I'd come that way because it has a padlocked chain the whole way across the end of the path. When Peter and Bessie turn up, and my new friends can see from a collective inspection of the lorry's interior that he and I at least have a place to sleep, they go and fetch Signor Grosso Formaggio (I'm sure my Italian is improving) who graciously escorts us to the sports stadium and shuts us all in there for the night. It turns out to be an excellent place to stay; the air's as fresh here as it was in San Martino, and in the morning I find Leo dozing peacefully in the sunshine instead of stamping irritably round in circles, trying to shake the flies out of his ears. Later in the day when I pass a wall thermometer I realise the drop in temperature is something of an illusion – it's actually 35°C, but the difference is that the humidity has gone.

With the corresponding fog blanket absent from my brain I decide to concentrate on the complicated Topo map, and manage to follow a *strada antica*, an ancient trail through the woods. It even has Via Francigena signposts, though they usually turn up about a mile after the track has divided, and meanwhile I'm relying on guesswork and the compass. The map is decorated with symbols of windmills and two of a figure of a galloping horse and rider in a blue square – the index helpfully tells me that this means Cavallo/Horse/Cheval, but I haven't the slightest idea if the horse and rider are zipping round a racecourse or out of control in an equestrian centre. Either way, there are no windmills, stables, race tracks or even hoof prints to be seen, but it's bliss to be out of earshot of traffic and civilisation, working our way through a forest full of ferns, huge trees, and swallowtail butterflies instead of the usual winged bloodsuckers.

On the other side of the woods Topo spits us out on to the road at the Ponte a Cappiano, where Leo's disintegrating shoes echo as we pass through the bridge's tower and on to its narrow, galleried span across the Usciana Canal. When we get to Fucecchio I'm thankful we didn't reach it last night as there would have been nowhere to stay – it looks like a boring urban sprawl and if you happen to be on a horse it inspires only one focus, which is to get through it as quickly as possible and escape to the lanes on the other side of the River Arno.

By contrast, the village of San Miniato is a delight. It sits on a hill crowned by a tower built by Frederick II in the thirteenth century, which at 120 feet is so visible that I have no trouble finding my way there. The tower survived centuries of battles and rebellion until it was blown up by the Germans in 1944, and after the war ended an exact replica was built brick by painstaking brick until by 1958 it was keeping a lookout over the Arno river plain once more.

I ride Leo into the town centre so I can go to the *municipio* and get my passport stamped. There are two other women there who to my surprise are doing the same thing. They're the first pilgrims I've talked to since I've been in Italy; they look vaguely familiar and then I realise I saw them in Fucecchio, getting off a bus. It occurs to me they must have caught another one to San Miniato because they certainly didn't sprint past me on the way. They're earnest German ladies, and they assure me gravely in formal English that the roads to and from the cities are so extremely dangerous that it's much safer to take the bus. Given Leo's and my adventures yesterday I can certainly agree with that, and after a further satisfying moan about the Via Francigena's dreadful signage we wish each other *buen camino*, using the traditional St James farewell in Spanish, and go our separate ways.

Beyond San Miniato the countryside is transformed into the undulating hills of Tuscany that so far have featured only in my imagination. In a rose-tinted afternoon the roads and tracks are bordered by trees dripping with apricots, nectarines, apples, pears, walnuts and even bright blue plums; the few cars I meet slow right down so the drivers can shout *bravo!* and *bello cavallino!* and there are big ruined houses for sale, each waiting to be turned into a romantic expat's vision of a castle in the air.

In the villages, the householders loll over their gates and kindly point out that my horse needs new shoes.

Dogana's a long way on a long day; it isn't on the Via Francigena, which Topo sends gallivanting over the hills, but on a straight metalled lane which is better for Leo's feet. I can cut back to the Via tomorrow and hopefully get to San Gimignano by evening, and then we'll take a day off at that famous little town, full of Romanesque and Gothic architecture, which is such a magnet for tourists that maybe we'll find a horse trekking centre (and a farrier) nearby.

Dogana, meanwhile, is a small, plain town whose name translates as Customs. I find Peter and Bessie parked on the edge of an expanse of communal land fringed by houses, and Leo and I are despatched to find out if we can set up camp on the grass. After an animated conversation with three old women, entirely in mime, I'm sent off to see the fruit-and-veg man who seems to be in charge around here. He's very friendly and helpful, and indeed so is everyone else; we have an attentive audience who are fascinated by Leo, Bessie and our electric fence, and an old chap even takes the village pump apart to make the water run faster into the horse bucket. Signor Fruit-and-Veg brings us two apples, two giant peaches and an invitation to the coffee bar round the corner when we've finished supper.

Long after dusk has fallen we're still sitting in the street outside the bar conversing in a variety of gestures and languages with the villagers who, like Dee and Vincenzo, have welcomed us into their lives for the evening. The most talkative person is an enormous Signora; she's the wife of the fruit-and-veg man and she's an impressive matriarch. She also speaks good French and is a mine of local information about Dogana, so called because this is where the tax on wine and oil was levied and collected in the 1940s. She tells us its World War II memorial commemorates two Italians shot by the Americans (which event she doesn't hold against the Allies in general or, by association, Peter and me in particular – *ah, la guerre, c'est la guerre*); and then abruptly she veers away from history with a naughty suggestion out of the blue that perhaps she should lend me her husband for the night. I'm saved from having to look either honoured or horrified (it's not at all obvious which would be the appropriate response) because all the menfolk promptly suggest that Signora should spend the night with the horse. My own husband observes rather gloomily that he supposes he'll be sent off for a walk.

It's definitely time Peter and I retired to bed (in Bessie, and preferably with each other) so we go off giggling, but when Signor Fruit-and-Veg comes knocking on Bessie's door very early next morning I decide not to open it just in case he's come to joke about his *droit de seigneur*. However, when I look out cautiously a bit later, to my relief it seems he was just being hospitable – he's left a box of apples and carrots for the *cavallo*, and lemons for Peter and me to cheer up the last of our gin.

Dogana's residents assemble to wave goodbye, and no one states the obvious as I leave to the usual accompaniment of loosely clacking horseshoes. I'm keeping my fingers crossed that they'll stay on Leo's feet for the twenty–odd miles to San Gimignano, and as we head towards the Via Francigena the map shows we're now beside the River Sanguigno, which sounds like a good omen.

But it isn't.

I'm just turning left at a crossroads when the percussion of Leo's footfalls changes from its usual four-four time into a three-four of clack-clack-clack followed by a muffled thump. This turns out to be because one of his front shoes has fallen off in the middle of the road with all its sharp nails pointing upwards.

'*Leo!* whoa, just eat in the verge for a minute, I'll have to pick it up before someone runs it over.'

I push him to the side of the road, dart back and retrieve it before the next motorist finds he's got a flat tyre with six holes in it. Standing on the verge with the shoe in my hand, I can see there's no way I can hammer it back on to Leo's ragged hoof. And he can't carry on barefoot, particularly when the foot that's bare is a front one. About 80 per cent of a horse's weight is supported by its forelegs, and in his case the soles of his hooves are so flat that without a shoe to raise them off the tarmac he'd be moaning within yards.

Somewhere in a saddlebag there are some equi boots, the equivalent of rubber galoshes. They're the sort of emergency equipment you carry in the hope you never have to use it, and they've travelled 1700 miles to Santiago de Compostela and now another 1200-ish towards Rome without ever being removed from their packet. However, I'm going to have to use one of them now – it's that or phone Peter and wait for him to come and rescue us with Bessie.

But bloody-mindedly I decide that we'll manage on our own, so I extricate a boot out of the bag, wiggle it over Leo's hoof, tension it to a close fit with its clumsy system of wires and levers, and set off down the road again with all my fingers crossed.

25

A Dose of Culture: San Gimignano and Siena

Clunk-clunk-clunk-shuffle-slide-scrape.

Leo's galosh is useless. It was the correct size all those years ago, but now it seems too big for his unshod foot and it swivels round to left or right as the camber of the road changes. I dismount to straighten it, get on, get off again, try walking beside him, and eventually take the boot off altogether to see how his hoof's getting along inside it…

And it's immediately obvious we'll have to stop.

I notice for the first time that the inner surface of the galosh is lined with little metal claws. I suppose their purpose is to grip the foot but in Leo's case they're tearing chunks out of it, and now his hoof is far more tattered than it was when the shoe fell off. We're still miles short of San Gimignano, and if I go any further I'm going to end up with a very lame horse.

So it's phone Peter time. He turns out to be ahead of me at the campsite there where the fastidious proprietor is busy packing him off to a horse trekking centre at Sant'Andrea, a sideways step from the Via Francigena. By the time he tracks me down, Leo and I have fallen asleep under a tree. It takes an hour to decant our belongings out of Bessie and on to the road so we can clear a space in the horse section, load Leo and then heave everything back again in a mess on the other side of the central partition, and we're pretty hot and worn out by the time we get to Sant'Andrea.

But we're not complaining, these days – since the humidity sogged off we've been a lot more cheerful, even more so today when it turns out the centre is a proper Agriturismo farm with accommodation for guests, a swimming pool and a reputation for fantastic organic food. The owner is a bosomy lady with a big laugh as well as an unforgettable name: Tiziana, pronounced Titsiana. She lets us put Bessie by the pool and raises no objection when we tell her sheepishly that really we need to sleep in the lorry because we can't afford to stay in her beautiful lodgings. As for Leo, he has mixed feelings about his own lodgings in a paddock that's bare earth because it hasn't rained here for months, but he's pacified by the presence of equine neighbours and an unlimited supply of hay.

Selim from Senegal is in charge of the horses. He's quiet and gentle with his animals who all look up to him, quite literally, because he's seven feet tall, his height accentuated by his thinness and the finely sculpted features of his face. I crick my neck trying to have a conversation with him, but at least there's no language barrier; thanks to Senegal's colonial legacy, Selim speaks French, and in no time at all he's found a farrier who'll come and put four new shoes on Leo on Monday morning. Today's Saturday, and I'm just contemplating the joyous thought of a day's rest tomorrow and a tourist trip to San Gimignano when I remember there's the small problem of a break in the continuous thread of our pilgrimage. There was no alternative to cadging a lift in Bessie today but I need to make up the mileage somehow, and 'somehow' means Minnie the bike.

That's going to require energy, fuelled by a large supper tonight for a start, and since we have no will power to resist Tiziana's dinners, we join the other guests for a calorie-laden meal of lasagne, prosciutto, barbecued beef, an interim course of cheese with three kinds of honey – an unusual culinary combination for Peter and me – and a last gasp of *budino cremoso*, a rich and wobbly Tuscan crème caramel.

The wines flow with the courses, a constant reminder that we've arrived in the Chianti region. My recollections of its wine go back to the days when it was served in London's bistros, its bulbous bottle squashed into a raffia basket called a *fiasco* – but I don't recall a lot about the taste.

Tonight's organic wines are in slender bottles and they're produced on this farm – pale gold Donna Iolanda, and Chianti Colli Senesi that's as densely red as garnets and tingles on the tongue; we work our way through samples from various different years, and all of them are the subject of much rolling round the palate and earnest discussion. However, it's hard to be earnest for long because the entertainment going on outside the dining-room is very distracting. It seems that Tuscans like to take their dogs on holiday with them, and while we humans are agonising over the merits of the *vino*, the canines are having a wonderful time. As Tequila the Beagle waltzes past the doorway trying to hump a fluffy Pomeranian and then comes spinning back attached to the ankle of Maggie the Bernese Mountain Dog who's much bigger than he is, it's enough to make you choke on your drink.

San Gimignano on the skyline looks like a small scale Chicago from the Middle Ages, and for centuries it's been a stop-off point for pilgrims on the Via Francigena. In the old days there were seventy-two towers pushing up into the sky, but as the decades rolled by most of them were reduced to house height and now there are just fourteen, still enough to give the little walled city an extraordinary silhouette.

We find it is indeed bristling with Romanesque and Gothic architecture, just as the brochure says – not just the towers, churches and museums but the tall houses too – and its streets are paved with truly ancient flagstones. It's also jam-packed with tourists, but it's quite a welcome novelty for Peter and me to be mixed in with them wearing that same label, and in my case wearing a blue paper shawl that's been handed to me at the door of Santa Maria Assunta church. This isn't for draping over my shoulders – it's to tie round my waist to conceal the fact I'm wearing shorts, and it leaves me wandering to and fro in a blue mini skirt instead, just one of a gang of female visitors trying to cover up their irreverent naked legs.

The exterior of the church is so plain that the fanfare of colour inside is an astonishing contrast, the nave filled with Romanesque arches in striped bands of black and white marble, the vaulted ceilings sparking with gold and red and lapis lazuli. Most brilliant, most vivid of all are the frescoes that coat the walls with tales from the Old and New Testaments: Adam and Eve, Noah building the Ark, Pharaoh's army drowning in the Red Sea, the Nativity, the Last Supper – and many more apparently dating from the fourteenth-century Sienese School of painting, the images and colours so intense, so vital, they look as though they were created yesterday.

After a deeply satisfying potter up and down the aisles, we go and poke around in the tourist shops filled with carvings in alabaster and olive wood, hand painted bowls and ferociously expensive leather handbags, none of which are of any use to pilgrims. So before I can be tempted into any impulse buying we climb up to the city wall and drink in the view across the patchwork of green woods and fields and vineyards, all interwoven in a perfect snapshot of a Tuscan summer. Then there's a strictly practical visit to a proper shop, an *alimentari*, to stock up on food supplies. The tourists are in here too and there's a pushy American woman behind me who doesn't want to queue - when I tell she'll have to wait until Signor's finished putting my shopping in a bag, she complains that the grapes in her hand are too heavy for her to hold. Well, try lugging these five kilos of potatoes back down the hill then, Madam. Except of course I don't say that, I just smile as Signor flicks a glance at her and immediately slows down the packing of my groceries to a snail's pace.

And after that I can't think of any more displacement activities to delay the inevitable: putting in some pilgrim miles on Minnie, which means not only struggling to keep my balance in the first place but stopping her leaping out of gear. The first part of the journey is actually quite relaxing – it involves climbing a hill so steep there's no question of pedalling up it, so I walk. But then it's a Big Dipper of a road all the way back to Sant'Andrea, and by trial and a lot of error I find the easiest way to manage the bike is to freewheel down from the crest of the first hill and hope to build up enough speed to get up the next one without having to pedal at all. Unfortunately Minnie's rear wheel wobbles uncontrollably if she achieves more than 5 m.p.h., and by the time I get back to the farm my legs are also wobbling uncontrollably owing to fatigue and desperate efforts to stop myself careering into passing cars. But at least my guilty conscience has been assuaged.

Monday is all mapped out: the farrier is due at 8 a.m. and I reckon it'll take him about an hour to re-shoe Leo, and then I can leave Sant'Andrea by ten, return to San Gimignano and maybe ride the sixteen miles or so to Abbadia a Isola, our next planned stop on the Via. So I get up early, catch Leo and have him fed, watered, and waiting by 7.45 a.m. – and four hours later I turn him out in his field again, bored, impatient and still unshod. Needless to say, the farrier turns up within minutes.

By then I'm ready to curse all Italian blacksmiths, but Irwen's both charming and disarming, not Italian anyway to judge by his Welsh-sounding name, and he speaks fluent English. I don't think it has occurred to him that he's more than a bit late so I haven't the heart to mention it, and it takes him a further three hours to trim Leo's moth-eaten feet and fit them very gently and carefully with new shoes. After he's finished I feel I should invite him for lunch since it's now nearly 3 p.m., so Peter and I share out our Bessie provisions and the meal stretches through a leisurely discussion about the lack of a British constitution, the disparate characters of Irwen's thirteen horses, the problem of the badgers in his garden which eat his tomatoes, and his wife's job teaching Italian for NATO in Belgium.

We also talk about Siena, which he describes as his spiritual home, a place where the crime rate is low and families stick together. He says the city has Etruscan roots, and when that mysterious civilisation was absorbed by the Romans, according to legend the city was built by Senius and Aschius, the sons of Remus whose brother Romulus founded Rome. Christianity arrived there in the fourth century AD, and before long a stream of pilgrims began to flow through on the Via Francigena.

By the time Irwen leaves it's so late there's no point in my riding anywhere today, so we decide to take Bessie on a trip to

Siena which means I can bypass it with Leo in a couple of days' time instead of having to plough my way through the middle.

However, parking the lorry within walking distance of the pedestrianised centre isn't easy because horseboxes aren't allowed to drag down the tone of the tourist coach park, and we're not inclined to pay the 20 euros flat rate for an overnight stop we don't need in the camper van section. Eventually Peter manages to tuck her into a space as tight as a coffin on a street just outside the city walls, and we muddle through the cobbled lanes on foot, hoping we'll be able to find our way back again later.

There isn't exactly a flood of pilgrims in Siena this afternoon, even though it's an important destination for them; they'd probably be recognisable by their oversized hiking sandals and battered rucksacks, but I don't see any likely candidates at all. There are plenty of noisy holidaymakers, though, in fact so many that we decide against joining the crush of them waiting to get into the cathedral, even though by all accounts it's spectacular. It's less effort on a hot day just to admire its ornate façade and gaze up at the dramatic *campanile*, the soaring bell tower striped liked a zebra from top to bottom in black and white marble, the symbolic colours of Siena with an intriguing equine origin – mythology tells you they represent the white coat of the horse Senius rode, and the black one belonging to Aschius.

The cathedral baptistery, the Battistero di San Giovanni, is more appealing if only because it's far less crowded. It's dominated by a fifteenth-century hexagonal font made of marble, enamel and bronze, showing scenes from the life of John the Baptist. The most famous sculptors of that era created it but unfortunately none of their names means anything to me apart from Donatello, whose panel of the Feast of Herod has some wonderfully drunken revellers slumped round the table.

Like the church in San Gimignano, the vaulted ceiling and the ancient paintings catch the eye, all riotous with brilliant colour; and expecting more of the same, we hand over 6 euros each to visit the crypt. But what a disappointment – this is the most uncrypty crypt I've ever been in, just a big room with chipped frescoes traced over the walls. Peter and I are prepared to be very unimpressed, not least with the mystifyingly expensive entrance fee, until we read its history.

It seems this was never a conventional crypt, more a kind of ante-room with stairs leading up to the nave, and its walls were decorated with elaborate scenes from the New Testament which must have taken years to paint. But all that talent, all that effort went to waste because the place was later demoted to a store-room, filled with building materials, and finally sealed off altogether and forgotten for nearly 700 years.

The room was rediscovered during excavation work in 1999, its frescoes now reduced to fragments but some still glowing with their original bright blues and reds, the halos of the saints still burning gold. It took three years to clear the room completely, and when the world's experts turned up to check it out, they pronounced the frescoes to be some of the most important examples of mediaeval painting in the whole of Italy.

Peter and I start to take a second and more respectful look at them, but the fact is we need to leave now or we'll be driving the forty miles back to Sant'Andrea in the dark, always a problem with the unwieldy Bessie and her squinting headlights. We set off on a guesswork route through the pencil-thin streets hoping we'll find her eventually, but first there's an irresistible stop in the Piazzo del Campo where the sun's just setting behind the majestic Palazzo Pubblico town hall. Tall buildings fringe the huge shell-shaped square, and the Torre del Mangia bell tower rises to the incredible height of 300 feet; for the energetic (with time to spare) there are 500 steps to climb inside it for the reward of an awesome view over the city and probably half of Tuscany as well. It seems odd that such a lofty and dignified building should be called the Tower of the Eater, and it isn't until much later that I find out that the name is in memory of its greedy first guardian in the fourteenth century.

As for the Piazzo del Campo, even an ignoramus like me has heard of that because of the famous Palio horse race. This is held here twice a year, on 2nd July and 16th August, the riders representing the different neighbourhoods of Siena, the *contrade* – and it's not staged for the benefit of the tourists. It has taken place every year since 1656 and it's a deadly serious competition, filled with passion and danger as the riders gallop their horses bareback round the Piazzo. Fortunately for Leo the second race is still a week away so we'll miss it, along with any opportunity for him to be commandeered by some wild-eyed opportunist jockey.

By the time we track down Bessie it's completely dark, and the road home is a nightmare of bumps and ruts left over from frosty upheavals in the tarmac last winter. The lorry's headlights jump and point at the sky, the verge, in fact anywhere but the way ahead, with the result that we miss the turning to Sant'Andrea, arrive on the motorway by mistake, and find ourselves almost in Florence before we can turn round.

So it's a late night followed by an early start for Leo and me. As I leave our lovely Agriturismo I spot Selim bent double in a field as he struggles to pull up some weeds, and he stands up to wave goodbye, unfolding gracefully to his extraordinary height. It's been a wonderfully bucolic and indeed alcoholic couple of days; Peter has a stash of Tiziana's 2003 vintage red stored in Bessie's booze department for future reference (a necessity, not a luxury, of course) and our bill for two dinners turned out to be four times the cost of two nights' accommodation for one lorry, two people and a horse. It was worth every single *centesimo*.

26

The Vexatiously Frustrating
Via Francigena

> For an occupation that's truly crap
> Try puzzling out an Italian map;
> Don't think you'll get to anywhere soon –
> You might as well steer by a map of the moon.

And that's what it feels like. I start off so well with a short cut back to San Gimignano that I decide to stick to the red-and-green-starred Topofrancigena route winding temptingly across the chart towards Abbadia a Isola. Ignoring the rest of my motley map collection and any potentially pioneering paths, I manage this very successfully for the short distance from San Gimignano to Santa Lucia where a VF sign appears right on cue, stuck to a lamp post. It instructs pilgrims to carry straight on – but what it actually means is Turn Right Immediately, since the alternative is Melt Through This Stone Wall Right In Front Of You.

Having worked that one out and picked up the Topo trail again, it behaves quite well for some miles and provides a treasured, rare reminder of our days on the Camino Francés in Spain as it wanders through woods and valleys, doubling back, fording a river … but the difference is that finding arrows or signs, never mind any that point in the right direction, is down to pure luck. And as for the river, it has no orderly Camino-style stepping stones – it's over a foot deep and any pilgrims without a handy horse would be soaked to the knees. Not surprisingly, I don't meet anyone all morning.

Lunch follows its usual routine: I sit with my back against a tree while Leo stands over me, his muzzle right in my face as he helps himself to all the Marmite crusts, half my orange and a whole Mars Bar. We could easily doze off here, digesting in a companionable stupor, but we've still got a long way to go, so back off a bit, Leo, give me room to get up…

Oh God, that's really unfortunate. As I climb to my feet I realise my riding trousers have split in sneaky silence right across my bottom – simply disintegrated, rotted away after sweaty weeks in the saddle, and there's now nothing to conceal the expanse of pink knickers underneath.

And there's no keeping a low profile for long either, because we're forced to stop in the village of Quartaia. The VF map tells me to cross the road but on the other side there are no more signs at all, and while I'm busy looking for them, the storm that must have been playing grandmother's footsteps behind us suddenly falls out of the sky with a crash. We scuttle into a covered market for shelter but I'm already soaked, knickers and all, and so is the sheepskin on top of the saddle. The rain continues for a good half hour and when it finally eases up I make a hasty exit from the town in any old direction, hoping we'll be out of sight before anyone has time to notice a peculiarly indecent pilgrim.

Eventually the Via turns up again, but only because I find it by using the compass – we're a mile out of Quartaia before the first arrow puts in an appearance. To my relief it follows a remote cross-country route where I see no one apart from one red squirrel, two squashed toads, one pheasant and numerous English foxhounds baying in their kennels. All is well as far as Gracciano, which looks like a sensible short cut to take until I discover it's a sizeable town while realising simultaneously that although most of me has now dried off, the still soggy sheepskin has left a large and persistent wet patch on my bottom to go with the split trousers and pink pants. Meanwhile the VF signs have vanished again, but I'm not going to stop and ask for directions because I'm getting some funny looks just riding by.

On the other side of Gracciano another arrow appears but it's angled due north, towards the Florence motorway. Well, I can't be bothered to go searching for a track to Abbadia a Isola any more, I'll just stick with this little road and hope no cars come driving up too close behind me. And it turns out to be a delight, a sunken lane that I'm sure is every bit as pretty as the starred route, making its way eastwards between dry stone walls with olive trees whispering a silvery lullaby in the orchards on either side.

Peter and I meet at an old farmstead just short of the village, and when I call in there (now with a baggy jumper judiciously wrapped round my bum), the very elderly owner shows me a field for Leo and a space for the lorry beside some derelict pig sheds. So that's us fixed up with everything we need for the night, and I even find another pair of riding jeans in Bessie that are still intact.

But there's more to come. Signor dodders into a barn to fetch an armful of alfalfa hay to boost Leo's supper, and his son strides purposefully into the pig sheds and emerges with a very un-porcine item – a two litre bottle of unlabelled Chianti. He gives it to Peter, who obviously looks needier than me, and tells him that since it's only 11° proof, he can drink the whole lot tonight and he won't get a headache. Peter looks doubtfully at the bottle which has about an inch of amber-coloured liquid sitting heavily on top of the wine. 'Ah,' says Signor Minore, 'don't worry, this is how we preserve it.' And he removes the cork and shakes the bottle violently, spraying a liberal dose of what turns out to be olive oil all over the grass. My husband downs the rest of the contents during the evening, no trouble at all.

Abbadia a Isola's name means Abbey of the Island, a reference to the solid ground it was built on 1000 years ago above the marshland at the junction of the roads to Volterra and Florence. These days the swamp is all rolling farmland, its rich earth ploughed into gingerbread chunks, but this little hamlet is still a prominent staging post on the Via even though all that's left of its original Benedictine abbey is the church with its clean lines and rounded arches. The frescoes inside have dimmed with the passage of time except for the big triptych altarpiece, lit so the paintings of a solemn Virgin and Child surrounded by saints are set in gold. It's very striking, and to me the whole village is a special place.

While riding away next morning I take a casual snapshot from Leo's back, pointing Peter's old camera at a stone archway as I pass by without really noticing what I'm aiming at; but when the print's developed months later to my surprise it's so evocative that it transports me straight back to Abbadia's sense of time standing still. The arch frames two old ladies in blue dresses sitting outside a crumbly house, a sprawl of roses drooping from the balcony and soporific washing dipping from the line; the women are facing each other in quiet companionship, hands folded in their laps as though they've sat that way every morning for years, and behind them the jumbled fields and woods ramble off into the distance.

From the other side of Abbadia I can see the walled town of Monteriggioni with its fourteen watchful turrets on a faraway hill. In front of me, amazingly, there's an authoritative-looking red-and-white Via Francigena sign pointing to a track across the countryside. This passes close to Castello della Chiocciola, a name that looks as though it should translate as Chocolate Castle, with three distinctive towers of varying heights, two of them square and the third a tall cylinder with a flag waving off the top. To my disappointment it turns out that the word

Chiocciola has nothing to do with chocolate – it means snail, in itself a puzzling name for a castle until I learn that *scala a chiocciola* means a spiral staircase, in this case the one that winds up inside the cylindrical turret.

By now the trail has gone haywire again and the day becomes a mixture of delight in the fabulous countryside and absolute frustration at the terrible signage that has me peering at the map or the path every few minutes. After Chocolate Castle, Topo directs me over a stream and straight ahead the other side … well, I would if I could but again there's no straight ahead, it's left or right and nothing to say which. So I guess at left, which turns out to be correct, and then there's a whole mess of distracting GR tracks through tangled woodland and oh God, Leo, this would be such a fantastic day if it wasn't so infuriating.

When the VF arrows suddenly start proliferating I realise I must be close to Siena, and then I'm almost on top of the motorway that runs parallel to it. The signs are sending pilgrims towards its centre now, but Leo and I turn off to travel along a ridge to the west with an amazing view: as we walk along, the city unrolls into a long tapestry of churches and towers and ancient houses on the other side of the valley.

Less impressive are the livery stables where we ask for a night's lodging. It's not far from a hamlet called Grotti which should have been warning enough, though the people who work at the stables obviously think that it's Peter and me and our grubby pilgrim horse who are going to lower the tone. The proprietor is away and the remaining Jobsworths don't want us mixing with their clients. However, I stare them down obstinately until in the end we're allowed to park on open ground which I can see has served as a giant muck heap for at least twenty years. But it has clumps of wild alfalfa growing on it, so Leo has no complaints.

And in the end, Peter and I have none either. When darkness floods the landscape the full moon rises above Siena, and the cypresses lining the lane become sentinels of the night with their pencil-thin shadows; the countryside's voluptuous curves shift and glimmer as the moon sails on, and there isn't a sound to be heard.

It's Day 100, 10th August, and Topo says I'm only about 140 miles from the Vatican, though it's a case of so near and yet so far in terms of time. If I can follow the map easily, it shouldn't take much more than a week – if not, Christmas sounds about right. The authentic and most direct route of the Via Francigena sticks to the Via Cassia for much of the way from Siena to Rome, but that's the main road and I imagine every pilgrim whether on foot, bike or horse tries to keep off it. Topo's recommended and excursion paths weave across it from one side to the other in extended loops, and maybe the best I can hope to do is shuttle between them, ironing out a few of the bends. That's if there are any arrows to point me in the right direction …

My idea of pursuing my own version of the Via has now pretty much died a death and instead I've become quite obsessed with following one of the official paths, having realised they're littered with buildings and sometimes whole villages of historical interest I might otherwise miss. So now I spend my time doggedly hunting down arrows and signs that are sometimes attached to fallen posts/chucked in the ditch/dumped in the undergrowth/ pointing the wrong way or altogether absent, and hardly have a moment to think about anything else. All thoughts of the fund-raising aim of the pilgrimage and even my mother have drifted into the background, though I'm sure she wouldn't mind; even so, a small voice does warn me that while I'm searching fanatically for proper pilgrim routes, Peter's probably hoping equally fervently that we just get to Rome and go home soon.

As luck would have it, today turns out to be one of the best riding days of all in Italy, beginning with a sideways hop to the fortified farm at Cuna. This is an untidy complex of red brick buildings which in the twelfth century included a pilgrims' hospice; the farm itself was probably built 200 years later, and it was then reinforced to protect the grain and cereals in its granaries. Over the years it has sprouted two towers, two circles of walls, and so many houses to fill the gaps between the walls and the farm buildings that now, centuries later, I'm staring at a massively fortified mini-village.

It even has a church, an unpretentious little building which is dedicated to St James and St Christopher, so I feel I ought to have a look. And inside there's a big surprise, one that plunges me back again into memories of the road to Santiago, and to a village in Spain called Santo Domingo de la Calzada which is home to an unusual legend.

The story concerns a mediaeval family from Germany: father, mother and son who were making the pilgrimage to Santiago Cathedral and who stopped in Santo Domingo for a night. The next morning the son was falsely accused of stealing a bag of money and was promptly hanged, leaving his sorrowing parents to carry on without him. On their way back a few months later they found he was still suspended from a tree and, far from being in an advanced state of decomposition, he was very much alive. So they rushed to the judge who had sentenced him to death and were told scornfully, if understandably, that their son was no more likely to be alive than the well-cooked cockerel and hen on his plate. Whereupon, of course, the chickens flapped off the table squawking, thus proving the boy's innocence, and he was cut down, reprieved, and presumably trudged back home to Germany with his mother and father.

The surprise I find in the church at Cuna is a very old fresco illustrating exactly the same story. I suppose this might be an international legend that lives on in multiple forms in multiple countries, but to me it's an extraordinary link between the Camino Francés and the Via Francigena, with St James as the lynchpin.

After Cuna, the Via's path joins an ordinary hiking trail and I can find my way along it quite easily by compass and by sight; there are big views across hills of stubble, all precision cut in corduroy stripes and buttoned with rows of cypress trees, and the track keeps well away from the roads. For a few blissful miles I can doddle along thinking of nothing in particular, soaking up the sunshine and the breeze, immersed in the pleasure of just mindlessly *being* for a change.

And then ... what's this, Leo? Topo says the Recommended Via turns left here and we should be going to Lucignano d'Arbia. But that will mean joining the Via Cassia, so after a short consultation with my conscience I stick with the hiking trail, Via 500c, which goes straight to Ponte d'Arbia. This is a village further down the line on the Via Francigena where, predictably enough, there's a bridge over the River Arbia, and where Via 500c suddenly sprouts some VF signs of its own. We walk along beside a rusty railway line, and I'm just thinking its proximity doesn't matter because it doesn't look as though it's been used for years when the ghost of an old train comes trundling along, all chipped green paint and no passengers, and the driver gives Leo and me a haunting toot on the horn.

He signals the start of an other-worldly sort of evening. Buonconvento is the next notable town on the Via Francigena, a place I'd like to skirt round (whatever its delights) because the Via Cassia runs through the middle, but that's a problem for tomorrow, and now I pause at the entrance to a farm that's almost as large as Cuna to phone Peter who is checking out the local *agriturismi*. While he's telling me he's drawn a blank at every one, I'm automatically assessing the spot where Leo and I are standing now ... hmm, a bit of grass, big Scots pines for shade, wonder if there's water anywhere ... and at that exact moment the owner walks by. So I ask him with expansive gestures if we can stay right here for the night and he tells me to help myself, waving a hand towards the vast farm buildings coated in Virginia creeper, from which I deduce he means there's a tap somewhere around. And then he disappears, never to be seen again.

When Peter arrives I smother Leo in fly spray since swarms of the pests have suddenly homed in on him; I imagine they're already here because Signor has a herd of cows, but in fact I never do see any signs of livestock, crops, stored grain or anything more useful than a proliferation of yarrow, a wild white herb that supposedly stops nosebleeds.

There's a tap in a strange building that looks as though it was a house once, lodgings for farm workers who have long disappeared. It has a cobwebby dining-room where the refectory table is all laid up with plates and cutlery layered in grime. Worse, there's an ancient bag of flour, alive with weevils, sitting in the middle, and as for the fridge ... I home in on it with a grisly fascination and try to open the door. God knows what's inside, but luckily I never find out because the disintegrated rubber seal has jammed it shut.

Water still coughs out of the tap, so I fill up Leo's buckets and rush away quite unnerved, back to the reassuringly solid Bessie as a gloomy dusk descends. Peter seems unmoved by the eerie atmosphere here, or maybe he's too tired to notice it. When I climb into bed he's already conked out, dead asleep in the bottomless pit of exhaustion, whereas I toss and turn, jittery in this peculiar place where the ordinary sounds of the night are becoming more and more muted and muffled, as though someone's wrapping the lorry in blankets of creeper.

In the morning, of course, it turns out there's a perfectly ordinary explanation: the world is cloaked in fog, something we haven't seen or thought about for weeks. It all adds to the spookiness though, and when there's a crash on Bessie's roof I jump out of my skin. But it's only a giant pine cone dropping out of a tree, and then it leaps off the roof and into Leo's breakfast bowl, narrowly missing his nose which might otherwise have needed patching up with the yarrow.

I'm in a rush to get away now before anything else happens, so I put the cone in Bessie as proof that this strange farm really does exist and then we head off through a peasouper that writhes clammily round Leo's fetlocks, on an invisible route to God knows where.

27

Where Our Only Neighbours are the Gentle Dead

I haven't been able to pinpoint a convenient little lane that might divert me round Buonconvento on any of the maps, so my invisible track inevitably ends at a road junction where a prominent VF sign points towards the town. Unmissable even in the fog, it's a modern signpost depicting two stick people who've inexplicably got left behind in the 1950s - the bloke is manfully toting a rucksack while the woman trots dutifully behind him wearing a dainty headscarf and a most impractical skirt. I decide I might as well follow it because I know there's a church in the town that is dedicated to Saints Peter and Paul, and maybe I ought to visit it as a counterbalance to the St James church at Cuna; but the centre turns out to be seething with tourists and it's another place that's far too busy to leave Leo tied to a lamp post while I go sightseeing.

Worse, Topo says there's an unavoidable stint on the Via Cassia coming up, though the mist is clearing now so at least I'll be able to see the lorries. The map quickly directs pilgrims on to a loop away to the left of the main road but then I notice they're planted back on it again, and that's quite enough to send me out of Buonconvenuto in a completely different direction – towards the Crete Senesi, the clay hills of Siena. As I ride along, an appetising view of Montalcino appears in the distance and I pass close to its sloping vineyards where roses bloom exuberantly at the end of every row of vines, fragrant barometers for the health of the grapes. They're prone to the same diseases, and they're a useful early warning system – if the roses keel over, the vines will be next. The Sangiovese grapes here are translated into the warm, earthy wine for which Montalcino is famous, and they're already plumping up in the August sun, reminding me that the seasons are sliding by and soon it will be autumn. It seems a long time ago that I rode through the wakening vineyards of springtime Burgundy.

I get back on the Via Francigena when it veers away from the Via Cassia on to a smaller road to Torrenieri, but this town has none of the obvious charm of romantic Montalcino on the hill; it's full of new-build houses, and though I know it's an established and probably significant halt on the pilgrim road, the only reason it'll stick in my memory is because of its rude donkey. Leo and I have just crossed over the River Asso on the far side of the town when a real live Asso in a field spies him and thinks he must be competition for its two wives. In seconds it has rounded them up and jumped on the nearest with an ear-splitting bray of 'She's Mine, She's Mine!' while Signora Jenny Donkey rolls her eyes in an Oh-No-Here-We-Go-Again way. Meanwhile Leo's eyes are popping out of his head with either lust or admiration, and I keep him on a tight rein in case he's contemplating a leap over the fence to join in.

Further down the road we arrive in San Quirico d'Orcia which is a lot more appealing than Torrenieri, and a reassuring VF sign of the plump-mediaeval-pilgrim variety points me down its tiny streets to the church of Saints Quiricus and Julietta, a solid twelfth-century building with three arched portals. The main one is particularly fetching, flanked by columns balanced on the backs of lions and with an unusual pair of stone crocodiles facing each other over the door, while above them a traditional rose window is set into the wall. The church's architecture slides seamlessly from Romanesque to Gothic and its interior is filled with a harmony of styles that's now become familiar to me, quiet and serene except for the burnished gold of the rococo altar.

Leo waits patiently while I get my passport stamped and ask if there's anywhere nearby for a horse to stay. There ought to be – San Quirico was once full of hospices for overnight travellers, some of whom must have been on horseback. But no longer, it seems; today's town hall officials shake their heads in unison and we have to set off again, this time into the mountains on a VF excursion route that leaves me with no particular expectations that any of the blue symbols indicating water, church towers, a cemetery and even a bed will yield anything useful to a tired rider. But while I'm trying to identify a distant village, St James comes crashing up the track in a Jeep and clunks to a stop beside me. He has blazing blue eyes and a taste for Mozart, if the sonata notes dancing out of his car window are anything to go by, and he's absolutely positive the manager of the hotel where he's staying will welcome a horse into the garden.

I have my doubts, but my new friend is turning his car round and escorting me to the village which turns out to be an entrancing place called Bagno Vignoni, where the main square is made not of paving stones but of water – a whole thermal spa of it. It seems that hot water has been welling up here for more than 2000 years, pouring in from the geothermal area around Mount Amiata, an extinct volcano I think I noticed vaguely when approaching San Quirico. The bath-mad Romans were the first to exploit Bagno Vignoni's possibilities and since then it's been popular with visitors from all walks of life, from the rich and famous to the smelly travellers on the pilgrim road.

The hotel manager is summoned, but he confesses the garden is too small to accommodate a peckish horse and he invites us to use the rough grass beside the car park instead. Having positioned Bessie tactfully out of the way, we take up St James' invitation to join him for a drink in the hotel. His real name is Helmut Schober, and he's an artist from Austria who creates images of light in acrylic paint, all inspired by the music of Mozart. I'm not a great fan of abstract art but the book of his paintings that he gives me is absolutely arresting, his flights of imagination soaring out of every page.

From an Austrian painter to an Austrian hiking map: I abandon the Topofrancigena chart in favour of a large and detailed Kompass version, which might make it easier for me to keep away from the Via Cassia around here. Confusingly, it also shows some variations of the Via Francigena that Topo doesn't mention, but really I now need to stop obsessing about historically accurate routes and concentrate on getting to Rome in one piece and as soon as possible, for Peter's sake if not my own. Anyway, I'm beginning to wonder how precise any of the maps are – Kompass shows Mount Amiata in a completely different place from where I thought it was on the Topo chart, and unless the defunct volcano has suddenly re-ignited overnight and slithered its fiery way several miles to the south, that wasn't Mount Amiata I was looking at yesterday.

Today's meander round the countryside takes in a pimpled landscape of conical volcanic hills crowned by forts that guard the Via Francigena in all its forms, with the dominant battlements of Radicofani king of them all, easily visible miles away to my left on the other side of the Via Cassia. The air freshens as Leo trundles uphill through the forests to an altitude of nearly 4000 feet while I search for non-existent VF signs and puzzle over a couple of strange hiking itinerary maps attached to posts. The reason they're strange is because they're identical and tell the hiker *You Are Here*, even though they're planted at least two miles apart and the *Here* arrow is in exactly the same place on each one, pointing to a straight stretch of road even though I'm actually at a dirt track crossroads on both occasions.

But in the end we come down from the hills and creep round the edge of the town of Abbadia San Salvatore, which I think really does have Mount Amiata planted close beside it, and after our tortuous journey of at least twenty-five miles we bump into Peter and Bessie just short of the walled village of Piancastagnaio. I know this town doesn't feature on the Topo route but if it did, I'm sure its cemetery would be usefully picked out in blue – it turns out to be a very suitable place for a pilgrim horse. The main road to the village is fairly narrow, but there's a wide dual carriageway to the graveyard with a verge on either side (an unusual luxury in Italy) that's full of clover, as Leo soon discovers.

The Italians seem to take their dead very seriously. In this enormous cemetery, laid out in the shape of a cross, the deceased are interred in little houses, or incinerated and their ashes placed in individual alcoves in a high wall with a rolling ladder to facilitate visits to those in the upper storeys. According to a lady who's up the ladder replacing some flowers, you can only rent an alcove, and if you don't keep up with the payments, Signor from the Council comes along and removes your relative. I'd like to know what then happens to the ashes, but it seems an improper question to ask Signora as she balances on a rung with a fistful of lilies. Anyway, this spotless necropolis is obviously lovingly tended: every alcove is overflowing with fresh flowers and not a single one is empty, so presumably everyone pays their rent on time. I'm not sure we should even be asking if we can camp on the edge of the carriageway just outside, but no one seems to object and by nightfall, when the living have all gone home, the whole wall is a-flicker with soft little lights in every shrine and our only neighbours are the gentle dead.

Guilt nudges at me as I admire the matter-of-fact way they're treated here; with respect and tenderness but no particular mystique, as though caring for them is just part of life's daily routine. They remind me that I haven't been back to visit my mother's grave since her funeral – not because I don't care, but maybe because I care too much. I hate to think of her mortal remains disintegrating underground even though I'd like to believe that she herself, the essence of Ma, has survived somewhere else. Cremation seems more liberating somehow, as though the souls of the departed take flight more easily, unfettered by their bodies.

My parents were both brought up to be church-goers, though Ma was no great lover of the rituals of organised religion; she preferred to be regarded as a pantheist, and believed divinity and immortality were all around in the environment. Meanwhile, my more conventional father did his best to keep her on the straight and narrow, making sure she attended the services at Easter, Christmas and Harvest Festival at least, and reminding her she was on the rota for renewing the church flowers. My mother could never remember when it was her turn to do them, and my sisters and I used to phone her and unkindly impersonate the vicar's wife so we could tell her off for forgetting. In the end she realised what we were up to, and then came unstuck when the vicar's wife really did phone and Ma addressed her crossly as Penny-Susie-Tessa-Meef-just-stop-that-will-you, as she could never tell which one of us it was.

At her funeral, however, Pa did move away from convention: he insisted her grave should be dug deep enough for him to be interred on top of her when his own time came, as he thought that was a lot more cosy than just lying by her side. And he also agreed to an unorthodox request from all his daughters that a head-and-neck image of Ma's pony, The Fiddler, should be carved on her gravestone, possibly causing passing visitors to wonder if there's a horse buried there as well.

Piancastagnaio's cemetery gates open on the dot of 7 a.m., and fifteen minutes later there's a steady stream of cars arriving. Today is Sunday but no one seems to be at Mass; in fact those who aren't visiting dead family members are shopping in the local *alimentari*, as far as I can see. The sun is out and the air's sparkling with bonhomie: as Leo and I clatter round the outside edge of the village, there's a chorus of *bon viaggio, bravo*, and even a stray exclamation of *hi!* from a youth hanging out of an upstairs window. And for the first time, I see an ordinary signpost on an ordinary road pointing to Rome.

This probably involves the Via Cassia, so I turn Leo towards the stubble field hills instead, heading roughly south-east. There are various types of little signs littering the tracks: enigmatically, they say IF or IFL or even IVF. I decide the last one probably doesn't stand for In Vitro Fertilisation but for Itinerario Via Francigena, but they all lead to one road in the end which inevitably is the Via Cassia, though it turns out to be so quiet on a Sunday that I follow its abundance of supersized VF signs all the way to Acquapendente. This town's name translates as Hanging Water and it comes from the miniature waterfalls twinkling in the River Paglia nearby, a river I cross without realising at the time that it's a liquid boundary marking the end of Tuscany and the beginning of our final stretch through the region of Lazio.

Another road sign is pointing to Rome, this one giving the distance – 132 kilometres, a bit more than eighty miles. For the first time, I don't feel as though I'm on a never-ending expedition, but one that almost has a finish date attached to it. Perhaps even Friday this week...

On the other hand, there's yet another distraction I can't resist, even though it means a delay on what's already a long day – it's the pink and cream façade of the Basilica del San Sepolcro, Acquapendente's cathedral. I leave Leo in its car park while I go and take a look inside.

First impressions are a disappointment – an art exhibition is covering the walls and obscuring nearly all the architecture; the paintings are naff and banal to my eyes, pinned up, propped and plastered over every available space. More interesting is one of the permanent fixtures, somebody's effigy in a glass case which from a distance looks as though he or she has stabbed himself with a quill pen, though on closer inspection the person turns out just to be holding it at an unfortunate angle. Close by there's a sad little photo of the cathedral's façade of stucco and terracotta taken in about 1943, showing the terrible damage inflicted by wartime bombs.

I set off for the crypt, a dangerous excursion down sixteen stone steps in pitch blackness. I've read in the blurb that there's a little temple here that's an identical copy of the Holy Sepulchre in Jerusalem, but in the end I don't go looking for it as I'm likely to break my neck in the darkness. All I can make out is a pair of small windows glowing a ghostly green from the weeds outside crawling over the glass, and then my eyes take in two people on the inside sitting right in front of them, so silent and motionless that I wonder if they're still alive. In the end I can't resist approaching them to find out, and they're not alive at all, and indeed never were – they're carved out of wood, staring dead-eyed at the greenery.

The noticeboard outside the cathedral gives a potted history of the building in English. It seems the crypt is the oldest part, and the church itself has been demolished and rebuilt several times.

The translation takes some unscrambling: *'according to tradition,'* it says,

> *a certain Queen Matilde – probably Matilde of Westphalia (895-968), the wife of Henry the First of Saxony, mother of Otto the First, who availed himself of the patrimony transferred to him by Henry to found monasteries. Queen Matilde then, who was headed towards Rome in order to build a church dedicated to the Holy Sepulchre, stopped at the Roman Gate in Acquapendente, off the stream Quintaluna, because the mules loaded with gold refused to continue, indeed often knelt and, in a dream, the queen was asked to build a church in that spot.*

I suspect the mules mutinied because they were exhausted by having to cart so much heavy gold all the way from Germany, but I like Matilde's explanation that they triggered a dream that led her to cut her journey short and use the gold to build her church here instead of in Rome.

Meanwhile my own equine companion is dozing gently in his parking spot, fortunately still upright on his own four feet, while an enterprising Italian father bounces his baby up and down on the saddle. When the infant has been prised off and we manage to leave, my decision to stay with the Via Cassia for the rest of the day makes it surprisingly easy to find a place for the night – we haven't gone far before an Agriturismo materialises close to the road, complete with a restaurant serving excellent dinners and a proper field for Leo, with a ginger mare on the other side of the fence who thinks he's wonderful.

If it wasn't for the fact that I've reached the end of my large scale Kompass map and I haven't got any more of them, I'd almost be confident that the last leg of the journey to Rome will be quite straightforward. After all, Matilde referred to the

Quintaluna stream nearby, which could have been named for the time it takes travellers to walk from here to the Vatican. That would tie in with my own estimation of Friday, if *quinta luna* translates as five days. Tonight, scrubbed clean, full of food and feeling positive, I'll assume it does.

28

Pointing Primly at my Wedding Ring

Leo's in a grump.

'Oh, come *on*! We've got to get going, it's not that far now, it'll only take another few days…'

It's not that he's tired – he just doesn't want to be parted from his new flame-haired lady friend. He drags his toes and keeps on looking back hopefully at the Agriturismo, but I urge him down the road unsympathetically with voice and legs, and the fickle mare doesn't even bother to whinny an equine *arrivederci*.

Hmmph! We go stodging along the Via Cassia for half an hour before switching to a track across farmland peppered with late sunflowers. Arriving in the village of San Lorenzo Nuovo, an official VF sign catches my eye – but following it proves to be a big mistake. It turns out there are four versions of the Via Francigena around here, and I've chosen the worst one possible; it goes all round the houses of San Lorenzo and some neighbouring troglodyte caves as well, and then across the marshes to a ruined octagonal church. Not far from here I find one more sign – but it's pointing straight into Lake Bolsena, the enormous flooded crater of a dead volcano. What are we supposed to do here, Leo, swim across and search for signs the other side?

Now I'm the one in a grump, particularly when we have to double back to the main road and follow it for mile after boring mile to the town of Bolsena, the road no longer full of HGVs (for which I suppose I should be thankful) but crawling with coaches, caravans and cars instead. Campsite after campsite has colonised the shores of the lake; the town itself is heaving and Leo slows down to tortoise speed.

Eventually a pilgrim signpost turns up, prominently painted on a telegraph pole. It seems to accord with the start of another Topo trail, so rather than keel over with *ennui* on the Via Cassia, we go off on a long, rambling, pretty but possibly pretty pointless deviation through the woods and up a hill to a fountain whose significance escapes me entirely. I have to admit though that the view from here is amazing: Lake Bolsena is laid out like a giant's oval table top, eight miles long, and its colour on this sunny day is incredible – cobalt blue, made even more intense by the sheer volume of water that fills the plunging volcanic cone.

At the bottom of the hill two different types of sign send us straight back to the Via Cassia, and Leo nods his way along it for more tedious miles until we're nearly in Montefiascone, a town dominated by its distinctive basilica. The streets are packed with mediaeval houses, and it looks far too spotlessly preserved for there to be a messy horse hostelry within miles.

But while I'm wondering where to go next, yet another kind of VF sign swims into focus, a version I haven't seen before – it's a milestone pointing up a road to my left, with the red outline of a pilgrim on it and the magic word ROMA. When I follow it to the hamlet of Asinello, Peter and Bessie suddenly materialise in a layby next to a big circle of grass, nicely horse-sized, which is owned by the civil defence department. The hospitable *Protezione Civile* invite us to park here for the night and even neatly solve the problem of No Water For The Horse by siphoning off a supply from their truck.

The morning brings a brief but welcome switch from the Via Cassia to a Cassia Romana, an original Roman road running dead straight through the olive groves with paving stones that are still level, tight-fitting – and as smooth as inverted saucers from centuries of use. It's not easy for Leo to walk on them but he does his best, slipping along for a stretch so I can angle the camera to take a picture of the ancient slabs framed by his ears, a Leo Was Here shot for posterity.

Back on the ubiquitous Via Cassia, which at any rate is deserted on today's public holiday to mark the Feast of the Assumption, I'm gripped by the urge to get a move on now we're getting close to Rome, and I don't stop in Viterbo even though it looks like a wonderful old town begging to be photographed while I'm still in camera mode. The fact is, as a foot pilgrim (whether you're relying on two feet or four) you're never going to see everything unless you're as fit as a flea, have no ties or time constraints and are probably less than forty years old. Maybe the best you can do is to muddle through on the principle that you'll try and take a look at what's most important to you personally – a compromise between treating the journey as a race to Rome (or Santiago) which means you won't see anything much except what's right in front of your nose, and toddling off to explore every landmark in your pilgrim guide book. I'm reminded again that if you really want to immerse yourself in history, you need some (motorised) wheels and a mind-set that isn't dominated by the weather, complicated maps and the nightly problem of finding somewhere to stop.

Erring today on the side of the race to Rome principle, I ignore Topo with its alluring but probably lengthy deviations towards Vetralla and take a rural lane to the congenial village of Tre Croci, which has the three holy crosses of its name standing in the main square alongside a bar.

The lads in the pub are extremely helpful. They escort me up the road to the *campo sportivo*, a chunk of land in tatty condition which has a lot of weeds. It'll have to do. They give me the key to the gate padlock with a reminder to lock up in the morning and then they go back to their beer, telling Peter who has by now arrived in the square that they've installed his mother and her horse in the sports field. How very unamusing. My husband's face, however, wears the faintest hint of a smirk when he turns up at the *campo*.

Signor Officious arrives on the scene shortly afterwards, and *his* face is a thundercloud. By now Peter and I have erected 100 yards of electric fencing and when we're told we can't stay here after all (no reason given), we both turn mulish. It's been another day when our normal limit of twenty miles has been exceeded by at least another six, which may not sound like much but involves an extra hour and a half of riding. So Signor Unhelpful (who could be the mayor, for all we know) finds himself on the receiving end of reciprocal grouchy looks from both of us, whereupon he relents and says we may remain in the field for one night only. Then he goes off to the bar, no doubt to berate the boys for handing me the key, while Peter loudly threatens to empty Porta Potti in a GB motif all over the football pitch.

Water for Leo is no problem here either. There's a pump right by the gate, next to a wheelie bin that spews out a mob of scavenging kittens when I go to fill up the bucket. The presence of the pump pricks my conscience into action on the subject of clothes washing; now that we're nearing the end of the pilgrimage, I'm finding it hard to summon up the energy for sessions of sock scrubbing. We haven't had a domestic blitz since San Gimignano, and with a disgusting slippage of standards I've been recycling my socks from the filthy to the slightly less filthy. This evening we do make the effort to wash a shirt each, but Peter's reward for his industriousness is a terrible fright when he goes to hang them up in Bessie's horse section; he reels back under a deluge of panicking kittens who've abandoned their wheelie bin in favour of the back of the lorry.

The shirts drip steadily from our makeshift washing line, plinking on a biscuit tin with letters inked across the top: Francesca's Chocolate Brownies. Francesca is the wife of Jason the English farrier and the tin has nothing edible in it, just the last of the horseshoes he supplied, a reminder of a time before we left for Rome which now feels like a previous incarnation. I haven't given any thought at all to what it will be like to go back to England.

Meanwhile, plan ahead … only four more charts to cross, and then we'll be in Rome. I pore over the pages. I might get as far as Monterosi tomorrow night where Topo has an elegant golf course symbol sketched in close by, something that will please Peter. And the excursion route runs in a relatively straight line, so I may be able to follow it without too many problems. I notice the guide sends pilgrims back to the main road beyond Monterosi for a while, but I'm becoming quite blasé about that these days, and anyway there's probably another way I can go if I look at Peter's Michelin map…

Shit! Surely not… Topo's calling it the SS2 Veientana now, but Monsieur Michelin is adamant it's a big dual carriageway section of the Via Cassia.

It can't be. I scour both maps, but there's no alternative route. Panic's setting in as I dig out the phone number of a member of the Association Via Francigena in England, and to my relief he reassures me it'll be all right – there's a separate concrete path beside the motorway for pilgrims to walk on. It still sounds dangerous to me, but the only other way would be a convoluted diversion round the edge of Lake Bracciano, another huge drowned crater, which would take me away from the path of the Via Francigena altogether until I was practically in Rome. Anyway, when I check my only large scale map of the overall area to see if it would be feasible at least in principle, the answer's a definite No. It's based on a map created in 1879, so it's probably not that useful except as a wall poster.

Maybe the Via Cassia will be OK.

The next day's also a public holiday, which means the main road's quiet when I'm skirting round Vetralla. From here it's easy enough to pick up the VF signs again and follow them across country ... until they disappear in a gigantic nut orchard. The only arrow I can find points straight on, but once again there's no straight on – in the leafy jungle of hazel trees there's no path at all, and I get whacked on the head by so many branches wearing rows of nutterdusters that I have to get off or get knocked out.

'Leo, this is getting ridiculous.'

I drag him on through the vegetation, and right in the middle of it there's a strange sight: the ruins of an ancient chapel. Obviously it predates the orchard and I suppose there was a road leading to it once, but it takes me another ten minutes to fight my way out to some kind of rural *piazza* where two girls from Siena (of a rare breed called Real Pilgrims), are trying to work out how to get to Capranica, the next little town on the Via. Two forest roads and three metalled ones lead out of the square, and none of them is signposted. We wander from one to another, and eventually find a splodgy pilgrim painted on a tree a long way down one of the forest tracks.

In Capranica I learn the reason for today's fête: it's San Rocco's Day, commemorating his death on 16th August 1327, and the notice beside the little church and fountain dedicated to him advertises the superiority of the water pouring from the mouths of two stone lions. Leo and I, as parched as each other, agree that it's totally refreshing.

As it happens, I know a bit about this particular saint: also called St Roch, he was a pilgrim who walked from his native France to Rome and his statue often popped up when Susie and I were on the way to Santiago de Compostela. He cured victims of the plague, but his healing powers failed when he was himself struck down in Piacenza. Believing he was going to die, he took himself off to the woods – where unexpectedly he recovered, due not to divine intervention but to the kindness of a hunting dog, which brought him food from its rich master's table and applied canine antiseptic lick to the suppurating sore on his leg. But his luck finally ran out when he went home to Montpellier - he was arrested as a spy, and five years later he died in prison.

Sutri is another place I'd like to investigate, but everything's closed and I have to make do with a stamp in my pilgrim passport from a roadside bar. The town is built on a narrow hill of volcanic rock, and its ancient origins are more obvious here than anywhere else I've seen; as I ride along I come across an extraordinary Etruscan necropolis right beside the road. It's a maze of open chambers dug out of the *tufo* – volcanic ash that has solidified into rock – and a noticeboard records its history in the briefest possible way: cremations and burials here in BC, still in use in I AD, looted in mediaeval times, and a complex history.

The Via Francigena goes right past the golf course just before Monterosi. It turns out to be as good a place as any to spend the night, with plenty of grass just outside the gates and a spring that feeds a ceaseless supply of water into a tank. A lady leading a blind Dachshund across the course comes over to tell us about her poorly pet, which was stolen recently for porcupine hunting in the hills; unfortunately for the sausage dog it wasn't much good at it, and when it was blinded by quills it was left for dead in the street where luckily someone recognised it and returned it to her.

When we get round to discussing the less dramatic subject of taking a horse into the middle of Rome, she says the city is quite empty at the moment as everyone's gone to the beach. So maybe it won't be too difficult to ride Leo into the Vatican; I'd been hoping quite unrealistically to catch a glimpse of Pope Benedict, but it sounds as though he's also away on holiday, at Castel Gandolfo if not at the beach.

Half a mile beyond the golf course, I'm busy worrying about the stretch of dual carriageway beyond Monterosi when Leo and I are joined by a another worry – a loose dog, not of the squat porcupine-hunting type but an athletic German Shepherd with an unshakeable belief that we need an escort.

I manage to lose her again in the muddle of village streets, and presuming she's gone home my attention shifts back to the VF arrows which lead to the Via Cassia, just as I expected. What I didn't expect was that we'd be on the left hand side of the dual carriageway with the traffic storming straight towards us. There's a low wall to our right and I suppose we're in the pilgrim and/ or bicycle lane, but it's no real protection and there are long gaps in it where there's none at all. Meanwhile the lorries in the carriageway next to us are metal monsters right in Leo's face, their drivers waving and hooting, whether in sheer surprise at seeing us or to tell me off for taking a horse on such a dangerous road I've no idea.

But there's nowhere else to go. I must be grinding my teeth down to stumps with anxiety, though Leo's just shaking his head irritably as the side wind from the HGVs sweeps his forelock into his eyes, and then I hear a long hoot and shriek of air brakes on the other side of the motorway and the cursing of a driver through his open window...

Oh God, no, it can't be...

The central reservation also has a low solid wall, and poking up above it are a large pair of dog ears, followed by the whole German Shepherd as she scrabbles over the top and cuts straight across the traffic on my side of the road, heaving herself over our bicycle lane wall to fall in behind Leo, padding along at his heels.

What on earth am I going to do now?... Think ... and stop grinning, dog, or maybe you're panting with fright, you and me both, I can tell you...

A slip road comes into view. Thank God for that. I steer Leo up the slope, against the traffic joining the Via Cassia, and see there's a police car coming my way, maybe the officers will help. I flag it down, do my best to explain this is not my dog (and therefore can they please put it in their car and take it away before there's an accident) whereupon the hatchet-faced bastards tell me it's not their problem, and drive off.

I try a side road next but it leads straight back to the motorway, and I can see I'm going to have to scramble down the bank and ride Leo on the narrow hard shoulder itself with Miss German Shepherd still in tow, because the pilgrim path has vanished. To the left, however, there's a house. An entire family is pouring out of it to find out what's going on, so I try explaining my predicament in useless Italian: perhaps they could just hang on to my unwanted companion until Leo and I are out of sight?

Signor nods vigorously. He holds the dog round the neck while we go off, but I make the mistake of looking back just in time to see him shout and throw a stone at her, and then chase her back up the hard shoulder towards Monterosi. Seconds later she cuts across all the traffic again to get away from him.

She doesn't reappear. I'm convinced that's the end of her, but there's nothing I can do about it now, I've got enough on my hands just dealing with my horse. We try another slip road, ignoring its No Entry sign, and Christ, here's another police car coming towards me, this time flashing its blue lights, OK, OK, I know I shouldn't be here but there's no other way to go, I'm just following the pilgrim signs, you can see them for yourself.

One officer this time: he puts on his hazard lights and pulls up beside me, and I get ready for a telling off. But he's not interested in a horse hoofing up a dual carriageway slip road in the wrong direction – he just wants to know if I've reported a dog. I nod and point mutely back towards Monterosi, and in seconds he's floored it and the car's out of sight. Maybe Miss German Shepherd's owner realised she was missing, or maybe the first officers made a joke of it back at the police station and got an earful from their sergeant for refusing to help a silly woman on a horse with a dog she said wasn't hers. I'll never know, but at least that's one problem less; I just hope the dog's made it home in one piece.

Meanwhile, Leo, I've got to work out where we are. The exit road leads to a lane, and I need to stop and check the map properly to see if I can join a Topo route that leads away from the Via Cassia. As we're slowing down, I pass a car that's crawling along in the same direction. The driver winds down his window and says *Ciao*. I wait for the *bello cavallino* bit but he doesn't say anything else, so I just say *Ciao* back rather distractedly and pull up on the verge.

Signor stops his car alongside, so it seems a good idea to ask his advice. This involves my showing him various signs and roads and paths that I think may be OK, and Signor nodding and agreeing with all of them. I'm just congratulating myself on my excellent navigational skills and instinctive sense of direction when I realise he's started talking non-stop and the word *amore* is featuring in every sentence. He's also pointing to the field on my right.

Duh! Finally it dawns on me that he's asking me for a roll in the hay. This is very flattering as he's probably only in his thirties, in fact it makes up for being mistaken for Peter's mother the day before yesterday; really I should tell Mr Casanova to fuck off, but I've forgotten how to say it in Italian so I settle for pointing primly at my wedding ring instead. Signor is not at all perturbed, and it isn't until I get a fit of the giggles that he gets in a huff and drives away.

Perhaps he just fancied a turn with the dressage whip. When I tell Peter later about my encounter, he remarks uncharitably that I was probably just a case of any port in a storm. But in the meantime it's made my day, on a day that badly needed to be lightened, and for the next few hours Leo goes strolling down the lanes while I count all the different types of Via Francigena signs without a care in the world, until more by good luck than good judgment I end up at the luxurious golf complex near La Storta where Peter and I have arranged to meet.

The golf club is closed, in fact very closed, and security is tight. It takes a lot of pantomime on my part to persuade the armed security guards to swap their pistols for the mop bucket so they can get Leo a drink, but after that they're falling over each other to be helpful, and they manage to make arrangements for my horse to be installed at an equally smart private livery yard. We humans are allowed to stay as well, with Bessie parked in a familiar position next to the muck heap. There are no paddocks here for the show jumpers and dressage horses to relax in and kick up their heels, so Leo has no option but to put up with a couple of nights in a stable. Fortunately the yard manager understands equine psychology very well: when I tell her my horse can't bear being shut in, she leaves his door open and simply fastens a chain across the gap at chest height. Provided with an illusion of freedom, a heap of hay and more friends on either side, he's perfectly content: a seasoned old trooper who's carried me for nearly 1400 miles and would probably carry me for another 1400 without complaining.

But there's only one more day of travelling left to do.

Tomorrow: Rome.

29

A Fitting End to a Long Journey

In the dead of night I hear Leo tiptoeing past Bessie.

I'm out of bed and out of the door in a split second, grabbing my knickers and shoes ... if he gets on the golf course ... it doesn't bear thinking about – he'll be rolling in the bunkers, stampeding all over the greens.

What's going on? He's climbing up the muck heap, stopping at the top to peer around uncertainly, the darkness so intense that I can barely make him out even though his coat is basically white. That's odd ... I glance back at the line of horse heads nodding over their stable doors – and among them is the unmistakable pale silhouette of Leo, looking curiously in my direction. The horse on the dung heap is black, and when I scramble up to catch it the reason for its peculiar behaviour becomes obvious – it's wearing a fly veil that covers its head from ears to nose, and it can't see a thing.

With just a rope round its neck, it follows me obligingly up and down the rows of stables while I'm hoping I don't bump into any humans, given that it's wearing more clothes than I am. In its blind state it's very docile, so I push it through the only open stable door I can find and jam it shut, hoping the horse won't let itself out again.

And since by now I'm thoroughly awake, I spend the rest of the night wondering what it's going to be like taking Leo into the biggest city that he and I have ever visited.

Ironically, I've ridden so many miles on the Via Cassia that it feels like an old friend now, in spite of yesterday's horrors on the dual carriageway, and it seems fitting that I should stay with it all the way into Rome. The traffic's fairly heavy when I join it at Olgiata, close to where we're staying, but there are no lorries. As Leo walks along, the scenery changes dramatically from one mile to the next; from the pure suburbia of high rise flats, seedy hotels and communal wheelie bins scratching shoulders on the pavement, to a country road that's lined with trees pulling us into their shade, away from the scorching sunlight.

At La Giustiniana the road divides: the Via Trionfale to the right, the Via Cassia to the left. Both lead to the centre of Rome, and Peter and I have arranged to meet where the Cassia links up with the bicycle path running alongside the River Tiber. But needless to say, the Via Francigena signs all point down the Trionfale.

Well, I'm not going to follow them. The last of my Topo maps agrees that the historic route follows the busy Via Trionfale but recommends the old Via Cassia, which branches off from Cassia Nuova somewhere past Nero's Tomb. It even illustrates the final stretch on the cycle track with small blue bicycles speeding along beside the river, on to the Via Angelico and finally into St Peter's Square, the Piazza San Pietro.

Leo, we're going to stick with the recommended route. It looks much quieter and safer to me.

My horse doesn't care which way we go; he's in somnolent mode and ignores everything from the noise of the traffic to the rustling road map spread out across his shoulders, along with any idle chatter from me. Thick trees continue to shelter us and obscure most of the view ahead, and I have no sense of our proximity to Italy's capital city which possibly is just as well.

Nero's Tomb is planted quite inconspicuously at the roadside not far from where the Via Cassia splits in two. It's a stone sarcophagus on a plinth, majestic in shape but too weathered and smothered in graffiti for me to make out the inscriptions. Later I find out it was never occupied by Nero, but by Publius Vibio Mariano who was the Dean of Sardinia, and what he was doing there I've no idea. It dates from the third century AD, and a myth took hold in the Middle Ages that Nero was entombed in it even though the sarcophagus bears Mariano's full name. The romantic notion still persists, though you could hardly get dewy-eyed about the tomb's surroundings these days: the ugly apartments are back alongside us, along with more grubby bins and lines of parked cars.

The old Via Cassia bends away abruptly to the right and now it's like a country road again, with hedges on either side; as we go down the hill I have my first decent view of what lies ahead and it still bears no resemblance to the Rome I'm expecting. Tall buildings poke up here and there out of what appears to be a forest; we pass the junction with the Via di Villa Lauchili which is just a rural lane winding away across Clara's Vineyard … and then suddenly, yes, this must be Rome and what's more, Leo, we shouldn't be on this road now, we've just walked past a No Entry sign.

As we cross the Piazza dei Giuochi Delfici which is sprouting proper urban streets in all directions, the Via Cassia becomes one way only – for traffic driving out of the city, not into it. For a second I curse both the street map and Topo for not highlighting this fact, but then again, why would they? No one in their right mind would ride a horse to St Peter's Square. There's a perfectly good pavement for pedestrians but it's not wide enough for Leo, and the Via is becoming narrower, passing between stone walls and the tall sides of graceful old houses. Well, I'm not going to turn round and try and work my way through the back streets, we'll certainly get lost. At least the Via Cassia runs in a straight line all the way to the river.

Vehicles come rushing towards us, spread across both lanes. I keep Leo on the right hand side of the road and face them down to make them move over. I don't check the expressions on the drivers' faces – gobsmacked, probably, but nobody shouts or hoots; they all filter courteously into single file so their vehicles can pass us safely. It's the longest half mile I've ever ridden in my life, but I manage it undetected by the *carabinieri* which seems a reasonable achievement in itself.

The rounded dome of a church is coming into view, the Chiesa Gran Madre di Dio, and now there are cars parked on both sides of the street, taking up even more space which means it's all a bit of a squash, sorry, sorry drivers, sorry Leo – not that he needs an apology as he's still plodding along on auto pilot in the heat that's now bouncing off the walls. And that's it, the Via Cassia spits us out abruptly into the quite enormous Piazzale di Ponte Milvio, which presumably means we've arrived at the river. All of a sudden there are red traffic lights ahead, followed by a stark choice of three lanes that turn right or one that turns left, when what I need to do is go straight across to get on the bicycle path.

'Leo, WAKE UP! We're going to have to streak across here in a minute.'

'Eh, what?'

He flings his head up as he realises we're in a queue.

'Lights! I don't do waiting at lights! I'm going now!'

And luckily they change, and in the short pause before all the multiple lanes of traffic start pouring across in front of us, he leaps into a trot and shoots across to the safety of the bike lane. I stop briefly to look back at the Ponte Milvio arched across the

Tiber's green waters and then we set off again, more calmly now, to meet up with Peter and cover the final couple of miles of a journey that according to my diary has taken us 108 days.

As the river bends away to the left, the cycle path joins the Viale Angelico and becomes a proper little road on its own, with a dotted white line up the middle. Leo and I carry on along it, and with Peter walking beside us we make our way quietly on to the Via di Porta Angelica and through one of its high stone arches to follow the curve of the colonnades round to St Peter's Square. It's all going worryingly well; Leo is able to have a long drink from the pilgrim fountain we pass on the way, and the Swiss Guards in their flamboyant uniforms of yellow, blue and red don't seem to regard us as a threat to papal security.

However, having not looked at the detailed central section of the street map too closely, I've assumed that once we get round the colonnades we'll be in St Peter's Square. Wrong. We arrive in the Piazza Papa Pio XII which has an attractively alliterative name, but it's not where I'm expecting us to be. From here there's a great view of the Basilica, the full range of columns, the Egyptian obelisk brought to Rome by the Emperor Caligula ... and the Piazza San Pietro itself, fenced off behind iron railings. On the other side of them there's a decorous line of tourists waiting to go into the church. In Piazza Papa Pio they're milling around all over the place, and while I'm looking for a gap in the fence so we can get where I want to be, I realise there aren't just humans in the square with us – there are horses and carriages as well, waiting to take visitors on a tour of the city.

Unfortunately Leo sees them at the same time, and wakes up again with a start.

'Look, look – *more* new friends! I need to talk to them!'

He's instantly transformed from a docile companion into a sweaty mass of excitement, slithering about on the cobbles and threatening to barge his way through the tourists. I try to keep him still enough so Peter can take some hasty photographs of an equine volcano about to erupt in front of the Basilica, and then I spy an Italian police officer on the other side of the railings. In the heat of the moment I'm convinced he'll let an unruly horse right inside St Peter's Square since this is obviously such an unusual and important pilgrim occasion, but the answer's No before the request is even out of my mouth.

'A photo then, Signor? With you in it beside my horse and me?

The officer agrees to that, particularly as the railings are safely between him and us, but his cheery smile vanishes as the camera clicks. Leo has had enough of the hackamore bridle pressing on his nose as I struggle to control him, and turning his head towards the officer he clears his nostrils in one tremendous snort, spraying the man's uniform with a jet stream of snot.

The thought surges through my overheated brain that this is hardly a holy and respectful manner in which to arrive at the Vatican; but maybe in our particular circumstances it's just as important that my mother, wise in the ways of horses, would have seen the funny side.

All the same, I think it's time we left.

Peter holds up the traffic so Leo can dance his way up the road to the nearest bridge and then across it to the lorry which is pulled in neatly to the kerb. By now I can't wait to get off him before I fall off with exhaustion, but in a moment's inattention I let go of the reins while I'm heaving the saddle off his back. I realise what I've done as he moves smartly away, and for a second I can see him contemplating a whirl round on one hoof to gallop back over the bridge to the carriage horses. But he doesn't; instead he sees that Peter has lowered Bessie's ramp, and he loads himself on to the lorry instead. Maybe he, too, realises it's time to go home.

✄

Day 109 is our only opportunity for sightseeing before we have to pack up and leave. When Peter and I drive back into Rome, however, our first priority is to track down Don Bruno Vercesi. He's the priest whose name and address were given to me by the Association Via Francigena, and apparently he'll be happy to apply the final stamp to my passport. We walk up a narrow street close to Porta Sant'Anna, past the Swiss Guards again, and I knock on a door. Don Vercesi answers, not at all surprised to see yet another pilgrim; he examines my *credenziale* with keen interest and then adds the very last stamp in red ink. He says I need to get my official *Testimonium* from the pilgrim office, but it's closed today so it seems I'll have to wait till we get home and then write a letter asking for it to be sent to me.

Rome is like a furnace and our decision to take a tour on an open-topped bus is probably a mistake; after two hours of struggling to take in glimpses of all the famous landmarks through the beaded curtains of sweat pouring off my eyebrows, I probably haven't noted much apart from the Colosseum which is so gigantic it would be difficult to miss it.

The last time I was here was nearly forty years ago, when I spent two weeks working at the city's sports stadium while I was employed by the American rodeo. It was a chaotic life, and when I wasn't exercising horses by cantering endlessly around the arena, riding one and leading two while waiting for the moment when the cowboys would let all the Brahma bulls in as well for a joke, I was being chucked out of a stagecoach twice a night in the supporting act while the competitors took a break from being bucked off. It was hardly surprising there was never time to go sightseeing, and today I have a distinct feeling of *déjà vu*.

But we do at least visit the Basilica, although there's a long queue to get in. Fortunately, the security X-ray machine seems to be having a siesta, because it fails to register both the curved hoof pick and the Swiss Army knife in my bag. It's a pleasure

297

just to escape into the coolness of the massive church, but the staggeringly ornate interior is such an assault on the senses it would be difficult to absorb it all in less than a week. Although my own preference is for the unembellished, it's impossible not to admire the sheer amount of painstaking and elaborate work that's been carried out here over the ages, the columns and statues and paintings and acres of gold leaf; and the soaring inspiration of Michelangelo and the designers who came before him, all poured into a stunning Renaissance creation for the glory of God.

In the confusion of impressions, for me two works of art stand out. One is Michelangelo's *Pietà*, the statue of Mary cradling the crucified Christ across her lap. It's hard to believe her robes are carved from unforgiving marble rather than cloth; they flow and drape across her knees as she supports the body of her dead son. Her expression I can only describe as one of bleak serenity, but what's most striking is that her face is no older than his, her youthfulness symbolic of her purity.

The other is even more intriguing to me, due to my total misinterpretation of what I'm looking at because it's in a very dark corner of the church where the lights are turned off. All I can see is a high oval window with pale yellow light streaming through it; in the distance it looks like the face of a clock with sections divided by twelve lines, and hands pointing at ten to two. I don't bother to check if that's really the time. The rest of this part of the apse is so pitch black it's impossible to make out what might be there, and it isn't until I research the internet months afterwards that I discover it isn't a clock at all, it's an alabaster window above the very famous Cathedra Petri, the Chair of St Peter. The twelve sections are a tribute to the Twelve Apostles, and what I mistook for clock hands are the outstretched wings of a dove, the symbol of the Holy Spirit.

The Cathedra Petri itself, had I been able to see it, is an intricate and complicated piece of work by Bernini, instigator of Baroque sculpture and architecture, who enclosed the original Chair in a gilded throne poised above an altar of marble and jasper. Four enormous statues are gathered round it: Saints Ambrose and Augustin of the Latin Church, and Saints Athanasius and John Chrysostom of the Greek Church, while above them a pushy crowd of golden angels frames the window along with fat feathery clouds and rays of light.

To judge from the photos, it's an amazingly sumptuous creation; but at the time I didn't see any of it and in a way I'm glad I didn't. The only photograph I took inside the church was of that pale glimmer of the window and it caught my eye because, in all the majesty and extravagance of the Basilica itself, this was just a simple light in the velvet darkness, perhaps an unconscious symbol for me of the lifting of responsibility at our journey's end.

But we still have to drive Bessie well over 1000 miles home to England, with the additional weight of a horse on board. Fortified by the last of the mountain of sliced prosciutto that Peter bought several days ago, we set off in the rumbling, grumbling horsebox for Lucca. It seems odd to be travelling on the Via Francigena in reverse, with no qualms now about having to stay on the historic route of the Via Cassia; familiar landmarks keep trundling past and already the same nostalgia that engulfed me after leaving Santiago is threatening to catch up with me again. By evening we're back enjoying the hospitality of Dee and Vincenzo, a mere eight hours' drive instead of a tortuous horse ride in the opposite direction that took sixteen days, and after that Bessie roars up the Via Aurelia to Massa and then switches to a sprint along the motorway at almost fifty miles an hour.

Time seems to be flashing past now, too quickly for me even though I'm looking forward to seeing my father and family again; we're almost at the Italian/French border when we stop at a campsite at Bardonecchia, west of Susa and close to the Fréjus Tunnel which means that tomorrow we can drive under the Alps instead of over them.

But stop, stop ... I'm not ready to go back to living in a house, wearing a skirt, sitting in a stuffy court room all day long ...

Before we leave, I take Leo out for one last ride in the mountains on a beautiful sunny morning, in the pure and unpolluted air that only altitude can bring. I dawdle my way back reluctantly to the lorry and we drive the short journey to the tunnel. And maybe St James listened to me moaning because here he is again, this time disguised as a lady official who stops us at the entrance. In rapid Italian she tells us we can't go through Fréjus – it seems that Bessie's too old, her engine too hazardous/polluting/unreliable, or all three. She has a point.

So it's a chug along the valley to Susa, followed by a crawl in second gear up the mountains to the pass at Mont Cenis at five miles an hour instead of fifty, with a line of cars behind us that stretches out of sight. There's no room for anyone to overtake, and Peter's face is such a study that I can't resist taking a photo of his granite profile, followed by one of the motorised centipede reflected in the passenger side mirror. But thank you, St James, I'm glad we had to come this way after all – the lake at the top of the pass is a brilliant aquamarine, very different from its dull grey sheen when we passed by five weeks ago, and it's a great welcome back to France on a glorious day.

As we drive north past Lyon, I keep noticing suitable patches of horse pasture, clear springs and wide verges to ride on just when I don't need them anymore, and sadly St James can't find another reason to delay us. Our penultimate night is spent at one of my favourite places of all – Vézelay, in northern Burgundy. We stayed here in 2002 with Susie and Apollo, just a few hundred miles into our pilgrimage to Santiago de Compostela when the experience of travelling long distances on horseback was still quite new and strange. The Romanesque Basilica at the top of the village is the antithesis of the Basilica of St Peter; it's positively a hymn to simplicity, filled with gentle arches and flooded with light pouring through windows that have no stained glass at all.

Peter and I book ourselves into the pilgrim quarters on the top floor of the Hotel Le Compostelle, where we have an unusual view through the Velux window of hot air balloonists floating past, and the obliging owners let me shut Leo in their garden. Now we're back on comfortably familiar Chemin de St Jacques territory, and it brings home to me what a totally different experience the Via Francigena has been. The last few months have been a trip into the unknown, much more problematic and occasionally dangerous; sometimes awesome in the beauty of the scenery, and frequently maddening with the crazy inconsistency of the signage. I never saw a single VF pilgrim signpost in France, and in Italy there were often far too many of them, all pointing in different directions. I expect that's why I met hardly any pilgrims – perhaps they were lost in the undergrowth … though the more likely explanation is that my taking the Via's secondary route meant I was off the beaten track (if there is one) for at least half the journey.

But it's been a huge adventure, real pioneering stuff with no well-marked trail of yellow arrows to follow, no cosy *refugios* laid on for tired travellers; and in some ways, although I suspect I'll remember the pilgrimage to Santiago more fondly and with more nostalgia, it seems to me that the Via Francigena has been the greater achievement.

I know I won't have netted as much money in sponsorship for the Alzheimer's Society as Susie and I did for the East Kent Pilgrims' Hospices four years ago, which was mainly thanks to my ace-networking-and-fund-raising supremo sister, but it will still run into several thousands of pounds, a small contribution towards the search for a way to prevent the dreadful disease that invaded my mother.

Meanwhile, I know what I'm going to do first thing tomorrow – get up early and wander round the church. I'm not quite sure why this seems important, given that I'm not a believer in a conventional sense, but I can't shift the feeling that we've all been looked after on the Via Francigena, and that while I've only light-heartedly (and variously) held St James, St Peter, St Paul, my mother and the prayers of sister Susie responsible, it might not have been coincidence that an unexpected solution has turned up for every small crisis. Maybe some benevolent power really is keeping an eye on us all, and maybe our souls do live on forever in some way. Ma used to say occasionally that reincarnation would be a useful form of recycling, and add flippantly that she wouldn't mind coming back as a guinea-pig, of the free range sort that didn't have to live in a cage. But personally, I hope there's a heaven and she's in it, restored to the independent, adventurous, funny and loving personality she used to be.

In the morning I follow the line of brass scallop shells sunk in the cobbled street up to the top of the hill, and the entry in my diary that evening reads: *'for me the pilgrimage really finished today, when I went up to the Basilica, said thank you to Saint James, and then went down to the crypt and lit a candle for Ma. That, for me, was a fitting end to a long journey...'*

And indeed it was.

EPILOGUE

On 12th June 1945 my mother wrote a letter to Pa, marked Central Mediterranean Force, which she posted to his regiment for forwarding. She didn't know exactly where he was, only that he was in mountainous country somewhere, taking a very long time to get home now that the war had ended. In her letter she wrote:

What a wonderful part of the world you seem to have struck my darling, and what a wonderful life could we but share it – I can picture those mountains and those pine woods, valleys, flowers and sunshine, and I people them with a crying and longing heart with the picture of you and I, riding through happiness. Something that I long to do before we are too old my dearest, is to ride on a holiday across those parts of Europe, sleeping out and fending for ourselves – will you take me?

In the course of their busy lives my parents never had the chance to pursue her dream. It wasn't until I returned from Rome that this particular letter came to light, and I read it with astonishment. The pilgrimage had, of course, been partly to satisfy an ambition of my own, but now I'd like to think that it really was a proper ending for Ma, far more than I knew at the time, and that in some way it helped to fulfil her dream too.